REMAINS of a
REVOLUTION

REMAINS of a REVOLUTION

ANTHONY BURTON
Photographs by Clive Coote

ANDRE DEUTSCH

First published 1975 by André Deutsch Limited
105 Great Russell Street London WC1

Copyright © 1974 by Anthony Burton
Black and white photographs copyright © 1973 by Clive Coote
Colour photographs copyright © 1973 by *The Daily Telegraph*

This edition published by arrangement with
Sphere Books Limited

Maps by Derek Dooley
Designed by Kieran Stevens
Set in Monotype Baskerville

Reproduced, printed and bound in Great Britain by
Morrison & Gibb Ltd, London and Edinburgh

ISBN 0 233 96609 9

CONTENTS

'Amongst all the heroes and all the statesmen that have ever yet existed none have ever accomplished anything of such vast importance to the world in general as have been realized by a few simple mechanics.'

James Sims, *The Mining Almanack for 1849*

Introduction

It is hardly necessary to labour the importance of the industrial revolution that occurred in Britain between the middle of the eighteenth century and the early part of the nineteenth century, or to stress its importance in the history of the world. Many hundreds of thousands of words have already been expended on that subject. However, it is only recently that we have come to appreciate the value of the physical remains of the period. Written documents were studied for a long time while the study of buildings and machines was ignored, treated in a cursory manner, or pushed aside into a special compartment labelled 'history of technology'. This is no longer the case, and a new study has grown up that has been given the somewhat unsatisfactory name of 'industrial archaeology'. This book is an attempt to indicate ways in which the work of industrial archaeologists can illuminate and add to the documentary evidence of traditional research. The study of history is as much an act of imagination as it is an act of scholarship, and just as a visit to the battlefield of Waterloo is an immense aid to understanding the events of that battle, so to stand among the machines of a spinning mill is a help towards understanding the class war that had its roots in eighteenth-century Britain.

The book is not intended, however, as simply an illustration of historical fact. Social change often sprang from specific technological decisions, and, many times, evidence from buildings can act as an irrefutable confirmation or refutation of documentary sources. The book also has another aim – to give an idea of the often surprising beauty to be found in early industrial architecture and of the delight to be discovered in seeing machines at work, performing tasks for which they were designed two centuries ago. The photographs, therefore, form an integral part of the whole, and one of the problems we faced in compilation was in deciding what we could omit from the many hundreds of photographs taken by Clive Coote. Hopefully, we have been able to include enough to give the reader an impression of the wealth of material still to be found in Britain, even though that material is reducing at an alarming rate.

The problem of space has also led to a necessary selectivity in the text. A complete history of all the industrial developments of the period was simply not possible – nor was it necessarily desirable. Instead, I have tried to concentrate on what I consider to be the main lines of development, those that have had the most far-reaching effects in terms of social and economic change. Thus, there is a good deal of emphasis on textiles, while some industries such as gas, chemicals and glass have been completely ignored. I can only apologise to all who are offended by the omissions, and repeat that the examples chosen are those which, in my judgement, most clearly show the interaction between changes in technology and the everyday life of the people of the time and their successors for many generations to come.

I

A Green and Pleasant Land?

Utopia is a country with no existence in the present – it is a vague dream of a state for the future or of one that has passed away, a Golden Age, Arcadia, Merrie Englande. For a generation brought up in the slums of Manchester or Nottingham, working twelve and more hours a day in factory, mine and mill, the days before the industrial revolution of the mid-eighteenth century took on a rosy, retrospective glow. They dreamed of a time when the Yeoman of England had his cottage, his share of the common pasture where he could graze his cow or goat, a strip of land for his vegetables, and when he and his family could add to their income by the husband working at his loom while the wife sat at her spinning wheel. Most of all, they looked back to a time when a man was his own master, able to work in his own way at his own pace – and if he chose to honour Saint Monday (or even Saint Tuesday), then he could make up the lost time by working twice as hard for the rest of the week. There are a few elements of truth in this picture, rather more elements of distortion. If we are to understand the monumental changes in the organization of society and the economic life of the nation that we call the industrial revolution, then we must first establish at least the general outlines of the society that preceded it. To what extent was Britain in the first part of the eighteenth century the green and pleasant land of popular mythology? How far down into an earlier age did the roots of the industrial revolution pierce?

In part, the description was true. Britain was basically a green land, one in which the majority of the population lived in the countryside and took their livelihood directly or indirectly from agriculture. The 'pleasant' part of the equation soon begins to look a little less convincing under scrutiny. When Gregory King made his estimate of the numbers and conditions of the people of England and Wales in 1688, he placed them in two broad categories: those who increased the wealth of the nation; and those who decreased it. The decreasers of wealth were not the idle, the holders of sinecures or those who lived from revenues and inherited wealth, but those who worked as hard as they could but were unable in spite of their efforts to keep themselves and their families above starvation level, and who had to rely on charity to keep alive. They were the 'labouring poor'. Out of King's estimated population of five and a half million, more than half were 'decreasing the wealth', a statistic hard to reconcile with the sturdy, independent worker enjoying the roast beef of Old England.

But already, by the early years of the eighteenth century, change was affecting the British countryside. The cottagers who scraped a living by gleaning turf and wood from the commons, by keeping flocks of geese or, more rarely, a cow, were disappearing. The Enclosure Acts, which put the old common lands under the control of private landowners, and the improvements in agricultural techniques, were beginning to change the face of the country. Land drainage turned wastes into arable lands; new crops and the breeding of new strains of sheep and cattle meant far greater availability of food supplies for the nation as a whole and increased profits for the landowner with money to invest in improvements. On the other hand, the changes brought fresh difficulties to the smallholder with little or no capital, and for the bulk of the poor it meant a life of irregular and unpredictable bouts of work as agricultural labourers. The situation was worst in Scotland. Daniel Defoe, describing southwestern Scotland in his *Tour through the Whole Island of Great Britain* of 1722-4, wrote: 'The common people all over this country, not only are poor, but look poor; they appear dejected and discourag'd, as if they had given over all hopes of ever being otherwise than what they are.'

This book is primarily about the growth of industry, but this must be seen against the background of a country still, in the first part of the eighteenth century, reliant on agriculture as the main occupation of the people. Indeed, the improvements in agriculture are the dominant factors in the economic life of the period and were also a vital factor in the dramatic industrial growth that was to come, for without an agricultural industry able to produce enough food for the markets, the growth of industrial towns would have been an impossibility. But what of industry at this time? The Arcadian tale is of a domestic industry, where the husband worked partly in his fields and partly at his loom, while the wife sat spinning, her children clustered round her feet. John James in his *History of the Worsted Manufacture in England* (1857) described such a scene in the West Riding of Yorkshire as described to him by a 'venerable authority'. Bradford-dale 'was then crowded with hand-loom weavers and spinners ... the women and children of Allerton, Thornton, Wilsden, and the other villages in the valley, flocked on sunny days with their spinning wheels to some favourite pleasant spot to pursue the labours of the day'. The story goes that this idyllic scene was shattered when the new inventions in textile machinery forced these people into the towns to work in the new powered factories and mills. This is true in part, but only in part. Invention alone would have been insufficient to cause the great upheaval of the revolution: new machines and buildings require finance, an increase in textile production is no use unless there is a market for the new goods, an increase in trade requires a decent transport system to move raw materials and finished goods, new techniques and new machines require new materials for construction, notably iron, and an industrial revolution requires fuelling, and this means an increase in production of the primary fuel, coal, and that in turn means new ways of working deep mines by new draining methods. And so we go on and on in an apparently endless chain of interdependent factors. Such a complex series of developments could only have sprung from a complex social, economic and industrial base. To try and see this picture more clearly, we shall take a much more detailed look at some of its parts.

The obvious starting point is textiles. Throughout the period of the industrial revolution, it was the textile industry that set the pace, that produced the greatest social changes among its work force, and that exhibited most dramatically the rocketing production figures that economists call the take-off into self-sustained growth. Cotton may have dominated the later period, but in the early eighteenth century it was wool that predominated, and the main centres of the industry were not in Lancashire, but in the south-western counties of England. Celia Fiennes, an apparently indefatigable traveller who took her tour *Through England on a Side Saddle* in 1695, was blessed with a lively curiosity about everything she met on the way. She not only noticed the textile industry of the south-west but took the trouble to jot down this lively account of the serge trade of Exeter:

'The whole town and country is employed for at least twenty miles round in spinning, weaving, dressing and scouring, fulling, and dying of the serges. It turns the most money in a week of any thing in England. One week with another there is £10,000 paid in ready money, sometimes £15,000.... There is a prodigious quantity of their serges they never bring into the market, but are in hired rooms which are noted for it, for it would be impossible to have it all together. The carriers I met going with it, as thick, all entering into town with their loaded horses: they bring them all just from the loom, and so they are put into the fulling-mills, but first they will clear and scour their rooms with them, which, by the way, gives no pleasing perfume to a room.... Then they lay them to soak in urine, then they soap them and put them into the fulling-mills, and so work them in the mills dry till they are thick enough; then they turn water into them, and so scour them. The mill does draw out and gather in the serges. It is a pretty diversion to see it – a sort of huge notched timbers like great teeth.... The mills draw in with such a great violence that, if one stands near it and it catch a bit of your garment, it would be ready to draw in the garment in a trice. When they are thus scoured, they dry them in racks strained out, which are as thick set one by another as will permit the dresses to pass between, and huge large fields occupied this way almost all round the town, which is on the river side; then, when dry, they pick out all knots, then fold them with a paper between every fold; and so set them on an iron plate and screw down the press on them, which has another iron plate on the top, under which is a furnace of fire of coals – this is the hot press. Then they fold them exceeding exact, and then press them in a cold press. Some they dye, but the most are sent up for London white.

I saw the several vats they were a-dyeing in of black, yellow, blue, and green.... They hang the serges on a great beam or great pole on the top of the vat, and so keep turning it from one to another – as one turns it off the vat, the other rolls it out of it; so they do it backwards and forwards till it is tinged deep enough of the colour. Their furnace that keeps their dye-pans boiling is all under that room made of coal fires. There was in a room by itself a vat for the scarlet, that being a very changeable dye, no waste must be allowed in that. . . . The length of these pieces is or should hold out 26 yards.'

Serge mills can still be seen in the area around Exeter, for example at Sticklepath, but by the early eighteenth century the main centres of the cloth trade had moved farther east to Wiltshire and Gloucestershire. Defoe, whose accounts of trade and industry in his *Tour* are unsurpassed, was clearly impressed by what he saw on his Wiltshire visit. Of Frome, for example, he wrote that it 'is so prodigiously increased within these last twenty or thirty years, that they have built a new church, and so many streets of houses, and those houses are so full of inhabitants, that Frome is now reckoned to have more people in it than the city of Bath, and some say than even Salisbury itself'. When he came to the Avon valley and the towns of Trowbridge and Bradford-on-Avon, he found even more signs of a busy and expanding trade:

'The finest medley Spanish cloths, not in England only, but in the whole world, are made in this part. They tell me at Bradford, that it was no extraordinary thing to have clothiers in that country worth, from ten thousand, to forty thousand pounds a man.'

The wealth of the clothiers of Bradford and Trowbridge can still be seen in the towns, where the magnificent homes they built for themselves provide convincing evidence. In Bradford, for example, the rows of fine stone houses known as the Torys dominate the hill-side overlooking the river (plate 1). These men were not manufacturers in the sense that we now understand it – that word was then used to describe the humble cloth-workers not the employers – but acted more in the role of traders or merchants. They had no need to tie up capital in factories and machines, but relied almost entirely on the domestic workers.

The starting point of the industry is the raw material, wool. The Spanish fine medleys referred to by Defoe were so called because they were made from Spanish wool, but later, although English wool was introduced, the name stuck. English wool was generally reckoned to be superior to foreign, and Parliament was frequently bombarded by complaints about the export of local wool, which the protestors claimed enabled the European cloth-manufacturers to compete with the British in the important overseas trade. The improvement in English wool was due, in part, to the spread of the enclosure movement which enabled the stock-breeder to improve the quality of his flock. This was all recorded in a curious poem, describing the wool trade, John Dyer's *The Fleece* (1757):

> 'But lightest wool is theirs, who poorly toil,
> Through a dull round, in unimproving farms
> Of common-field: inclose, inclose, ye swains,
> Why will you joy in common-field, where pitch,
> Noxious to wool, must stain your motley flock,
> To mark your property?'

The clothier bought his wool from a variety of different sources. At the end of the seventeenth century, many clothiers bought direct from the farmer at shearing time, but, later, as the quality of the cloth changed and improved, they found they required a whole range of different types of wool. In these circumstances, there were obvious advantages in buying wool ready sorted, and the clothiers began buying from the trade's main centre, Blackwell Hall, in London, or from the 'broggers', men who attended country fairs, buying up wool and sorting it.

Once the wool was bought, it had to be cleaned and scoured,

which usually meant washing it in a stream and soaking it in urine. It was then dried in a specially built wool stove, close to the clothier's house or mill. A few of these old stoves remain in Wiltshire and Gloucestershire, and one of the best examples is to be seen at Frogmarsh mill at Woodchester, Gloucestershire. The mill itself is of mixed date, but the oldest, gabled section was almost certainly used in domestic manufacture and has the small square mullioned windows that are typical of the early period. The walls have been patched over the years with everything from brick to concrete, but the original uncoursed stone rubble can still be seen and wooden beam ends protrude through in places. Across the road from the mill is the wool stove, which is typical of this type of building: a circular tower, with lancet arched openings and a conical slate roof (plate 1). Anyone looking for these towers should take care not to confuse them with the circular lock cottages on the nearby Thames and Severn canal, although it seems a reasonable guess that the designer of the cottages drew his inspiration from the wool stoves which would then have been seen all over the Stroud area.

After the drying process, the wool was either dyed or left to be dyed later in the piece. Oil was added and the wool was ready for scribbling and carding. The aim of these processes was to pull out the separate strands of wool so that they were all lined up in the same direction. In carding, the wool was pulled between two hand-held cards studded with wire. Scribbling was a very similar process, but was normally carried out under the clothier's supervision. Here the wool was drawn over a frame set with iron teeth, using hand cards, and where dyed wool was used this had the additional effect of mixing the different colours together.

The wool was, at last, ready for spinning. At the beginning of the eighteenth century the spinners worked at their wheels in their own cottages much as they had done for many hundreds of years. These wheels were not usually the small wheels where the spinner sat at her task, but the 'great wheels' which stood some five feet high. But whatever type of wheel was used, its function was the same: to enable the spinner to stretch out the fibres of wool and simultaneously twist them together before working the yarn back on to a spindle. There were no special buildings concerned with spinning, but it is reasonable to suppose that the great majority of cottages in a cloth-making area would have had their wheels.

The spun yarn was returned to the clothier and was now ready for the loom. The weaver normally had his loom inside his own house or, more rarely, in a small out-building. The loom was a large machine which required a good deal of space (plate 2), and weaving was an occupation that required plenty of light. From these two requirements the workshop with the 'weaver's window' developed, which is such a familiar feature in all cloth-making areas. Sometimes they were established in towns, where it became usual to build terraces of cottages with workshops on the second floor, above the living accommodation. A few of these are still to be seen in the south-west. In Trowbridge, for example, there are rows of this type in Timbrell Street and Duke Street (plate 3). In both cases the weavers' workrooms can be clearly identified by the long row of windows on the second floor. The weavers, however, were also spread right out through the surrounding countryside. As trade grew, more workers were attracted to the region and occasionally squatted on common land, building up their own communities. The village of Dilton Marsh, Wiltshire, is a good example of a squatters' village, and a walk down the main street shows the haphazard way in which the cottages straggle out along the road: some cottages are detached, in some cases a group of weavers have joined together to build a short terrace, some cottages are built of stone, others of brick and the rest are a mixture of the two. Looms were housed in lean-to's, separate workshops, or in the houses themselves. Plate 4 shows a group of cottages that stands next to the schoolhouse and a small weaving shed. Weaving communities are to be found in many parts of Britain, though they are not always so easy to recognize. In Scotland, for example, there is little to distinguish the weaver's cottage. At Torbex, a tiny village on the edge of Stirling, there was once a weaving community, but the old cottages are simply terraces of single-storey buildings built in the simple Scottish vernacular style of the mid-eighteenth century (plate 5) and only a few isolated out-buildings hint at any sort of industrial activity. In Kirkcudbright-shire, the village of Kirkpatrick Durham was built around the weaving trade, and although it follows the same traditional pattern of housing, the single-storey cottage with a central door and rooms on either side, there are more signs of workshops built into the terraces (plate 6).

There was no great skill involved in weaving, though the work was hard and the hours long. The hand loom itself is a basically simple machine (plate 2). The warp of yarn is wound on to a roller to form a sheet of threads. Alternate threads can be raised or lowered, leaving a large gap in between, known as the shed. A shuttle, trailing a thread of wool, can be thrown through this space. This thread is then pushed firmly into place and the process repeated. The weaving of broadcloth, however, produced an added complication, for it was too wide for one man to both throw and catch the shuttle. Dyer gives the traditional Arcadian view of broad-loom weaving:

'Or, if the broader mantle be the task,
He chuses some companion to his toil.
From side to side, with amicable aim,
Each to the other darts the nimble bolt,
While friendly concourse, prompted by the work,
Kindles improvement in the op'ning mind.'

The hand-loom weaver holds a very special place in the history of the industrial revolution. In the Golden Age view of the past he epitomizes the happy, self-employed artisan whose way of life was destroyed by the machine age, which reduced him to wretchedness, poverty and even starvation. The second part of the equation is all too appallingly true, but the weaver of the early eighteenth century did not lead quite the idyllic existence that has been accorded to him. Establishing wage rates and standards of living for this period is notoriously difficult, but it seems that the weaver could expect to earn something in the region of twenty pounds a year, which puts him more on the level of the cottager and farm labourer than that of the skilled artisan or craftsman. He could, however, find ways to add to his income. He could, for example, take in a parish apprentice. This provided him with a double benefit: he received a premium from the parish for relieving them of the expense of maintaining the child and he acquired an unpaid helper. The cost of an apprentice depended on the means and conscience of the weaver, who was expected to provide shelter, food and clothing for the child. Other members of the weaver's household would add their share of work – the wife spinning, the children helping the parents. For those who, in King's phrase, were 'decreasing the wealth of the Nation', the children's work was an essential contribution to family income, and the sight of young children at work was generally welcomed as a sign of reasonable prosperity. Defoe quotes, with obvious satisfaction, the remarks of a Taunton manufacturer on his weavers' families: 'He farther added, that there was not a child in the town, or in the villages round it, of above five years old, but, if it was not neglected by its parents, and untaught, could earn its own bread.'

The weavers were nearly all occupied full time, working at their looms, though they would take advantage of periods such as harvest time when there was a great demand for labour, to temporarily quit weaving for the high seasonal wages. Comments such as this, by a frustrated Wiltshire clothier, are common: 'The remainder of your order shall be sent as soon as possible, but at present the workmen are in the fields hay-making.' In general, one has a picture of a group of workmen, far from prosperous, but with sufficient to live on and independent. Cottages, such as those at Dilton Marsh, are well-built and sturdy, though one has to remember that they served as workshops as well as homes.

The next stage in the manufacturing process brought the cloth to the fulling mill to be shrunk and scoured. The cloth from the loom was of a very open weave and still contaminated by the oil and grease from the spinning. In the mill the grease was removed by scouring with urine, and the cloth was shrunk and thickened by pounding it with water-powered hammers called fulling stocks. Very few of these fulling mills survive with their machinery intact. Some served a double function, being used for both corn-grinding and fulling, Arlington mill at Bibury in Gloucestershire being a good example. Corn mills have been recorded on this site as far back as Domesday, though the present buttressed building only dates back to the seventeenth century. In the early eighteenth century, it was used for fulling, but then reverted again to grinding. The mill is open to the public, but only the grinding machinery remains.

Many fulling mills were incorporated into the larger factories as new machines came to be introduced. One of the best remaining examples of a woollen cloth fulling mill, complete with all its machinery, is to be found oddly enough in Lancashire, in the middle of an area usually associated with cotton. Helmshore higher mill (plates 8 and 9) is of a rather late date and the machinery was nearly all installed in the early nineteenth century, but in principle it is identical with the fulling mills of the south-west.

The machinery of the mill is powered by a water wheel. The water collects in a quarter-mile-long mill pond, before being allowed to fall on to the wheel, a seventeen-foot diameter pitch-back wheel – that is a wheel in which the water drops on to the 'back' of the wheel, driving it in an anti-clockwise direction (plate 8). A wheel of this type generates immense power, but also requires immense quantities of water, in this case a staggering million gallons a day. Originally, there appear to have been two wheels, and the arch under which water flowed to the second wheel can still be seen from the outside of the building. It has been estimated that the original pair generated something in the region of 10 h.p.

Gears on the rim of the water wheel transmit the drive to a horizontal shaft on which are mounted tappit wheels. As the shaft turns, projections on the wheels strike the ends of the fulling stocks, which are lifted and then fall back into place under their own weight. So, the big wooden stocks hammer away at the cloth contained in the trough (plate 9), keeping up the pounding for two days, during which time a medley broadcloth might shrink by as much as half its width and a third of its length. The scouring in this mill was by urine – earthenware pots were kept in discreetly dark corners for the workers to furnish the raw material, and according to local tradition pots were handed out to the villagers who received a penny when they returned them full. Did Helmshore villagers, one wonders, have their own euphemism and announce coyly that they were 'going to earn a penny'? The cloth was then given a further washing.

Working conditions at the mill must have been far from ideal: the din of the water wheel, the pounding of the stocks, and the cramped space can still be experienced though, thankfully, the modern visitor doesn't have to put up with the stench of urine. The building itself, however, is a good honest piece of work – built of stone in 1789 with a slate roof, its stone-mullioned windows give it an appearance very similar to many Gloucestershire mills. Helmshore mill was built by the Turner family, whose excursions into the cotton industry will be dealt with in chapter 8 (see p. 144).

The fulled cloth was taken to the tenter field, where it was spread out to dry, suspended on tenter hooks, and the fields round the fulling mill were often bright with coloured cloths. Once dry, the last stages in the production were reached. The nap of the cloth was raised by stroking it with teazles set in a 'handle' – and, in fact, no better substitute for the naturally growing teazles was ever found for this job. Finally, the most skilled of all the cloth-workers, the shearers, cut the nap to provide the even, smooth-textured cloth needed by the tailors.

So, in reaching the state of finished cloth an enormous number of workers has been involved, even if one does not take into account the subsidiary workers – the men who moved the cloth around the countryside from one group of workers to the next, the iron-makers and wire-drawers who made the wire for the cards and scribbling frames, the teazle-growers, the mill-wrights and so on. John Haynes in his book *Great Britain's Glory* (1715) was one writer who marvelled at the numbers involved:

'I cannot forbear taking notice of the number of people employed in working a pack, or two hundred and forty pound weight of wool, into stuffs for the Spanish trade. . . . To make such a pack of long combing wool into fine stuffs, serges, sagathies, calamancoes, &c, would upon moderate computation, employ for one week three hundred and two persons, who will earn £43 10s, thus:

	£	s	d
7 Combers	3	10	0
Dyeing	5	0	0
250 Spinners	18	0	0
20 Throwers and Doublers	5	0	0
25 Weavers and Attendance	12	0	0
	£43	10	0

The west of England cloth was of a high quality, largely intended for the expanding home market, though some went for export to the

Levant or the East India Company. In the early eighteenth century there was little thought of competition from the north-east where the Yorkshire trade, although considerable, was in a far coarser cloth. But Defoe, in one of the best-known passages of his *Tour*, described the West Riding in the 1720s as an area of great industry and prosperity:

'We found the country, in short, one continued village, tho' mountainous every way, as before; hardly a house standing out of a speaking distance from another, and (which soon told us their business) the day clearing up, and the sun shining, we could see that at almost every house there was a tenter, and almost on every tenter a piece of cloth, or kersie, or shalloon, for they are the three articles of that country's labour; from which the sun glancing, and, as I may say, shining (the white reflecting its rays) to us, I thought it was the most agreeable sight that I ever saw, for the hills, as I say, rising and falling so thick, and the vallies opening sometimes one way, sometimes another, so that sometimes we could see two or three miles this way, sometimes so far another; sometimes like the streets near St Giles's, called the Seven Dials; we could see through the glades almost every way round us, yet look which way we would, high to the tops, and low to the bottoms, it was all the same; innumerable houses and tenters, and a white piece upon every tenter.'

He found, too, the cloth trade organized on rather different lines from those he had observed in the south-west, for here the master-manufacturer employed directly, controlling a large work force on what might be called a semi-domestic basis:

'Among the manufacturers' houses are likewise scattered an infinite number of cottages or small dwellings, in which dwell the workmen which are employed, the women and children of whom, are always busy carding, spinning, &c. so that no hands being un-employ'd, all can gain their bread, even from the youngest to the antient; hardly any thing above four years old, but its hands are sufficient to itself.

'This is the reson also why we saw so few people without doors; but if we knock'd at the door of any of the master-manufacturers, we presently saw a house full of lusty fellows, some at the dye-fat, some dressing the cloths, some in the loom, some one thing, some another, all hard at work, and full employed upon the manufacture, and all seeming to have sufficient business.'

Colonies such as Defoe described can still be found in the West Riding. At Almondbury, for example, a community that once stood in isolation on the moors above Huddersfield, but which has now been swallowed up by the spreading town, the close relationship between the master's house and the clustering workers' cottages can be very clearly seen (plate 7). The main house is stone-built, with carved decorations round its mullioned windows and on the gable ends, giving it an air of some opulence. The cottages round it are altogether plainer and the workmanship is much cruder. They must also have been quite cramped, for the loom shops with the familiar weavers' windows appear to have occupied the whole of the first floor, leaving only the ground floor for living space. Complete small industrial communities such as this are rare, though there are many examples of weavers' cottages in the valleys and on the hills round Huddersfield. In the Colne valley, there are rows of cottages where the weavers' windows indicate a continuous workshop running over the whole of a terrace. Some cottages have the continuous second-floor workshop but no direct access from the houses below. So the 'independent' weaver had to leave his home to go to work, even if his journey was no longer than from his front door, out into the street, and up a few steps to the workshop. At Golcar, a weaver's house and workshop have been preserved as a small museum.

Even a brief glance at these textile communities of the West Riding indicates a quite different working arrangement from that found in the south-west; something, in fact, much closer to the capitalist-worker relationship of the latter part of the century. If there is anyone combining the roles of farmer and textile-worker, then it is the master-manufacturer, not the weaver. It is not surprising, then, to find the kind of labour problems usually associated with nineteenth-century industry. John James in his *History of the Worsted Manufacture* (1857) quotes an anonymous pamphlet of 1741 on the Combers' Combinations:

'Our combers have for a number of years past, erected themselves into a sort of corporation (tho' without a charter), their first pretence was to take care of their poor brethren that should fall sick, or be out of work; and this was done by meeting once or twice a week, and each of them contributing two-pence or three-pence towards the box to make a bank, and when they became a little formidable, they gave laws to their masters, as to themselves, viz:– that no man should employ any comber that was not of their club, if he did, they agreed one and all not to work for him; and if he had employed twenty, they all of them turned-out, and often times were not satisfied with that, but would abuse the honest man that would labour, and in a riotous manner beat him, break his comb-pots, and destroy his working-tools. . . .'

In other words, the picture of a contented and entirely domestic industry existing before the new inventions revolutionized the scale and methods of textile production, comes a long way from being an accurate portrait.

The wool trade was of far greater importance than the cotton industry in this early period – 'cotton cloths' were, in fact, manufactured using linen yarn for the warp. The cloth made in this way was used as lining material for the clothes of the rich or as coarse fustian cloth for the poor. The expansion of the trade was held up by a number of factors – a shortage of the raw material which, unlike wool, had to be imported, the inability to spin a strong enough yarn to act as both warp and woof, and the slowness of the spinning process. Once these barriers were removed, the cotton industry took off in a spectacular flight of rising productivity. This process, which was central to the whole growth of eighteenth-century industry, is dealt with in a later chapter.

There was, however, one area of textile manufacture where mechanization had been established long before the eighteenth century – the hosiery industry. Towards the end of the sixteenth century, a young clergyman, the Reverend William Lee of Calverton near Nottingham, invented the stocking frame, a machine for knitting hosiery. There are a number of stories surrounding the invention: the most popular, if not the most likely, has the young curate courting a local lady who infuriated him by showing more interest in her knitting than in his passionate vows of undying love. Lee swore that he would make sure that, in future, young ladies would be forced to abandon their pernicious knitting that took their minds away from the serious business of romance, and set to work to build a machine that would do the knitting for them. He was successful and the first machine was completed in 1589. The basic knitting action of pushing threads through loops was performed by rows of hooks which could be made to open or close to either release or hold the thread. The components were held in a strong wooden frame which gave the machine its name 'stocking frame' and its operators the name 'framework-knitters'. The knitters sat in front of their machines and used both hands and feet to work it.

The stocking frame was destined to play an important role in the development of industry in the midlands, but not during the inventor's lifetime. Lee gave up the Church to develop his invention but proved no more fortunate in business than he had in love. He sought royal patronage, and Queen Elizabeth i came to see his work but refused him a patent, partly because she claimed it would throw the hand-knitters out of work and partly out of disappointment in finding the machine could only produce coarse woollen stockings and not the fine silk hose that might have aroused more enthusiasm in the potential patroness. Lee did eventually succeed in making silk stockings, but still received no patent. Disgusted, he left for France in 1603, taking with him workmen and nine frames, but found no greater success and died in poverty in 1610. James Lee, William's brother, came back to England and slowly the framework-knitting industry began to grow. In 1663, the knitters, who were mainly established in London, were granted their own Charter, which, among other clauses, specified how quality was to be preserved – the Society's deputies were empowered to enter any knitter's workshop and cut up any unsound goods and fine their manufacturer. An important clause limited the number of apprentices that might be employed by any master-knitter – an essential condition if adult workmen were not to be replaced by cheap child labour. Following the Charter, the knitters were incorporated as a Company in the City of London – which not only brought the pomp of gilded barges and sumptuous banquets, but introduced a new class of employer to the trade. These new employers had no previous connection with the industry, but bought their way into the Company for a hundred pounds. The apprentice rules were frequently breached, but no one paid much attention until the trade recession of the early eighteenth century brought widespread unemployment to the journeymen knitters. Gravener Henson, himself a knitter, wrote a history of the industry in 1831, and he described how angry knitters descended on the shop of a Mr Nicholson, where they found twelve apprentices working by candlelight. The men set to and smashed the frames. It was the beginning of the decline of the London trade, and also the beginning of a long history of oppression of the knitters, punctuated by outbreaks of framebreaking.

The decline of the London trade was followed by a move away from the capital, and the restrictive rules of the Charter and the Company. Henson reports that 'so great was the change that no less than eight hundred frames were brought from London to Nottingham, from the year 1732 to 1750 and sold for less than half price; a similar quantity had been removed to Leicester, whilst numbers were laid up as useless or were sold for old iron'. So the framework-knitting trade returned to the area from which it originated, and there it prospered. John Blackner, who wrote a history of Nottingham, claimed that at the time of writing, 1815:

'So much is this town dependant upon the engine, known by the name of the stocking frame, and its appendant machines, that, if it stood still, all other businesses must stand still also. The town may in fact be compared to one vast engine, whose every part is kept in motion by this masterpiece in the mechanic art.'

For the earlier period, he reported that whereas in 1641 there were only two stocking frames in Nottingham, by 1739 there were fifty framework-knitters, fourteen frame-smiths, twelve needle-makers, eight setters-up and five sinker-makers. By the end of the century, the industry had developed to such an extent that there were something like twenty thousand frames in Nottinghamshire and Leicestershire.

The organization of the midlands industry was mainly domestic, based on the putting-out system. The knitters gathered at the master's shop or warehouse to collect yarn, deliver the finished stockings and receive payments. In some few cases the knitters were employed directly in workshops, but the putting-out system continued right up to the twentieth century. Appropriately, one of the many villages where knitting was established was Calverton, where the Reverend Lee first worked on his invention. Many of the old knitters' cottages remain. Framework-knitting, like weaving, was an operation that required a good light working area, so the large window became the mark of the knitter's workshop just as it had of the weaver's. A terrace of such cottages, all that remains of Windles Square, can be seen in Calverton. The workrooms occupy most of the ground floor, and the very large windows at both front and back contrast strikingly with the minute openings in the rest of the cottage – with that much expense going into providing large workroom windows, economies had to be made elsewhere. Even with these large windows, there was not enough light to cover the whole of the long working day, and glass globes were hung near the frames to concentrate what light there was on to the work. There are other cottages in the village, but this row shows most clearly how work space dominated living space in the knitters' homes. Calverton also has an example of a knitters' workshop, in the building which is now a printer's. It is a simple two-storey building, having the same type of windows as the cottages (plate 10).

Although up to now we have been concentrating on textiles, the connections with other industries have been indicated. Iron, for example, was an important material in textile-working, used as wire for cards or for the hooks and other parts of the knitting frame and, of course, iron found many other uses in everyday life. Iron was needed to shoe horses that were the main carriers of goods and people, and for simple objects like nails, needles and tools. There was also a large demand for the metal from the military. It is also evident to us, looking back on the period, that iron was destined for an increasingly important role in the manufacture of machinery. But the iron industry at the beginning of the eighteenth century needed a major technological breakthrough if it was to be capable of expanding to meet the new demands.

Iron occurs naturally as an ore, from which the metal has to be extracted. This is done by heating to a high temperature with carbon in some form – if the metal that results from this process is free of carbon, it can be easily rolled, stretched and bent and is known as wrought iron, if some carbon remains, the resulting metal can only be used for casting, and is therefore known as cast iron; if too many impurities remain then the iron is useless. The first technological problem which was overcome many centuries ago was that of heating the metal and the carbon to a high enough temperature. At first, this was carried out in small hearths, where the wind was used to increase the temperature, but the resulting metal was still very impure and had to be beaten with a hammer to remove the slag. But already by the sixteenth century major improvements had been made. The hearth in which the ore was heated was made part of a much larger, and higher, structure, which could produce a stronger up-current of air. These were called 'bloomeries'. Later an even more powerful current of air was supplied by using bellows, powered by a water wheel, and the strength of the blast was impressive enough for these to be known as blast furnaces. This was a real breakthrough and represented an enormous increase in efficiency of iron production. It still, however, suffered from one very serious disadvantage: the only form of carbon that could be used as fuel in the furnaces and which would not introduce impurities was charcoal, and the supply of charcoal depended on the availability of timber. So we find iron-making flourishing in areas which possessed two natural resources, plenty of wood and plenty of water for the bellows. This gave a clear advantage to countries such as Sweden, and in Britain it meant that the early iron industry was found in areas which no longer have any connection with the industry, and often indeed have given up any connections at all with heavy industry. One such area was the Weald of Sussex which Defoe visited and commented on the problem which was vexing the iron-masters of the day:

'I had the curiosity to see the great foundaries, or iron-works, which are in this country, and where they are carry'd on at such a prodigious expence of wood, that even in a country almost all over-run with timber, they begin to complain of the consuming of it for those furnaces, and leaving the next age to want timber for building their navies.'

Defoe thought the complaint 'perfectly groundless', but the problem was a real one, and if there was to be any great expansion in iron production then it would have to be overcome. Another area of Britain which, today, seems even more remote from even the suggestion of industry is the beautiful wooded valley of the Wye. The area surrounding the romantic ruins of Tintern Abbey was one of the busiest iron-producing areas of the seventeenth century, and even in the next century it was still bustling with activity. Stebbing Shaw described the area as he found it in his *Tour of the West of England in 1788*:

'We now left the great road at the village of Turlington, and passed thro' hollow and uncouth tracks, seldom appointed by any carriage but those of the natives; after a few specimens of pleasing recluse scenery, we enter a profound dell for several miles; a gurgling brook winding thro' the umbrageous cavity which supplies a number of large iron works above the village of Abbey-Tintern: Mr Tanner is the ostensible manager; the Duke of Beaufort the great proprietor. We inspected the principal furnace, and saw the ore, which is mostly brought from that vast source, at Furness in Lancashire, dissolved by the blast of immense bellows, worked upon the modern construction of cylinder pumps. They have a method of separating the best quality from the dross, by a water wheel and hammers, from which they collect considerable quantities of pure metal, and the powder sells to the glass houses for their use. Lower down are various forges, for the purpose of striking this mutilated ore, into every requisite size and form of the broadest bars to the finest wires.'

The traces of this once active industry have all but disappeared back into the umbrageous cavities, but a few remains can still be found to form a standard of comparison for the changes that were to come. The Coed Ithel furnace, near Llandogo, is one of the finest examples of a seventeenth-century charcoal blast furnace to be seen today (plate II). It was built on a platform of ground, formed behind strong masonry walls. The outer cladding of the furnace has almost completely disappeared, revealing the curved walls of the furnace itself rising up from its hearth. In winter, the lines of the pit where the water wheel once turned can be seen, but in summer this is almost completely hidden by the undergrowth.

The manufacture of goods from the iron was still a largely local affair. There were extensive wire-works round the Tintern furnaces, but elsewhere the iron was worked in small individual forges and smithies, or even on the domestic scale, by the thousands of nail-makers, who hammered away in their own homes or in small work-shops. The main production was in wrought iron, but some cast iron was produced in the larger foundries, and it was in one of these that one of the vital developments of the history of industry occurred (see chapter 3).

The iron industry was by no means the only metal industry in Britain. In Cornwall, the mining of tin and copper had continued for centuries, and the tin trade was so important that it was regulated by its own sets of laws and rules – the Stannery Laws. Many early writers enthused over the great wealth of the industry. Richard Carew in his *Survey of Cornwall* of 1602 wrote:

'But why seeke wee in corners for pettie commodies, when as the onely mynerall of Cornish Tynne, openeth so large a field to the Countries benefit? this is in working so pliant, for sight so faire, and in use so necessarie, as thereby the inhabitants gaine wealth, the Merchants trafficke, and the whole Realme a reputation: and with such plentie thereof hath God stuffed the bowels of this little Angle, that it overfloweth England, watereth Christendome, and is de-rived to a great part of the world besides.'

He describes how the tin was recovered by 'streamworke', sifting the ore out of the hill streams and by 'Load' or underground workings. Of the workers underground, he writes:

'In most places, their toyle is so extreame, as they cannot endure it above four houres in a day, but are succeeded by spels: the residue of the time, they weave out at Coytes, Kayles, or like idle exercises. Their Kalendar also alloweth them more Holy-dayes, than are warranted by the Church, our lawes, or their own profit.'

The ore is brought to the surface – 'brought to grass' – broken by hammers and then pulverized under water-powered stamps, 'where three, and in some places sixe great logges of timber, bound at the ends with yron, and lifted up and downe by a wheel, driven with water, doe break it smaller'. The ore is then taken to the blowing houses for smelting – simple stone buildings with thatched roofs. Dust and ashes collected in the roof 'for which cause the owners doe once in seven or eight yeeres, burn those houses, and find so much of this light Tynne in the ashes, as payeth for the new building, with a gainfull overplus'.

By the time Celia Fiennes was visiting the tin mines almost a century later, the industry had expanded but already there was evidence of the problem that was to bedevil the Cornish miner as he pushed his shafts ever deeper – water. This was the scene near St Austell:

'There were at least twenty mines all in sight, which employs a great many people at work almost night and day, but constantly all and every day, including the Lord's Day, which they are forced to prevent their mines being overflowed with water. More than a thousand men are taken up about them; few mines but had then almost twenty men and boys attending it, either down in the mines digging and carrying the ore to the little bucket which conveys it up, or else others are attending the drawing up the ore in a sort of windlass as it is to a well.... They have a great labour and great expence to drain the mines of the water with mills that horses turn, and now they have the mills or water engines that are turned by the water which is conveyed on frames of timber and trunks to hold the water, which falls down on the wheels as an overshot mill... they do five times more good than the mills they use to turn with horses....

'Thence I went to ———, six good miles away, and passed by a hundred mines, some of which were at work, others that were lost by the waters overwhelming them.'

At the beginning of the century, the problem of water drowning out the mines was becoming acute. Long tunnels, or adits, were dug into hillsides to meet the shafts in order to act as drains, and elaborate systems of water-powered pumps were constructed. But in spite of all the activity the main impression is of an industry in a state of crisis. The old Stannery Laws were neglected – a 'Body of Tinners' petitioned in 1744 for a revival of the Stannery Parliament which they claimed had not met for thirty-one years and for a restoration of tinners' rights which were 'become precarious and uncertain, and in great Danger of being lost'. The main difficulty, though, was the rising costs of mining which the petitioners felt was now so desperate that 'the working and searching for Tin, in deep Mines especially, is in great Danger of being discontinued'.

Like many other industries, progress in tin- and copper-mining was dependent on some form of technological breakthrough. The same was certainly true of other mineral mines – the Derbyshire lead mine described by Defoe hardly sounds like a modern, progressive industrial concern.

'We went ... to a valley on the side of a rising hill, where there were several grooves, so they call the mouth of the shaft or pit by which they go down into a lead mine; and as we were standing still to look at one of them, admiring how small they were, and scarce believing a poor man that shew'd it us, when he told us, that they went down those narrow pits or holes to so great a depth in the earth; I say, while we were wondering, and scarce believing the fact, we were agreeably surprized with seeing a hand, and then an arm, and quickly after a head, thrust up out of the very groove we were looking at. It was the more surprizing as not we only, but not the man that we were talking to, knew any thing of it, or expected it.

'Immediately we rode closer up to the place, where we see the poor wretch working and heaving himself up gradually, as we thought, with difficulty; but when he shewed us that it was by setting his feet upon pieces of wood fixt cross the angles of the groove like a ladder, we found that the difficulty was not much; and if the groove had been larger they could not either go up or down so easily, or with so much safety, for that now their elbow resting on those pieces as well as their feet, they went up and down with great ease and safety ... the man was a most uncouth spectacle; he was cloathed all in leather, had a cap of the same without brims, some tools in a little basket which he drew up with him, not one of the names of which we could understand but by the help of an interpreter. Nor indeed could we understand any of the man's discourse so as to make out a whole sentence; and yet the man was pretty free of his tongue too.

'For his person, he was lean as a skeleton, pale as a dead corps, his hair and beard a deep black, his flesh lank, and, as we thought, something of the colour of the lead itself, and being very tall and very lean he look'd, or we that saw him ascend *ab inferis*, fancied he look'd like an inhabitant of the dark regions below, and who was just ascended into the world of light.

'Besides his basket of tools, he brought up with him about three-quarters of a hundred weight of oar, which we wondered at, for the man had no small load to bring, considering the manner of his coming up; and this indeed made him come heaving and struggling up, as I said at first, as if he had great difficulty to get out.'

Defoe found the condition of the miner's family even more start-ling, for they had no house to live in, only a cave among the rocks:

'There was a large hollow cave, which the poor people by two cur-tains hang'd cross, had parted into three rooms. On one side was the chimney, and the man, or perhaps his father, being miners, had found means to work a shaft or funnel through the rock to carry the smoke out at the top.... The habitation was poor, 'tis true, but things within did not look so like misery as I expected. Every thing was clean and neat, tho' mean and ordinary: there were shelves with earthen ware, and some pewter and brass. There was, which I observed in particular, a whole flitch or side of bacon hanging up by the chimney, and by it a good piece of another. There was a sow and pigs running about at the door, and a little lean cow feeding upon a green place just before the door, and the little enclosed piece of ground I mentioned, was growing with good barley; it being then near harvest.'

Defoe questioned the woman, and discovered that her husband earned a mere fivepence a day as a miner, and though she helped out when she could by washing the ore, she only contributed a

ool-drying tower at Frogmarsh mill, Woodchester

2 *Above* The broad loom with Kay's flying shuttle. The handle hanging down in the centre of the frame has strings attached leading to the pickers at either end of the shuttle board

Weavers' cottages: 3 *Above right* Town cottages in Duke Street, Trowbridge; 4 *Right* Small workshop attached to a cottage in Dilton Marsh

5 *Above* Scottish weavers' cottages at Torbex, Stirlingshire

6 *Below* The planned village of Kirkpatrick, Durham, built round an old weaving community

7 *Above* A working unit:
clothier's house and weavers'
cottages at Almondsbury near
Huddersfield
Helmshore higher mill:
8 *Right* The water wheel;
9 *Far right* The massive
fulling stocks

10 *Above* Framework knitters'
workshop at Calverton – the
Dovey Workshop

11 *Above* The Causey
Arch: the world's
oldest railway bridge
12 *Left* Abandoned co
chaldrons by the staith
at Seaham harbour
13 *Right* The engine
house for the New-
comen-type engine at
Elsecar colliery: part
of the engine's beam
can be seen with pump
rods attached

14 *Far left* The open-topped cylinder of the atmospheric engine at Elsecar colliery

The charcoal-smelting iron furnace at Bonawe: 15 *Above* The division between furnace and charge house can be clearly seen; 16 *Left* The wheel pit

17 *Below* A small beginning to a great enterprise – the bellied pots produced at Coalbrookdale
18 *Above right* The lintel of the old furnace at Coalbrookdale, under which the first coke-smelted iron poured
19 *Below left* From cooking pots to railways, the changes at Coalbrookdale mark the advance of the industrial revolution

20 *Above* The excavated remains of the
Bedlam furnaces
21 *Right* The vertical blowing engine in its
engine house by the site of the blast
furnaces at the Blists Hill Industrial
Museum

Textile machinery at Helmshore higher
mill: 22 *Above left* The spinning jenny;
23 *Below left* Arkwright's water frame
Cromford: 24 *Above* Part of Arkwright's
original mill; 25 *Right* One of the sturdy
terraced houses in North Row, with a
second-floor workshop

North mill, Belper : 26
Above the attic, once also
serving as school room fo
factory children. The flo
throughout this fireproof
mill are, as here, brick
27 *Left* The base of the
structure, the gigantic st
blocks in the basement w
support the iron pillars a
brick arches

further threepence – the man, wife and the five children had to be supported on a maximum of eightpence a day.

Like the miners of Cornwall, the miners of Derbyshire have worked the ore beneath their feet for centuries. 'T'owd man', as later generations called the early miner, can be seen depicted in a carving in Wirksworth Church. This shows the miner with his pick and kibble, the basket he used for carrying the ore, and is believed to date from the twelfth century.

While it is true that the Derbyshire mines were often operated by individuals or small groups, nevertheless there were significant technical advances in the industry which required far more capital than Defoe's poor wretch could ever have mustered. In the seventeenth century the problem of draining the mines, which beset most mining operations, was tackled by building extensive adits, referred to in Derbyshire as soughs. The first of these appears to be the Longhead Sough, driven in the 1630s under the direction of the famous Dutch engineer, Cornelius Vermuyden. By the eighteenth century the mining area was riddled by these tunnels, the most impressive of which stretched for miles under the hills. One of the more important soughs, Hillcar Sough, ran for nearly four miles before reaching its outflow above the river Derwent. The stone arch marking the end of the sough can still be found in Hillcar Woods at Darley Dale.* There is a certain interest in tracing the outflows of these old soughs, but simply finding the exit point gives no idea of the great engineering skill and even greater surveying skill that went into their construction. Exploration of soughs and other underground workings is strictly a job for the experts, but gives a unique understanding of the problems met by the miners and the skills they used to help overcome them. The other factor of importance in the construction of soughs was the cost involved, which was very considerable. As with the Cornish mines, the lead mines were in need of new techniques.

One major factor affected all industries – transport. Any expansion of trade depended to a large extent on the ability to move goods efficiently and at a reasonable cost. Neither condition was met in the early part of the eighteenth century to any great extent. The two

*A very full description of the Derbyshire soughs can be found in Frank Nixon's *Industrial Archaeology of Derbyshire* (1969).

main forms of transport were overland by the highways or pack-horse routes, or on water by the river and coastal routes. Of the two alternatives, transport by water was the more efficient. Celia Fiennes noted, for example, that on the Severn there were 'many Barges that were tow'd up by strength of men six or eight at a tyme', and at Gloucester she found 'a very Large good Key on the river'. The Severn was in fact one of the major trading routes of the country, and Bristol a port second only to London. Work on improving river navigation, to enable barges such as those seen by Celia Fiennes to penetrate deeper and deeper into the heart of the country, had begun long before the start of the eighteenth century. On the Wey Naviga-tion, for example, built from Weybridge to Guildford between 1651 and 1653 by Sir Richard Weston, we can already see all the new techniques of navigation improvement being used. There are ten locks used to overcome the fall of the river, and four weirs, and the seventeen-mile navigation contains no less than seven miles of arti-ficial cutting, dug in order to avoid particularly difficult sections of the river. Eighteenth-century river improvement saw even more impressive engineering work – for example, on the Aire and Calder Navigation in Yorkshire, still a busy commercial route, and the Kennet Navigation from Newbury to Reading. The latter route had to deal with a fall of one hundred and thirty-eight feet in an eighteen-and-a-half mile route, an average of seven foot for every mile. This involved the construction of eighteen locks, which are most unusual in having turf sides instead of the more usual brick or masonry.

These river improvements were an important contribution to the general improvement of transport, but still left a great deal to be done. Whole areas of central Britain were untouched by the changes, and even the improved areas suffered from severe disadvantages. Moving from one privately owned navigation to another was often difficult, because of the intense rivalries between the different con-cerns. William Darvall of Maidenhead tried to take Thames barges on to the Kennet in 1725 and received this alarming reaction from the local bargemen:

'Mr Darvall wee Bargemen of Redding thought to Aquaint you before 'tis too Late, Dam You. if y. work a bote any more at

Newbery wee will Kill You if ever you come any more this way, wee was very near shooting you last time, we went with to pistolls and not too Minnets too Late. The first time your Boat Lays at Redding Loaded, Dam You, wee will bore holes in her and sink her so Dont come to starve our fammeleys and our Masters... so take warning before 'tis too late for Dam you for ever if you come wee will doo it – from wee Bargemen.'

More important than such dramatic, but comparatively rare, confrontations between boatmen, were the many complaints that the owners of the Navigations were abusing their monopoly position by overcharging for freight and neglecting to keep the channel dredged and locks and wharfs in good repair.

The coastal route was of obvious importance, but also suffered from a number of disadvantages, most importantly the dependence on the weather – storms and unfavourable winds could keep boats tied up in harbour for weeks. Serious disruptions could be expected in wartime, when apart from the risk of attack, merchant ships could be requisitioned by the government in an apparently arbitrary manner – and the sailors who manned them were also liable to be 'requisitioned' by the infamous press gangs.

If the movement of goods by water presented difficulties, the movement by land must often have seemed impossible. Road maintenance was the responsibility of local parishes, under a system that was set up in the Middle Ages. A surveyor of roads was appointed by the parish to maintain the section of the road that fell within the parish boundaries – and to get the work performed he could call on the men of the parish to perform their Statute Duty of six days' work each year. Not surprisingly, the system failed abysmally. John Hawkins described how he found it to work in practice in *Observations on the State of the Highways* (1763):

'Let us now see in what Manner the Law at present under Consideration is observed in those few Parishes, where the Inhabitants are disposed to yield obediance to the Letter of it; the Days for performing the Statute Duty are so far from being considered as Days of Labour, that as well the Farmers as the common Day-Labourers, have long been used to look on them as Holidays, as a kind of Recess from their accustomed Labour, and devoted to Idleness and its concomitant Indulgences of Riot and Drunkenness.'

The surveyor could, in theory, collect money instead of labour from the parishioners and use it to hire labourers, but all too often by the time he had eased the necessary funds from the parishioners' purses 'the wet Weather sets in, and there is an End of Road-Work for that Year'. To compound the difficulties, the surveyor usually knew little or nothing of road-building anyway, and Hawkins describes the scene of inept surveyor accompanied by his unwilling work force as 'a Contest between Ignorance armed with Authority on the one Side, and invincible Obstinacy on the other'. It is not too surprising then to find travellers such as Defoe complaining of the state of the roads on which they travelled – in fact the only surprise is that anyone managed to travel anywhere at all. Past Dunstable, on the way to Nottingham, for example, he found that

'you enter the deep clays, which are so surprisingly soft, that it is perfectly frightful to travellers, and it has been the wonder of foreigners, how, considering the great numbers of carriages which are continually passing with heavy loads, those ways have been made practicable; indeed the great numbers of horses every year kill'd by the excess of labour in those heavy ways, has been such a charge to the country, that new building of causeways, as the Romans did of old, seems to be a much easier expence.'

The pack-horse routes, which formed vital links in the commercial traffic of the country, were little more than rough tracks, but, by keeping as far as possible to hill tops and other dry stretches, they at least contrived to keep reasonably clear of the cloying mud and filth of the valleys. Many of these old routes can be followed, for example in the Pennines where the lines of the tracks can be seen high on the moorlands, only occasionally sweeping steeply down to some town or village. Looking down at Hebden Bridge, from Heptonstall, for example, the pack-horse route is clearly seen leading right down to the pack-horse bridge across the river (plate xxi). These routes were quite satisfactory for carrying goods such as wool or cloth, but were of no help in moving heavier commodities as they were unusable by carts and waggons. The answer, for improving the road system, was for Parliament to empower individuals or small groups to construct roads at their own expense and then charge travellers for the use of them. These road-builders were the Turnpike Trusts, who first began construction work in the seventeenth century. Initially, however, they met so much opposition from local travellers objecting to the tolls, that a century went by before the great age of turnpike-building really got under way (see chapter 5).

The major problem that even improved roads failed to solve was the provision of suitable transport for the bulk commodities essential to the development of an industrial revolution, and of these commodities the most important was coal, the fuel of the revolution.

2

Coal and the Miner's Friend

The development of the coal industry, which was crucial to the industrial revolution, hardly began in any large way at all until the sixteenth century. Its earlier use was so little known in some parts of Europe that Aeneas Sylvius, who visited Scotland in the middle of the fifteenth century as papal legate, was astonished to see the poor people begging for 'black stones'. By the end of the sixteenth century, no one would have been baffled by the sight of coal, which was well established as the most important domestic fuel in towns, and was beginning to find uses in industry.

The earliest coal mines had done little more than dip under the surface of the ground. Some workings were in the form of drift mines, tunnels dug horizontally into a hillside – a type of working still to be seen in the small, independent mines of the Forest of Dean. Other mines were worked by sinking a short shaft into the coal seam, and then working steadily out from that until the miners decided there was danger of a cave-in, when they would abandon that shaft and sink another. This type of working was called a bell pit, from the bell-like shape of the space cleared out around the main shaft. These workings have long been abandoned, but the bell pits have left behind distinctive scars on the landscape, in the form of round humps, marking the spoil thrown up from the pit, with slight dips in the centre where the shaft was sunk. Whole areas have been marked in this way – a characteristic of coal-mining areas was and is the mess left behind by the need to dump the unwanted spoil that has to be cleared to get at the coal. Bell-pit remains can be seen, for example, in the Scottish coal fields – one prominent set being at Muirkirk in Ayrshire. Later this method was replaced by the 'pillar and stall' method, in which the miners cut away at the coal, leaving large pillars of it as supports. This was the technique which Celia Fiennes found in use when her excellently curious mind led her to enquire into the workings of a mine:

> 'Here we entered Derbyshire and Went to Chesterfield 6 mile, and Came by ye Coale mines where they were digging. They make their mines at ye Entrance like a Well and so till they Come to ye Coale, then they digg all the Ground about where there is Coale and set pillars to support it, and so bring it to ye well where by a basket Like a hand barrow by Cords they pull it up – so they let down and up the Miners with a Cord.'

The actual mining methods were comparatively crude – the majority of the work was done using simple hand tools, and where extensive areas of rock were met, they were usually broken up by the old method of fire-setting, lighting fires to heat the rock and then throwing on cold water so that the sudden contraction would crack it. The need for an improvement in these primitive techniques was pressing, for there was a steadily growing demand for coal, particularly from the capital. This demand was largely met from the great coal fields around Newcastle upon Tyne – not because they were necessarily the easiest mines to work, nor because they could produce the best coal, but because they were best situated for transport to London. The river Tyne was thick with the massed ships of the colliery trade, and the association between Newcastle and the coal trade was so firmly established that the phrase 'sending coals to Newcastle' passed into the language as a description of an entirely pointless activity. Defoe described the area as he found it in the 1720s:

> 'From hence the road to Newcastle gives a view of the inexhausted store of coals and coal pits, from whence not London only, but all the south part of England is continually supplied; and whereas when we are at London, and see the prodigious fleets of ships which

come constantly in with coals for this encreasing city, we are apt to wonder whence they come, and that they do not bring the whole country away; so, on the contrary, when in this country we see the prodigious heaps, I might say mountains, of coals, which are dug up at every pit, and how many of those pits there are; we are filled with equal wonder to consider where the people should live that can consume them.'

Other areas contributed to the growing stocks of coal and, in Scotland, the area round the Firth of Forth rivalled Tyneside for output. Gradually the methods of finding, winning and shifting the coal began to improve – for when it was clear that money was to be made from coal, then money began to be invested in coal. Some of the money went into improvements at existing collieries, some into speculative forays; it was not uncommon to find an eighteenth-century gentleman testing for the possibilities of mineral wealth beneath his parks and fields. John Holland in *Fossil Fuel* (1835) quotes a writer of that period on the delights of test-boring: 'Of all branches of business, of all the experiments that a man of sensibility can be employed in, or attend to, there is perhaps none so amusing, so engaging, and delightful as a successful trial upon the vestigia or appearance of a seam of coal.' Holland comments wryly: 'He should have added that the mortifications attendant on disappointment are often proportionately trying.'

Underground working developed from the old cavernous bell pits into a series of ever-extended galleries as the miners followed the coal seams. This brought added labour and danger to the already hard and dangerous life of the collier. As the face moved farther from the shaft, so the distance the hewn coal had to be hauled increased and so also the problem of ventilation became more critical. The incidence of 'choke damp' which suffocated and 'fire damp' which exploded became more common. Roger North, quoted in Robert Galloway's *History of Coal Mining in Great Britain* (1882), described the situation in the north of England in 1676:

'Damps or foul air kill insensibly; sinking another pit that the air may not stagnate is an infallible remedy. They are most affected in very hot weather. An infallible trial is by a dog, and the candles show it. They seem to be very heavy sulphurous airs, not fit to breathe, and I have heard some say that they would sometimes lie in the midst of a shaft and the bottom be clear.'

The immediate answer to choke damps was, as North describes, to sink more shafts, but it was soon discovered that a more economical solution was to provide a flow of air through the workings. The simplest way of achieving this was to sink a second shaft and light a fire at its foot, creating a strong up-draught that sucked fresh air down the main shaft and along the galleries. The treatment of fire damp was considerably more alarming. Once fire damp was discovered, the fireman was sent for. Covered in sackcloth soaked in water, he crawled along on his stomach until he reached the pocket of gas. He then stuck a candle at the end of a pole, lit it and pushed it forwards towards the gas. The resultant explosion, in theory at least, passed over the prone fireman without harming him. The risk of explosions from fire damp was great, since the nature of the damp was not understood and miners continued to work using naked flame for light. In some areas particularly prone to fire damp, other methods of illumination were tried, including the use of the luminescent glow from putrefying fish – a cure that must have come close to being as unpalatable as the disease.

The working conditions in the mines were bad and, in Scotland, they were atrocious. Until 1775 the Scottish colliers were *ascripti glebae*, that is they were considered part and parcel of the colliery where they worked. Robert Bald described their situation in *A General View of the Coal Trade of Scotland* (1812):

'They belonged to the estate or colliery where they were born and continued to work and from it neither they nor their children could remove; so much so, that when an estate with a colliery came to be sold, the colliers and their families formed part of the inventory or livestock, and were valued as such; in short, they were bought and sold as slaves.'

Bald goes on to describe their actual work:

'It appears that in working the Scotch coal, which is very strong in the wall, it requires such constant exertion and twisting of the body, that, unless a person have been habituated to it from his earliest years, he cannot submit to the operation. For instance, it is a common practice for a collier, when making a horizontal cut in that part of the coal which is upon a level with his feet, to sit down and place his right shoulder upon the inside of his right knee; in this posture he will work long, and with good effect. At other times, he works sitting with his body half inclined to the one side, or stretched out his whole length, in seams of coal not thirty inches thick.'

The work of women in carrying the coal was an abomination that continued in Scottish pits right up to the time that Bald wrote in the early nineteenth century:

'In those collieries where this mode is in practice, the collier leaves his house for the pit about eleven o'clock at night, (attended by his sons, if he has any sufficiently old), when the rest of mankind are retiring to rest. Their first work is to prepare coals, by hewing them down from the wall. In about three hours after, his wife, (attended by her daughters, if she has any sufficiently grown) sets out for the pit, having previously wrapped her infant child in a blanket, and left it to the care of an old woman, who, for a small gratuity, keeps three or four children at a time, and who, in their mother's absence, feeds them with ale or whisky mixed with water. The children who are a little more advanced, are left to the care of a neighbour; and under such treatment, it is surprising that they ever grow up or thrive.

'The mother having thus disposed of her younger children, descends the pit with her older daughters, when each, having a basket of a suitable form, lays it down, and into it the large coals are rolled; and such is the weight carried, that it frequently takes two men to lift the burden upon their backs: the girls are loaded according to their strength. The mother sets out first, carrying a lighted candle in her teeth; the girls follow, and in this manner they proceed to the pit bottom, and with weary steps and slow, ascend the stairs, halting occasionally to draw breath, till they arrive at the hill or pit top, where the coals are laid down for sale; and in this manner they go for eight or ten hours almost without resting. It is no uncommon thing to see them, when ascending the pit, weeping most bitterly, from the excessive severity of the labour; but the instant they have laid down their burden on the hill, they resume their cheerfulness, and return down the pit singing.

'The execution of work performed by a stout woman in this way is beyond conception. For instance, we have seen a woman, during the space of time above mentioned, take on a load of at least 170 lbs avoirdupois, travel with this 150 yards up the slope of the coal below ground, ascend a pit by stairs 117 feet, and travel upon the hill 20 yards more to where the coals are laid down. All this she will perform no less than twenty-four times as a day's work.'

The worst treatment of all was that handed out to the 'Framed Bearers' or 'Fremit Bearers', that is the women who were not related to the miners whose coals they carried.

'These are at the disposal of the oversman below ground, and he appoints them to carry coals for any person he thinks proper, so that they sometimes have a new master every day: this is slavery complete; and when an unrelenting collier takes an ill-natured fit, he oppresses the bearer with such heavy loads of coal, as are enough to break, not only the spirit, but the back of any human being. . . .

'In surveying the workings of an extensive colliery below ground, a married woman came forward, groaning under an excessive weight of coals, trembling in every nerve, and almost unable to keep her knees from sinking under her. On coming up, she said in a most plaintive and melancholy voice: "O Sir, This is sore, sore work. I wish to God that the first woman who tried to bear coals had broke her back, and none would have tried it again." '

Some of this wretched work was eased in the early eighteenth-century pits when horse-gins or whim-gins came into use for raising coal from the foot of the shaft. The horse-gin was a simple machine, in which a horse, walking round a circular track, was used to turn a heavy wooden drum. Ropes fastened round the drum then passed to pulleys placed over the shaft, and as the drum turned, so the ropes could be used to lower or raise weights in the shaft. Soon the gin became the main surface feature to be seen in a mining area, but very few have survived to the present day. One of these machines, however, remained in use in the Nottingham coal field right up to the twentieth century, and when its days were finally ended it was dismantled, restored and re-erected at Nottingham's Industrial Museum at Wollaton Hall.

The photograph of the Nottingham gin (plate III) clearly shows the different features of the machine. The shafts for the horse can be seen at one end of the main horizontal beam that passes through the central drum, the circular track is marked and the pulleys can be seen above the top of the shaft. The photograph also conveys a great deal of the fascination which these old machines still exercise – the starkness of their outlines and the basic simplicity of the purely mechanical principles on which they operate make them easy to 'read'. No special instruction is required to understand their working, in contrast to most modern machines where only the expert in, say, electronics can make any sense of a complicated mesh of circuitries. Machines such as the horse-gin impress us by their scale and their functional simplicity, and it requires very little imagination to see the even greater impact they must have had on the scenery of the mining districts where they once stood astride countless pit-heads.

The greatest improvement in the transport of coal came with the introduction of railways, which came into general use in the north-eastern coal fields in the late seventeenth century. Roger North wrote of the Newcastle collieries in 1676:

'Another thing that is remarkable is their way-leaves, for when men have pieces of ground between the colliery and the river, they sell leave to lead coals over their ground, and so dear that the owner of a rood of ground will expect 20*L*, per annum for this leave. The manner of the carriage is by laying rails of timber from the colliery down to the river, exactly straight and parallel, and bulky carts are made with four rowlets fitting these rails, whereby the carriage is so easy that one horse will draw down four or five chaldrons of coals, and is an immense benefit to coal merchants.'

These early railways, or tramways, as they came to be known, soon spread throughout the colliery districts. It is hardly necessary to stress their importance to future transport developments, but it is often surprising to find that the construction of these early tramways involved quite considerable engineering works, not to mention a considerable expense. The builders of the Tanfield Tramway in the 1720s, for example, had to take their tramway over the Houghwell Burn, where it cuts through a deep and heavily wooded valley. They called in a local mason, Ralph Wood, who designed a single, graceful arch with a 103 foot span to carry the four-foot gauge wooden tramway. Today the Causey Arch, as it is generally known, enjoys the distinction of being the world's oldest railway bridge. This majestic span – which is difficult to find and, once found, difficult to see – is a plain, unadorned structure, and given its impressive scale and delightful setting is in need of no adornment (plate 11). It is, however, evident that if such a structure was considered economical, then the early railways must have made an immense contribution to the growth of the north-eastern coal fields. Indeed it is doubtful if the coal fields could have spread as they did without this efficient communications system to link them to the ports. Even then, Sir Frederick Eden noted in his Parochial Reports on *The State of the Poor* (1797) that many of the Tanfield collieries were unprofitable and that many had closed: 'The great length and expense of coal roads (several of the mines being six or seven miles distant from the Tyne) are heavy drawbacks.' But Eden reported two thousand inhabitants in Tanfield, most of whom were employed in the coal industry.

The termini of the north-eastern tramways were the coal ports, and there too a distinctive system developed – the coal staithes. Waggons, or chaldrons, ran out over high wooden piers above the wharfs, and from there coal-drops could be swung out over the ships, allowing the coals to fall straight down chutes into the holds. The staithes and coal-drops of Newcastle and Sunderland were once famous and impressive sites which have now gone. Seaham Harbour retained its coal-drops until quite recently, but although the original drops have gone – one has been dismantled and stored for re-erection at an industrial museum – there are still modern staithes at Seaham, and some of the old wooden chaldrons have been left behind. The photograph (plate 12) shows two of these chaldrons, and in the background, looking not unlike part of a roller-coaster are the modern staithes. A feature to note on the old chaldrons are the enormous levers of the hand brakes, which operated directly against the outer rim of the wheels.

The main obstacle to progress in mining was water, and various methods were tried for removing it from the workings. Adits and soughs, such as those already described for Cornish and Derbyshire mines, were dug. The Preston Grange colliery, near Edinburgh, for example, was drained by an adit that discharged 220 gallons a minute into the Firth of Forth, but even that rate proved insufficient and the workings were drowned out in 1746. Construction of adits represented a high expense for the mineowners and an abominable task for the workmen, as John Holland recorded:

'Few operations can be conceived more unpleasant and dangerous to the workmen, than the execution of these adits, especially when, as is sometimes the case, they are barely wide enough to allow the sinker to creep along. The dangers which are created by blasting the solid rocks with gunpowder in such confined spaces, will be easily conceived.'

The pumps that were installed to lift the water to the surface or to the level of an adit involved increasingly elaborate arrangements. The most remarkable of the seventeenth-century pumping systems was that of the Ravensworth colliery on the Tyne, where the simple chain and bucket pumps were arranged in three stages, each being powered by its own water wheel. All three wheels were moved by water from the same stream, the first wheel being raised above the level of the ground on pillars, the water from that falling on to the second wheel at ground level, and then finally passing to a third wheel below the surface. By constructing such a complex system, the miners were able to get down to a depth of two hundred and fifty feet. But there were limits to the use of adits and chain pumps for drainage, and as the demand for coal grew so the search for improved drainage methods became more intense. The solution to the problem was not only of vital importance to the whole of the mining industry, but marked one of the great turning points in the history of the world.

The first steps towards the eventual solution came in the labora-tories of the scientists of the seventeenth century, who worked on a number of possibilities for constructing 'engines that would use fire to raise water'. The basis for the research was the idea that if a vacuum could be created inside a suitable chamber, then water would be sucked in to fill the vacuum and could then be forced out again using steam or hot air. The scientists had no difficulties over the theoretical basis of such an engine, but were invariably defeated by their inability to match the theory to technological possibilities. In 1698, however, Captain Savery of the Royal Engineers took out a patent for a 'fire engine', and to show that he was very well aware of the practical value of his work, he headed his application for the patent 'The Miner's Friend', and attached this address to 'The Gentlemen Adventurers in the Mines of England':

> 'I am very sensible a great many among you do as yet look on my invention of raising water by the impellant force of fire a useless sort of a project that never can answer my designs or pretensions; and that it is altogether impossible that such an engine as this can be wrought underground and succeed in the raising of water, and dreining your mines, so as to deserve any incouragement from you. I am not very fond of lying under the scandal of a bare projector, and therefore present you here with a draught of my machine, and lay before you the uses of it, and leave it to your consideration whether it is worth your while to make use of it or no....
>
> 'For draining of mines and coal pits, the use of the engine will sufficiently recommend itself in raising water so easie and cheap, and I do not doubt that in a few years it will be a means of making our mining trade, which is no small part of the wealth of this kingdome, double if not treble to what it now is.'

Savery's engine had two cylinders, which were alternately filled with steam, which was then condensed, creating a partial vacuum. Air pressure then forced the water into the cylinder, and more steam, at a high pressure, was used to force the water out again towards the surface. This design suffered from a number of serious disadvantages: the engine had to be built underground, it required a great deal of steam and thus a great deal of fuel, and the pressure of steam needed to force out the cold water was high enough to make the problem of exploding boilers something more than a mere possibility. Nevertheless, however inefficient the Savery engine might have been, it did work, and as is often the case it was soon followed by a far more efficient, and more important, successor – Thomas Newcomen's atmospheric engine.

The first Newcomen engine was erected at a pit near Dudley Castle in Staffordshire in 1712. It was credited to both Savery and Newcomen, but the former's only claim to its design came from his establishment of the earlier patent, which was framed so loosely as to cover every possible use of fire or steam to lift water. The new engine replaced Savery's two cylinders by a single cylinder and piston. The piston was attached by chains to one end of a massive wooden beam, pivoted at its centre, to the other end of which were attached pump rods that went down the mine shaft. Steam was admitted to the cylinder, and then condensed by spraying with cold water. This produced a partial vacuum, and air pressure acted on the top of the piston to push it down into the cylinder, hence the name 'atmospheric engine' usually given to these machines. Once a position of equilibrium was reached between the pressure in the cylinder and the external pressure, then the weight of the pump rods would drag down the other end of the beam, the piston would come up and the whole cycle could be re-started. So the beam rocked up and down, moved alternately by the rods and the piston, and as it rocked, so the rods were moved up and down in the shaft to produce the pumping action.

Newcomen's success was greatly aided by his own ability in handling metals, for he was trained as a blacksmith. This illustrates one of the recurring themes of the industrial revolution – the contribution made by the craftsman-inventor. But, at the same time, one must not forget that Newcomen's work was possible because scientists had already investigated the phenomenon of the vacuum. We do not know to what extent Newcomen himself was directly aware of the work of the scientists, who were so gravely hampered by their lack of practical experience in construction – even the experienced blacksmith, Newcomen, found great difficulty in fitting the piston to the cylinder with any great accuracy. Nevertheless, Newcomen was able to build well enough to put into practice what had previously remained as theory in learned treatises.

The Newcomen engine possessed great advantages in comparison with the Savery engine. In the first place it did not require the use of high-pressure steam, which meant that simple boilers could be used with very little risk of explosion. Then, because it used rods to 'pull' the water to the surface, instead of pressure to 'push' it, the engine could be built above instead of below ground. Lastly, it was simple both to construct and to use, for the engine builders soon realized that by hanging rods from different parts of the beams, the motion of the beam could be used to move the rods up and down and so automatically close the different valves in the correct sequence. Its main disadvantage was that because the cylinder had to be alternately heated and cooled, it was an extravagant user of fuel. But this was of no great importance for a machine intended for use in a coal field where the shortage of fuel was, in the nature of things, hardly likely to be a problem. Cheap fuel, unsuitable for other uses, was quite good enough to keep a boiler fire burning.

The use of Newcomen engines spread rapidly through the coal fields of Britain. By 1725, the engine was so well known that it was considered a suitable subject for a riddle or 'Prize Aenigma' in *The Ladies' Diary*. The author begins with a truly excruciating couplet referring back to early experiments with the vacuum:

> 'I sprang, like Pallas, from a fruitful Brain,
> About the Time of Charles the Second's Reign'

and continues with what must surely be the first poetic description of a steam beam engine:

> 'On mighty Arms, alternately I bear
> Prodigious Weights of Water and of Air.'

By this time the use of the engine had also spread to Scotland. Engines were built under licence as recorded for one erected at Edmonstone colliery in Midlothian in 1725, where the licence was 'granted by the *Committee* in London, appointed and authorized by the *Proprietors* of the *Invention* for raising *Water* by *Fire*, to Andrew Wauchope of *Edmonstone*, Esquire'. The royalty to be paid was set at £80 per annum for eight years. The machine was ready for use in July 1727 at a final cost to the colliery of £1,007 11s 4d, carefully itemized by the accountants, who noted everything from 'To a cilinder 29 inches diameter, with workmanship, carried to London and all other charges and expences, £250', to 'Two copper pipes – £0–8–0' and 'To post letters – £0–1–0'.

The engineers, the Potters, who came to erect the engine, were kept on at a salary of £200 per annum, very handsome for the time, and once the initial costs of the engine were cleared they were to receive half the profits. But that confidence in this new and still slightly mysterious machine was less than complete is clear from a clause in the agreement that specified that:

'In case, by any unforseen accident, it shall happen, that the said engine shall not be able to draw the water, and make it a going work, then it shall be in the power of the said Jno. and Abr. Potters, to take away all such materialls as shall be furnished by them, and the said Mr Jas Smith shall only be lyable to pay them a reasonable allowance for their pains and charges in repairing the engine.'

The effect of the steam engine on the Scottish coal industry – and the statement was equally applicable to the industry of England and Wales – was summarized by Robert Bald:

'The steam engine produced a new era in the mining and commercial interests of Britain, and as it were in an instant put every coal field, which was considered as lost, within the grasp of its owner. Collieries were opened in every district, and such has been the astonishing effect produced by this machine, that great coal was shipping free on board, in the river Forth, in the year 1785, at 4s 10d. per ton, that is, after a period of seventy years, coals had only advanced 2d. per ton, while the price of labour, and all materials, was doubled.'

Bald quotes the relevant wage figures, which ranged in 1715 from 6d a day for labourers to 14d a day for colliers. These figures help to put the salaries paid to the two engineers into perspective, and to show how high a value was placed on the skills of the comparatively small number of men who were at first familiar with the new machines.

The Newcomen engine had a remarkably long life in the British coal fields, surviving long after far more efficient engines had been introduced elsewhere. Many collieries had a number of engines at work, and the scene that was once dominated by the gaunt open frames of the horse-gins was now also marked by the high stone engine houses and the smoke from their chimneys. Even the aristocracy joined the rush into the new technology, as John Byng found when he visited Neath in the 1760s:

> 'Just above the town is placed the house of Sir Herbert Mack-worth, called The Knoll.... He has 6 coal pits in his park, at full work whence 50 tons of coal are daily carried to his copper works, and several others that have overflow'd, but are now draining by fire engines.'

Another of the collieries owned by the aristocracy was that of Earl Fitzwilliam at Elsecar in Yorkshire. John Holland described it in its later life in the early nineteenth century:

> 'The collieries belonging to Earl Fitzwilliam at Elsecar and Raw-marsh, near Rotherham, are carried on with great spirit, and the whole of the arrangements for working them are on a scale of great magnitude.... There is, moreover, little or no fire damp, so that the colliers work with open lamps; and so clean and commodious are the board ways, in many parts, at least, that the ladies from Wentworth House sometimes go down to witness the operations.'

Elsecar is still a working colliery and, inevitably, the process of modernization has swept away much of the evidence of its early working days. This is true of mining sites all over the country. In some industries the centres of production move, leaving old sites to gradually crumble away, as at the Llandogo iron-works, and even that remains only because the main structures are stone and not metal that can be sold for scrap. But collieries must stay where the coal is to be found, and on the more productive coal fields replacement of old by more modern techniques leads to an inevitable process of continuing renewal. Often all that can be traced of old mining areas are the hollows that mark where shafts were sunk, and the spoil heaps that form such oppressive backgrounds to so many mining communities. Old housing is the other exception, for many examples of early housing are to be found, suggesting that there was rather more incentive for mineowners to provide new machinery than to provide new houses. At Elsecar, however, there is rather more to see. For, apart from retaining one curiosity in the form of Earl Fitzwilliam's private railway station, there is also a Newcomen-type engine. This is being maintained as an important historical monument – and it is important, for it is one thing to see an engine in a museum and quite a different experience to see it in its engine house, on the site where it passed its working life.

Engines such as these were normally made and assembled locally, and the parts, such as cylinders, which required more accurate casting were made by specialists in foundries. Boilers were not required to withstand any great pressure, so were built up from riveted wrought-iron plates as little more than oversize cooking pots. They were known, according to their shape as either 'haystack' or 'beehive' boilers. Unfortunately, the Elsecar boiler is not among the parts that have been preserved.

The starting point for the construction of an engine is the engine house (plate 13). This had to serve as more than a simple cover to keep the machine out of the rain: it also had to act as a rigid frame to hold the engine itself steady and to support the massive rocking beam. The photograph shows the solid stone, three-storey engine house, with half of the beam protruding through the wall. From the end of this beam, the first section of pump rods can still be seen suspended over the now disused shaft. The strength of the building can be gauged from the size of the gritstone blocks, particularly from the massive dressed stones used for the quoins and the string courses; and the thickness of the walls can be seen in plate 14.

The engine itself has been much modified over the years. Originally the beam would have been wood rather than the present cast iron and the pump rods and piston would have been suspended by chains from its ends. The old system of cooling the cylinder to condense the steam by spraying with cold water has been replaced by a new system in which the water is injected into the cylinder. Nevertheless, the main principles of the atmospheric engine are still there to be seen. The main point to notice is the distinctive cylinder with its top open to the atmosphere (plate 14). The photograph also shows that this is an unusually light and airy engine house, perhaps because it was built at rather a late date – recorded over the lintel as 1787, but almost certainly not completed until 1795. The other point which one notices is the comparative crudity of the construction and the simplicity of the operation – a combination which helped greatly towards the success of a machine that had to be built and operated in a world just beginning to master the new technology.

Behind the engine house, and visible in the photograph (plate 13), are the few remaining cottages dating from the period when the engine was installed. Most of the housing at Elsecar is nineteenth-century (see p. 197).

The development of the steam engine opened the way to a new age of deeper pits. The increased use of the engine also brought new demands for the iron industry to supply the necessary castings. It was the beginning of a close inter-relationship between the iron and the coal industry, which was to become even closer and far more important following developments that began in the iron industry of Shropshire.

3
The Darbys of Coalbrookdale

In chapter 1 we took a brief look at the process of smelting iron using charcoal. Although the process of charcoal-smelting was centuries old, it was only with the introduction of the blast furnace that there was any really notable increase in either scale or sophistication of techniques. In spite of the obvious disadvantages of the charcoal furnace, it continued in use well into Victorian times. The furnaces of this type were necessarily situated close to suitable supplies of timber, and those that survived were often in the more remote parts of Britain. One of these old sites can be found in an area which seems as remote from industry as the Wye valley – among the hills and lochs of the Scottish Highlands, at Bonawe on the shore of Loch Etive in Argyllshire.

In 1762, Richard and William Ford, James Backhouse and Michael Knot took a lease on the Bonawe site, and established an iron-works that was to remain in production until 1866. What is truly remarkable is that they were able to work using ore that had to be shipped around the coast from England. Little remains to remind us of what must once have been a busy scene with the boats unloading their cargoes of ore – the only vestige of harbour installation is a single jetty, now used by pleasure boats, taking tourists for rides on the loch. The remains of the works themselves, however, are very well preserved and rank amongst Scotland's most important industrial remains. Where the Llandogo furnace has lost its outer cladding, but retained much of the actual furnace, the opposite is true of Bonawe. The outer casing of the blast furnace is in first-rate condition, and even a cursory inspection shows it to be on a much larger scale than the earlier Wye furnace. The main furnace is a square stone structure, built against the hillside. It was built with care, and it was built to last, for although the stones are rough blocks, they have been put together by a mason who knew his craft. Strength was an essential for any structure built on such an exposed site.

The furnace building is in three distinct sections: the upper end is the charge house, where the materials to be fed into the furnace could be collected. The method of building against the hill meant that these could be wheeled straight in from the store sheds, and be ready for use at the top of the furnace itself. A short bridge connects the charge house to the furnace proper, topped by its squat square chimney. The metal was tapped at the foot of the furnace, where there are two hearths with metal lintels, which still carry the date of the opening of the furnace (plate 15). A small stream was channelled off towards the furnace to turn the water wheel which provided the power for the blast, and the wheel pit itself can be clearly seen at the side of the furnace (plate 16).

An iron-works in such a remote spot had to provide for the needs of its work force, and company housing was provided. The houses, some of which can be seen in the photograph (plate 15), were built as an L-shaped tenement block, one of the first examples of this type of housing to appear in western Scotland. The tenements were built in two storeys, access to the upper storey being by an outside stair-case. The accommodation they supplied seems cramped and claustrophobic, with very little head-room, but in a period when this area of Scotland was in a desperately depressed condition, they no doubt seemed at least adequate. Other buildings at Bonawe include the quite extensive storehouses where ore and fuel were kept, ready to be wheeled to the charge house. Altogether, Bonawe represents a well-organized site and, in effect, a complete industrial unit.

These distant outposts of the iron industry produced iron that was very expensive, largely because of the high transport costs involved, but survived for so long because they also produced iron of an extremely high quality. Yet, even when the works at Bonawe were first begun, they were already obsolete or, at best, obsolescent. In Coalbrookdale, in Shropshire, the Quaker iron-master Abraham Darby succeeded in 1709 in replacing charcoal by coke for smelting. This is an event of the greatest importance in the history of industrial development, for iron could now be manufactured using the apparently limitless resources of the coal fields instead of the severely limited supplies of charcoal. This in turn ensured that sufficient iron would be available for the increased use of the metal for machines, for building and for transport. The event is so important indeed that Coalbrookdale is sometimes referred to as 'the Birthplace of the Industrial Revolution'. Hopefully, enough has already been written to show that there is little justification for such a claim: just as 'the oldest pub in Britain' can be found in Nottingham, Berkshire and a few other places, so birthplaces of the industrial revolution are claimed for places other than the Darby iron-works. The industrial revolution grew from many roots – the development of the steam engine might be termed every bit as important as the invention of coke-smelting, and the inventions of the textile industry, which led to the evolution of the factory system, could certainly be said to be just as important in terms of their effects on the overall pattern of society. Having said that, it is nevertheless true that the Darby works were the scene of one event of crucial importance and of many later innovations, that add up to a unique collection of industrial 'firsts'. We are fortunate that the history of the area can be traced both through written records and through the physical remains.

Abraham Darby began his career working in brass-casting in Bristol, but soon became interested in the casting of iron. He visited Holland, probably in 1704, where he watched Dutch workmen casting brass pots. Darby tried to get them to do the same with iron, but they failed. Back in England, an apprentice, John Thomas, asked if he could try to see if he could do any better. He tried, and succeeded. The secret of casting iron pots was considered so valuable that, according to Thomas's daughter, Hannah Rose, Darby and her father 'were so private as to stop the keyhole of the door' when they discussed the process. Darby took even more vigorous steps to protect the secret: in 1707, he drew up an agreement with Thomas which, among other clauses, specified that:

> 'John Thomas consents to work and labour faithfully for Abraham Darby in the art and mystery of casting and moulding of iron potts from this day and date for the term of three years. . . . John Thomas . . . doth covenant that he will not at any time hereafter serve any other person whatever on or about the casting of iron pots in sand nor will he disclose the method to anyone.'

In the same year, Darby applied for and received a patent for his 'new way of casting iron bellied potts, and other iron-bellied ware in sand only'. The iron-bellied pots referred to in the preamble to Darby's patent were to be the main manufacture of the Darby works for many years. Samples can be seen (plate 17) in the small museum at Coalbrookdale – a curiously domestic beginning to a major industrial upheaval.

Darby realized that there was a great potential market for his cheap iron cooking pots, but his Bristol partners showed considerably less enthusiasm. So Darby set out to look for a suitable iron-works to take over and begin his own business. Arthur Raistrick in his authoritative work on the Darbys, *Dynasty of Ironfounders* (1953), suggests that Darby may already have been considering the possibilities of using coal, and that this influenced the choice of site. Certainly Darby would have been aware of earlier experiments with coal-smelting, particularly those of the iron-master Dud Dudley, who worked at the end of the seventeenth century. Dudley claimed to have successfully solved the problem – a claim it is difficult to substantiate. Darby himself had become aware of the advantages of coke as a fuel in place of coal from his own apprenticeship in the malting industry, where coke was widely used, and the Shropshire coal was ideal for coking. If he had already formed his plans, then the deep gorges of the Severn valley were perfect for him. The area had plentiful supplies of both iron and coal, and the geography of the area could hardly have been bettered. As you approach Coalbrookdale from the north, the sides of the valley begin to close in as the road runs down to the Severn. Water flows rapidly down, ensuring abundant supplies to turn the water wheels for the blast. A prudent man would also note that the sides of the hill are thickly wooded, so that should new experimental techniques fail, there was plenty of wood for charcoal for the old methods. Continuing downhill, a short journey brings you to the Severn, which at that time was one of the major trading routes of England. The area satisfied every requirement – plentiful supplies of raw material, adequate water for power, and easy access for transport. Premises were available and Darby moved in in 1708.

The old furnace he acquired was indeed old, and required a good deal of work and reconditioning before it could be put back into blast. The hearth and bellows, in particular, required extensive work. The furnace was tapped through an arch topped by metal beams, one carrying the date 1638, and this beam has been retained through the renovation and subsequent rebuildings. The foundations of the original furnace can also be seen at ground level. The development of the furnace, and the enlargement of the hearth to take ever larger castings, can still be seen in the old furnace at Coalbrookdale. The original hearth was extended, and the extensions are marked by three tiers of lintels, the original with two above, inscribed "Abraham Darby 1777" (plate 18). The main structure we can see today is the rebuilt furnace of 1777, but the visitor of a romantic disposition can stand under the arch of 1638 and recall that it was through this arch that coke-smelted iron first poured in 1709.

Although the old furnace is the obvious centre of interest at the Coalbrookdale works, a study of the whole layout is rather more rewarding. Darby showed quite remarkable foresight in planning the works in a logical progression, which minimized the labour needed in moving from one part of the process to the next. The furnace pools which provided the water for the wheels were built in a series down the hillside, so that all could be fed from the same stream. Coal and iron pits were above the level of the works, so that the journey to the furnaces was all downhill. The furnaces themselves were built against the hillside for easier loading. Furnaces and forges were built next to each other, from where the finished ironware could be carried, again downhill to the Severn.

Production at Coalbrookdale continued at first in domestic pots and pans, as Samuel Smiles recorded in his *Industrial Biography* (1863):

> 'It appears from the "Blast Furnace Memorandum Book" of Abraham Darby, which we have examined, that the make of iron at the Coalbrookdale Foundry, in 1713, varied from five to ten tons a week. The principal articles were pots, kettles and other "hollow ware", direct from the smelting furnace; the rest of the metal was run into pigs. In course of time we find that other castings were turned out: a few grates, smoothing-irons, door-frames, weights, baking-plates, cart-brushes, iron pestles and mortars, and occasionally a tailor's goose. The trade gradually increased until we find as many as 150 pots and kettles cast in a week.'

When Abraham Darby died in 1717, he left the works in a prosperous condition, but his son, Abraham Darby II was then only six years old and the business passed under the management of Richard Ford. It was not until Ford's death in 1745, that it again came under the control of the Darby family. Under Abraham Darby II, advances were made in iron-making almost as dramatic as those of his father's time. He introduced a steam engine to recirculate the water from the furnace pools – an immense saving in time and hence money, as drought could otherwise bring the works to a halt. The water-wheels needed a steady supply and, although there are no wheels left at Coalbrookdale, the remains of the wheel pit, near the viaduct, give some idea of the size of a wheel and the quantity of water needed to turn it.

The steam engine was beginning to play an important part not only as an aid to production but as an end product. The earliest Newcomen engines were made with brass cylinders, but although these could be produced to a much higher degree of accuracy than iron cylinders they were prohibitively expensive and iron soon became the norm. The Coalbrookdale works were adding engine castings to their pot and pan production as early as 1720, and as the century progressed they gained a reputation for manufacturing machinery to set beside their thriving domestic business. Soon they were supplying all kinds of heavy industrial castings, and their reputation spread throughout the country. Entries such as the following from the records of the Coventry Canal Company could be repeated for many concerns in many different parts: May 27, 1770 – pd John Parrish expences for himself and Horse 3 Days going to Coalbrookdale to procure Iron-Work for a Crane & Stops.'

However, the main problem facing Abraham Darby II was that of improving the quality of iron from the works. Although the coke-smelting process had long been established, the iron they were able to produce was only suitable for casting, not for forging. There was a growing demand for iron that could be slit into rods for the nail-makers and that demand was still being met by the charcoal fur-naces. At some time around the year 1750, Abraham Darby at last succeeded in using the coke-smelting process to produce pig iron that could be slit. His wife described his success in a letter:

'But all this time the making of Barr Iron at Forges from Pit Coal pigs was not thought of. About 26 years ago my Husband con-ceived this happy thought – that it might be possible to make bar iron from pit coal pigs. Upon this he sent some of our pigs to be tryed at the Forges, and that no prejudice might arise against them he did not discover from whence they came, or of what quality they were. And a good account being given of their working, he erected Blast Furnaces for Pig Iron for Forges. Edward Knight Esq., a capitol Iron-Master urged my Husband to get a patent, that he might reap the benefit for years of this happy discovery; but he said he would not deprive the public of such an Acquisition which he was satisfyed it would be; and so it has proved, for it soon spread and many Furnaces both in this Neighbourhood and several other places have been erected for this purpose.'

She then continued by indicating that the discovery came none too soon, for charcoal was becoming increasingly scarce and more and more expensive as the 'landed Gentlemen rose the price of cord wood exceeding high'.

One popular and persistent version of the story of the successful experiments has Abraham Darby spending six sleepless nights wait-ing for the results; as soon as the success was established, he collapsed and had to be carried home to his bed. True or not, Darby had triumphed, and his success could stand beside his father's as marking another major change in iron production at Coalbrookdale. The Darby family had come a long way from their beginnings as pan-makers, and in the next generation their work was to culminate in the masterpiece which still stands as the most fitting memorial to this extraordinary family.

In 1775 plans were finalized for building a bridge across the Severn, near Coalbrookdale. The necessary Act of Parliament authorizing the construction of the bridge and its approach roads was approved and, after consideration of a number of alternative plans for the bridge, the whole scheme was left in the hands of Abraham Darby III. The bridge that Darby proposed was to span the river in a single arch, and was to be constructed entirely from cast iron. It is, perhaps, difficult today to appreciate the audacity of the proposal. Here we have Darby proposing to construct the first bridge ever to be built out of cast iron and proposing, no small-scale experiment, but a massive structure with a span of a hundred foot, with a maximum height over the river of forty feet and having a width of twenty-four feet. The result as we can see today was no tentative attempt to come to terms with a new technique, but a splendid and majestic piece of civil engineering (plate IV). Many thousands of iron bridges have been constructed since then but this, the first, holds it place among the best of them.

Darby's methods of construction are particularly interesting. We are now accustomed to seeing iron constructions with the sections riveted or bolted together, but Darby, perhaps because he had no precedents to follow, treated the iron sections as if they were wood. So we find them fitted together in a series of mortice and dovetail joints, and where one member passes through another, the joints are made solid with iron wedges. These details can be seen in plate IV. Darby imitated wood for the joints, and also produced a variation of a design based on stone bridges. The circles above the arches simulate the new technique in stonework of piercing the spandrels of the arches of a bridge to lighten the load of the arches themselves. Such pierced spandrels can be seen, for example, in the Marple aqueduct on the Peak Forest canal.

Most of the commentators, who came to the bridge after its opening in 1781, were content to stand and admire, as did John Byng: 'But of the iron bridge over the Severn, which we cross'd and where we stopp'd for half an hour what shall I say? That it must be the admiration, as it is one of the wonders of the world.' One contemporary, however, Richard Gough, took the trouble to describe the construction in vivid and accurate detail:

'Over the Severn in this Dale was laid 1779, a bridge of cast iron, the whole of which was cast in open sand, and a large scaffolding being previously erected, each part of the rib was elevated to a proper height by strong ropes and chains, and then lowered till the ends meet in the centre. All the principal parts were erected in three months without any accident to the work or workmen or the least obstruction to the navigation of the river.'

For the casting of the seventy-foot sections, Abraham Darby rebuilt the old furnace, and the two lintels dated 1777 mark that rebuilding. The furnace that we can see today is substantially the same as that used for making the iron for the bridge, and is typical of furnaces of the period, though a few of the details are unique. Inside the square tower, the furnace itself can be seen to be circular in section: it might appear that there is a great deal of outer casing for comparatively little furnace, but the space in between is packed with brick, rubble and fire-resistant material to give sufficient strength for the structure to withstand the pressures set up by heating and cooling the furnace. The lowest part of the furnace is the crucible, where the transformation of ore into metal actually took place. This extends to the height of the 1638 beam. The furnace then begins to widen until it reaches a maximum width of 13 foot 9 inches – the area known as 'the boshes', before tapering in again to a diameter of just over seven foot at the top of the furnace. The upper section was used to hold the charge, which gradually slipped down towards the crucible. The actual blast for the furnace came through a pipe, called the tuyere, which joined the bellows to the furnace. In Darby's furnace, the pipe was, possibly, allowed to go right round the furnace before the actual opening was reached, which would have resulted in some heating of the air, and a greater efficiency.

The furnace itself was charged at the top, material being wheeled across the bridge from the stores on the hillside. The hearth was closed by a fire-proof plug, and the furnace was tapped by removing the plug and allowing the molten iron to run out into the casting moulds. These were prepared in the sand at the foot of the furnace, and were shaped in the forms of the different bridge sections. The success of this furnace can be seen from the success of the great bridge built from its iron.

It is possible to recreate something of the working life of the Coalbrookdale iron-works in the eighteenth century from the remains still preserved on the site. The furnace pools and wheel pits already mentioned show the source of power for the furnaces and for the machinery used in the works. The old furnace, and the 'new' furnace which was added in the 1790s, built against the bank by Wellington Road, show something of the scale of iron-making. The large warehouse, built in the 1830s, gives further evidence of a thriving and prosperous concern – though it was once a little plainer, the ornate clock tower being an addition of 1843. What these remains do not tell us is anything of the working and social conditions of the men who made the iron in Coalbrookdale. For that information we must turn back to the surviving documents.

The main factor which determined the relationship between master and men was a common religious bond, for the Darby family were Quakers, and it was among the Quakers that they recruited much of their labour force. The Friends' meetings were held in the company offices, and these occasions enabled the Darbys and their workers to meet as equals. Continuity of Darby management was matched by a continuity among the work force, and the wage books show the same names recurring as generations followed each other into the works. In spite of the great technological innovations associated with Coalbrookdale, the organization remained for a long time at a sort of half-way stage between the domestic craft industry and the impersonal large-scale production unit that developed in other regions (see, for example, the section on South Wales pp. 106–14). Yet the work was hard, and the regulations were strict. William Reynolds, who for a time was a partner with the Darbys, laid down a set of rigid rules of which the following extracts should be sufficient to give some idea of their nature:

1 The wealth of the west of England cloth trade is reflected in these fine clothiers' houses at Bradford-on-Avon

11 The remains of a seventeenth-century blast furnace in the woods near Llandogo

III A stark and dramatic outline: the horse gin at Wollaton
Hall, Nottingham

IV *Right* The world's first iron bridge

v Arkwright's Masson mill, standing
beside the river Derwent at Matlock Bath

VI Solidly attractive terraces in Long Row, Belper, built by
the Strutts to house their workers

(1) Each Person employed in the Works shall come to, and be engaged in the Employment appointed for them, and at their proper Places from the hour of Six in the Morning to Six in the Evening, Breakfast and Dinner excepted, or forfeit the Sum of One Shilling in Addition to the Time lost by Absence or Indolence, which will be deducted from his Weekly Wages.

(3) Those who stay longer at their Meals than the Time allowed, viz: half an Hour at Breakfast and an Hour at Dinner, shall forfeit a quarter of a Day's Wages.

(10) If any One is found in that part of the Work where his business does not call him, he shall forfeit One Shilling.

The works at Coalbrookdale represented only a part of the iron-making enterprises of the Darbys and their partners, of whom the most important was the Reynolds family. Between them they built more furnaces, some of which have survived. Among these are the Madeley Wood furnaces, which soon became known by the more romantic name of Bedlam furnaces, a name probably derived from the violent appearance of a blast furnace particularly if seen at night. The poetess Anna Seward expressed the horror that many felt at the sight of the bedlam of industry invading the countryside, when she visited the area in about 1785:

'Scene of superfluous grace, and wasted bloom,
O, violated COLEBROOK! in an hour,
To beauty unpropitious and to song,
The Genius of thy shades, by Plutus brib'd
Amid thy grassy lanes, thy woodwild glens,
Thy knolls and bubbling wells, thy rocks, and streams,
Slumbers! . . .
　　　　　 – Now we view
Their fresh, their fragrant, and their silent reign
Usurpt by Cyclops; – hear, in mingled tones,
Shout their throng'd barge, their pond'rous engines clang
Through the coy dales; while red the countless fires,
With umber'd flames, bicker on all thy hill,
Dark'ning the Summer's sun with columns large
Of thick, sulphureous smoke, which spread, like palls,

That screen the dead, upon the sylvan robe
Of thy aspiring rocks; pollute thy gales,
And stain thy glassy water.'

Though the style is very much of the eighteenth century, the concern over pollution strikes a remarkably modern note.

Anna Seward's 'pond'rous engines' were an important part of the scene at Madeley Wood, for by that time the steam engine was being used to provide a direct blast for furnaces. The engines have almost all gone, and no doubt the poetess would find it a more pleasant spot, but the Bedlam furnaces have recently been excavated and can be seen standing by the roadside at Madeley Wood (plate 20). Nearby, in what is now the Blists Hill Open Air Museum, can be seen a further part of the iron-works concerns, including a large engine house which holds an engine that was used for blowing a direct blast for the furnaces (plate 21).

The innovations of the Darby family at Coalbrookdale were remarkable, and continued well into the nineteenth century. As early as the 1760s, Richard Reynolds had taken the adventurous step of substituting iron for wood on all the company's railways, and the connections between Coalbrookdale and the railways was reinforced when Trevithick came to Shropshire to arrange for the casting of the boiler for his locomotive. The association between the Darby family and Coalbrookdale ended officially in the middle of the nineteenth century, but the family was remembered for a long time after. Mr R. Bowen, who began his working career as an apprentice in Coalbrookdale in 1899, still recalls the story of the casting of the bells for Coalbrookdale Church when, it is said, members of the family threw handfuls of silver into the molten iron. The bells, says Mr Bowen, 'surpass for tone any of the bells of other local churches'.

The main contribution of the Darbys, the introduction of coke-smelting, was slow to spread. This was partly because the early experiments only produced iron suitable for the humble cooking pot, and partly because in an age of slow and inefficient communications, news from a Shropshire valley took time to percolate into the outside world. Whatever the reason, half a century went by following

Abraham Darby's first success before the replacement of charcoal by coke gained general acceptance. Other innovations in other industries produced more immediate changes, and in the textile industry the results were so dramatic that they led to a claim from Derbyshire for another 'birthplace of the industrial revolution'.

4
Towards the Factory Age

Most people, if pushed to name two inventions in the textile industry, would probably come up with Kay's flying shuttle and Hargreaves' spinning jenny: they might be rather hard pushed to say exactly what the flying shuttle and spinning jenny were, or just why they were important.

John Kay of Bury began his career in the textile industry as an apprentice to a reed-maker, preparing the split canes that were used to separate the threads in the loom, and he soon showed his flair for invention by devising a method of replacing the split canes by wire reeds. This produced a considerable improvement in the quality of the finished cloth, and Kay travelled the country selling his new reeds. He soon built up a thriving business and no doubt it was his early success that led him to look for other potentially profitable improvements. In 1733, when he was thirty-one years old, he produced his flying shuttle, which brought him fame but no fortune.

The weaving of broadcloth, as explained in chapter 1, required two men to throw the shuttle to each other across the width of the loom. By his one simple invention, Kay halved that particular work force. His first improvement was simply to ease the movement of the shuttle, by placing it on a long board, known as a 'shuttle race', which was attached to the wooden batten that was used to drive the weft home, and by attaching small wheels to the shuttle itself. The next vital stage was to devise a method whereby the one weaver could move the shuttle backwards and forwards across the race. At each end of the race he attached a 'shuttle box', which contained a spindle to hold the thread and a 'picker'. The picker moved along a short rod inside the box, so that if it was jerked it would hit the shuttle and send it flying across the race board – it simply did what the weaver's hand had previously done. All that was necessary now was to attach cord to each of the two pickers and fasten the ends to a stick. The weaver could then hold the stick in one hand, and by jerking it one way or the other work the two pickers and keep the shuttle moving backwards and forwards. This left his other hand free to operate the batten that pushed the weft home, while the warp was controlled, as before, with foot treadles. So by a few simple additions the two-man broad loom was converted to a one-man broad loom.

There were two possible outcomes from the use of the flying shuttle – either the level of production could be maintained, but the work force could be halved, or the same number of weavers could be employed and production doubled. The ordinary weavers' immediate reaction was fear of lost jobs, and they opposed the introduction of the new machines. Clothiers and master-weavers, on the other hand, immediately saw the advantages of combining increased production with lower costs and began a period of unmerciful pirating of Kay's invention. When Kay tried to fight for his reward, the manu-facturers banded together in 'shuttle clubs' to oppose him. Faced by opposition from both employers and employed, Kay left the country and settled in France, where he eventually died.

The possibility of doubling cloth production depended on enough yarn being available to meet the increased demand, and the search for new methods of spinning began. The authorship of the first of the new spinning machines is in some doubt – the choice lying be-tween Lewis Paul and John Wyatt. Paul patented the machine in 1738, but Wyatt made firm claims to the invention, for example in a letter to Sir Leicester Holt: 'I am the person that was the principal agent in compiling the Spinning Engine.' The truth is almost cer-tainly that both were involved in the design. The basis for this machine was that the thread – in this case, cotton – was first carded and then passed between rotating rollers which drew it out into finer threads. The fine thread was then passed over a hook or 'flyer' which gave the thread a twist before it was finally wound on to a bobbin. The set of rollers was arranged on a circular pattern, an arrangement described in verse in Dyer's *The Fleece*:

> 'A circular machine of new design
> In conic shape; it draws and spins a thread
> Without the tedious task of needless hands.
> A wheel, invisible, beneath the floor
> To every member of th' harmonious whole
> Gives necessary motion.'

The most significant feature of this invention was that it was far too large and complicated ever to be used in a cottage, and required a special mill or factory to house it. Textile mills were not unknown in the eighteenth century, for Thomas Lombe had established a silk mill at Derby in 1724, but it was Lewis Paul who established the first powered cotton mill. His first venture was at Birmingham in 1741, where he installed his machinery and used donkeys to supply the power. More importantly, he established another mill at Northampton the following year, and this time used water as his source of power. The Northampton mill had the backing of a number of influential men, including Cave, the editor of the *Gentleman's Magazine*, but it failed and found no immediate imitators. The problem of supplying yarn for the improved looms remained.

James Hargreaves was the first to produce a successful spinning machine that found wide acceptance throughout the industry, and was used for spinning both cotton and wool. Like Kay's flying shuttle, Hargreaves' jenny was essentially a very simple device. The old spinning wheel was turned on its side and used to turn a number of vertical spindles (plate 22). Not surprisingly, the story soon appeared that Hargreaves had accidentally knocked over a spinning wheel one day and, in a flash of inspiration, conceived the idea for the jenny. It is probably untrue. The sequence of events following the invention, however, are known with more certainty and are very similar to those following Kay's invention. Hargreaves' machines were attacked by fearful spinners and copied without payment by ruthless manufacturers. There were, however, other results. The jenny soon found more general acceptance among spinners, and became used in the domestic industry, though some were also installed in small work-shops. Secondly, the example of yet another inventor gaining little or no reward for his efforts was not lost on the next character to appear in the story of textile innovation.

Richard Arkwright's contribution as an inventor is the subject of some controversy. His background was hardly what one would expect for an inventor of textile machinery, for he began his working life as a barber and wig-maker. He did, however, work in the textile area of Lancashire, so must have been familiar with the problems of the industry from the customers' chat. The story of his invention is clouded by rival claims put in by Thomas Hugh and John Kay (no relation to the Kay of the flying shuttle). The facts are obscure, though it does seem likely that Arkwright made use of the ideas and the expertise of others. It would be interesting to discover the truth of the invention of the Arkwright spinning machine, but it is not par-ticularly important. What is important is that Arkwright was able to exploit the machine to the full, and his success triggered off the sweeping changes that took textile production from cottage to mill and which saw such a dramatic rise in the production of cotton goods that exports in the trade rose from around £300,000 in 1780 to £10 million a mere twenty-five years later.

In essence, Arkwright's machine was very similar to that of Wyatt and Paul (plate 23). Rollers, moving at different speeds, were again used to draw out the cotton threads, and a flyer imparted twist. There was one important difference, and that was that the spindles on to which the thread was wound were pulled round by the action of the thread itself, instead of being independently driven. This meant that power could be supplied very easily by a belt drive from a single rotating shaft.

Arkwright at first went into partnership with a Preston man called Smalley, but the opposition that was aroused by all new inventions in that area decided Arkwright to try to set up business in an area where he was less likely to have to face opposition from worried spinners. He moved to Nottingham, where he quickly acquired new partners, both hosiery manufacturers – Samuel Need of Derby and Jebediah Strutt. Strutt had already built up a good business based on an invention of his own which adapted the Lee stocking frame for the production of ribbed stockings. Need had backed Strutt, and the two men were very interested in any proposal that would increase yarn supply, for shortages were affecting hosiers as well as weavers. A small mill was established at Nottingham, where a few machines were tried out, using horses for power, and Arkwright took the precaution of applying for a patent. The experiments were sufficiently successful for the partners to decide to build a new cotton mill. They looked at various sites, before eventually settling on the tiny hamlet of Cromford in Derbyshire, on the banks of the Derwent. Why did they choose Cromford? An obvious attraction was the availability of water power to turn the machinery, but adequate water supplies could have been found in many other places. A factor which could well have weighed heavily with Arkwright was the site's remoteness. He knew of the merciless pirating of Kay's and Hargreaves' inventions, and was determined to avoid a similar fate. A letter to Strutt of 2 March 1771 indicates his great concern with secrecy:

'Desire ward to send those other Locks and allso Some sort of Hangins for the sashes he & you may think best and some good Latches & Catches for the out doors and a few for the inner ons allso and a Large Knoker or a Bell to First door. I am Determined for the feuter to Let no persons in to Look at the works.'

Remoteness acted as an aid to secrecy, and also being distant from traditional textile areas, there was less chance of any outbreaks of rioting or machine-breaking to disturb the work.

Another consideration was that a work force would have to have been specially imported to work in the mills. There was not enough local labour available, and there was not sufficient accommodation for workers brought in from other regions. In other words, the partners had to build a mill village to accompany the new mill. Arkwright, at least, was determined to get the maximum possible production out of the new machines, and that meant putting an end to age-old working habits. There was no room for the irregular 'work to suit myself' attitudes of the old domestic workers, still less for the much-hallowed Saint Monday. Arkwright could well have considered that families brought from far away and settled in a mill house would be more easily persuaded or coerced into accepting the new discipline and strict hours of the factory. Andrew Ure in *The Philosophy of Manufacture* (1835) describes the development of the factory from the time of Arkwright up to his own day. He is much given to eulogies of the system, which he clearly regarded as having reached something very close to Utopia:

> 'The constant aim and effect of scientific improvement in manufactures are philanthropic, as they tend to relieve the workmen either from niceties of adjustment which exhaust his mind and fatigue his eyes, or from painful repetition of effort which distort or wear out his frame. At every step of each manufacturing process described in this volume, the humanity of science will be manifest.'

Factories, to Ure, are 'magnificent edifices, surpassing far in number, value, usefulness, and ingenuity of construction, the boasted monuments of Asiatic, Egyptian, and Roman despotism'. All this splendid structure had its beginnings in the 'Napoleon verve and ambition' of Arkwright who had his way in the face of 'prejudice, passion and envy'. Ure describes his struggle to lead the work force to the Promised Land, and notes, with evident surprise, that:

> 'Even at the present day, when the system is perfectly organized, and its labour lightened to the utmost, it is found nearly impossible to convert persons past the age of puberty, whether drawn from rural or from handicraft occupations, into useful factory hands. After struggling for a while to conquer their listless or restive habits, they either renounce the employment spontaneously, or are dismissed by the overlookers on account of inattention.'

Faced by the intractable nature of the human section of the new development, the dependence of the work force on the employer, not only for their work but for the roof over their heads, must have seemed another powerful argument in favour of forming a new community.

In 1771, work on the new mill at Cromford was begun, and advertisements for workers to construct the machinery began to appear, such as the following from the *Derby Mercury*:

'Cotton Mill, Cromford, 10th Dec. 1771

WANTED immediately, two Journeymen Clock-Makers, or others that understands Tooth and Pinion well: Also a Smith that can forge and file – Likewise two Wood Turners that have been accustomed to Wheel-making, Spoke turning, &c. Weavers residing at the Mill, may have good Work. There is Employment at the above Place, for Women, Children, &c. and good Wages.'

The advertisement emphasizes the dependence of the new technology on older crafts. The main job of work was building and assembling the machinery – the spinning machines at Cromford were to be powered by a water wheel, which gave them the name 'water frames' and gave the name 'water twist' to the yarn they produced. Arkwright also installed machines for carding the cotton, another invention for which he had taken out a dubious patent. He concerned himself with everything in the mill, down to the smallest details of machinery and management. He was an irascible and overbearing employer, and quarrels between himself and his partners and mill managers soon broke out. He quarrelled incessantly with Need, who he felt was too concerned with Nottingham business and insufficiently occupied with affairs in Derbyshire. When Need had the temerity to apply for the temporary loan of some of the Derbyshire workers, he received the terse reply: 'As to sending any hand from hear I can't think of doing.' Arkwright also disagreed over the principle of employing weavers at the mill, and on this occasion he soon had his way, and all the looms were cleared out. His relations with the Strutts were no happier. Jebediah received a letter in 1774 in which his son reported of Cromford that 'I was there last Sunday but one, & heard very unfavourable accounts of Mr A.'s behaviour. I suppose he is going to leave you.' The unfavourable behaviour included a number of quarrels with Smalley, to whom Strutt wrote offering sympathy and giving an account of his own efforts at peace-making:

'I said what I could to persuade him to oblige you in any thing that was reasonable & to endeavour to live on good terms at least . . . you must be sensible when some sort of people set themselves to be perverse it is very difficult to prevent them being so.'

Whatever personal difference might be troubling the Cromford works, the troubles did not show themselves in the balance books. The new spinning mill was mightily profitable, and the partners began on a period of rapid expansion of their interests. A new mill was built at Belper, south of Cromford on the Derwent, and they even tried to venture into the traditional textile area with a mill at Birkacre, near Chorley, in Lancashire. The last experiment was not a success, and Arkwright's water frames suffered the fate of other inventions in that area. The *Annual Register* gave this report of the events of October 1779:

'Manchester, Oct. 9. During the course of the week several mobs have assembled in different parts of the neighbourhood, and have done much mischief by destroying the engines for carding and spinning cotton wool. . . . In the neighbourhood of Chorley, the mob destroyed and burned the engines and buildings erected by Mr Arkwright at a very great expence. Two thousand, or upwards, attacked a large building near the same place, on Sunday, from which they were repulsed, two rioters killed, and eight wounded; they returned strongly re-inforced on Monday, and destroyed a great number of buildings, with a vast quantity of machines for spinning cotton, &c. Sir George Saville arrived [with three companies of the York militia] while the buildings were in flames. . . .'

Arkwright retired back to Cromford, and prepared for the worst:

'Fifteen hundred Stand of small Arms are already collected from Derby and the neighbouring Towns, and a great Battery of Cannon . . . besides which, upwards of 500 Spears are fixt in Poles of between 2 and 3 Yards long.'

The worst never happened, and Arkwright was soon back at his main business of amassing a fortune. He was pushing hard to develop his trade, for already discontented voices were being raised in Lancashire, questioning the validity of the patents on which his monopoly depended. He fought the Lancashire textile men through the courts, in a series of contests notable for the amount of bitterness they aroused. New mills were begun in Derbyshire at Ashbourne (1781), Bakewell (1782), Wirksworth (1783) and Masson (1784). He travelled the country looking for new partners with whom he could develop his patent, even going as far as Scotland, where he joined with a wealthy Glasgow merchant, David Dale, to establish a new community based on cotton-spinning that was later to become world-famous – New Lanark (see pp. 164–9).

His first setback came when his patent for a carding engine – which was always based on a very doubtful claim of originality – was overthrown in 1781. The Birmingham manufacturer Matthew Boulton wrote to James Watt, describing Arkwright's anger:

'He swears ... he will ruin those Manchester rascals he has been the making of. It is agreed by all who know him that he is a Tyrant and more absolute than a Bashaw, & tis thought that his disappointment will kill him. If he had been a man of sense and reason he would not have lost his patent.'

Arkwright had received the support of many manufacturers, including Boulton and Watt, not because they sympathized with him personally, but because they feared a general attack on all patents, including their own. But, as Boulton pointed out, Arkwright was not a man of sense, and in 1783 he lost the remainder of his patents.

In spite of the removal of the protective cover of his patents, Arkwright had established a commanding pre-eminence among cotton manufacturers, and he continued to prosper. In 1788 he decided to build a suitably imposing house at Cromford, which would fit the dignity of his newly acquired knighthood. The house, Willersley Castle, overlooks the Derwent and the mills. John Byng gives an aristocrat's eye view of these doings of the *nouveau riche*:

'Went to where Sr R.A. is building for himself a grand house in the same castellated style as one sees at Clapham, and *really* he has made a *happy* choice of ground, for by sticking it up on an un-safe bank, he contrives to overlook, not see, the beauties of the river, and the surrounding scenery. It is the house of an overseer surveying the works, not of a gentleman wishing for retirement and quiet. But light come, light go, Sr Rd has honourably made his great fortune; and so let him still live in a great cotton mill!'

He died, however, in 1792 before he could move into his house. The obituarist in the *Gentleman's Magazine* seemed uncertain how to treat a man who combined fortune and trade, public success and personal disagreeableness. The result is a neat piece of ironical writing, that serves also to remind us that Richard Arkwright was a man of the eighteenth century:

'He has left one son and one daughter (a Mrs Hurst). Mrs Hurst it is said will have £200,000; Mr Arkwright an equal sum, with all the manufactories, worth as much more.... Sir Richard, we are informed, with the qualities necessary for the accumulation of wealth, possessed, to an eminent degree, the art of keeping it. His economy and frugality bordered very nearly on parsimony. He was, however, if not a great, a very useful character.'

The obvious starting point for any study of the effects of Arkwright's invention is Cromford, which can rightly claim to be the first cotton town of Britain – for it was cotton that called it into being, and cotton that caused it to flourish. Unfortunately, we can get very little idea of what the original mill looked like from the buildings to be seen today. It was built as a six-storey building, but two of the storeys have disappeared, and the rest is often obscured by later additions (plate 24). The water power was provided in part by a stream, Bonsall Brook, and in part by the Cromford Sough, which drained a nearby mine, the water being carried over the road on a wooden launder. A second mill was added in 1777, but this was burned down. A far clearer idea of the scale and style of these early mills can be obtained from the nearby Masson mill at Matlock Bath. Although, again, there have been later additions, the central block which formed the original mill is unchanged. The imposing array of Venetian windows, the dramatic contrasting of the red brick with the white stone for quoins and round windows and doors, at once indicate a desire to express, through the architecture, a sense of importance. The attempt succeeds. Just as impressive as the flamboyant statement of the styling is the scale of the works necessary to ensure an adequate supply of water for the wheel, shown in the weir built across the river (plate v).

The buildings tell us of an expanding industry, and of self-confident industrialists, but the old machinery has long gone, and we can learn nothing here of the working conditions found in Cromford and Masson. The mills were, in fact, worked day and night, for Arkwright was always conscious of the opposition to his patents, and was anxious to avoid the fate of earlier inventors. So, he accumulated what he could, while he could. Cromford, soon became a regular stopping-off place on the British Tour, which became such a feature of eighteenth-century life, and the tourists invariably made due note of the twenty-four-hour working and its cause. William Bray, for example, visited the 'mill for spinning cotton', which, he noted 'employs about two hundred persons chiefly children; and to make the most of the term for which the patent was granted, they work by turns, night and day.' While John Byng noted the phenomenon, and for once refrained from critical comment: 'I saw the workers issue forth at 7 o'clock, a wonderful crowd of young people, made as familiar as eternal intercourse can make them; a new set then goes in for the night, for the mills never leave off working.' It was not long, however, before Byng returned to his favourite refrain: 'Every rural sound is sunk in the clamour of cotton works; and the simple peasant ... is changed into the impudent mechanic.'

The continuous work of the mill made for a hard life for the operatives, but other factors, which were overlooked in the travellers' brief visits, had a more damaging long-term effect. Arkwright's son, Richard, giving evidence before Peel's Committee of 1816, set up to enquire into 'The State of the Children employed in the Manufactories of the United Kingdom', reported that in his father's time, children of seven to thirteen were mostly employed, who worked a thirteen-hour day. He claimed that their health was in no way impaired, though a few did become deformed. Andrew Ure, never the manufacturer's enemy, repeated the charge of deformity and added the reason: 'Arkwright's water frames were built very low in the spindle boxes to accommodate children, and consequently sometimes caused deformity.' Ure's statement can be borne out by an examination of a water frame. As can be seen in the photograph (plate 23), the spindles are placed very close to the ground and the young children, who had the job of changing spindles and mending broken threads, were forced to spend much of their working day bent low over the machinery.

Rates of pay are very difficult to determine for Arkwright's mills, though figures from Bakewell for 1786 indicate that the average weekly wage at that time was 3s 6d, though this only applied to adult workers. Wages fluctuated with trade conditions, but the spinners themselves were bitterly conscious of a steadily widening gap between themselves and their master, who 'from being a poor man not worth £5, now keeps his carriage and servants, is become a lord of a manor, and has purchased an estate of £20,000; while thousands of women, when they can get work, must make a long day to card, spin, and reel, 5,040 yards of cotton, and for this they have *four-pence or five-pence and no more.*'

On the living conditions of the Cromford workers we have far more evidence, much of it to be found in the buildings of the town. Arkwright's work force was mainly recruited from among the ranks of pauper families. Whole families were signed up on indentures, and could be – and were – sent to the House of Correction if they failed to work to their agreements. These families often came long distances, and had to be housed – and whatever one might think of inhumanity inside the mill, there is no trace of it in the housing. No doubt, the houses had to be made sufficiently appealing to attract families to move to Derbyshire, but given the position of the pauper families that would not have been too difficult to attain. The houses of Cromford rise well above that minimum, and one cannot help contrasting them with the squalid slums of the speculative builders and the damp cellars of the big cities such as Manchester in the following century. The best preserved example of Arkwright housing is to be found in North Street, Cromford, which was built in 1777 (plate 25). Whatever these houses might lack in elegance and refinement they more than make up for in robust, solid strength. The houses are built in a terrace, using the local gritstone, with heavy slabs for lintels over doors and windows. The street is wide and the outlook spacious. The houses are three-storey, but not all the space was intended for living accommodation. A large part of the employment at the mill was taken up by children and much of the rest by women, but it was never intended that they would provide enough to maintain the whole family. Extra work was needed by the majority of the men of Cromford. Looking along the top storey of the terraces of North Street, there are clear indications in the continuous lintel that they once had windows running the length of the street. These have now been mainly filled in, but the regularly spaced stone mullions can still be made out. These are the typical indications of an upper-storey workshop. In fact, the workshops over these rows were used for framework-knitting. The school at the end of North Street is a later, nineteenth-century, addition.

Cromford was Arkwright's town – he built the houses, he built the Church, and the handsome *Greyhound Inn* is a reminder that his town was a prosperous trading centre. It was from this inn that Arkwright played the bountiful squire. Byng reports that 'the landlord has under his care a grand assortment of prizes from Sr. R. Arkwright, to be given, at the years end, to such bakers, butchers, &c, as shall have best furnish'd the market'. In return, he expected to be given due recognition for his generosity, and the villagers complied by, literally, singing his praises:

> 'Come let us all here join in one,
> And thank him for all favours done;
> Let's thank him for all favours still
> Which he hath done besides the mill.
>
> Modistly drink liquor about,
> And see whose health you can find out;
> This will I chuse before the rest
> Sir Richard Arkwright is the best.'

The Cromford employees were overworked, underpaid, forced into a style and mode of working that was totally alien to them, and, in the case of some unfortunate children, permanently crippled. That is one side of the picture of life at Cromford. On the other side, we have to see that they came from far worse conditions, to live in a town that was pleasant and had well-built houses. One cannot help feeling, however, that it must have rankled to see their employer getting rich by their labour, and then forcing them into the roles of sycophants when he chose to make his annual display of generosity. In many ways, Richard Arkwright was the model for all those abrupt, dour 'where there's muck there's money' millowners of popular fiction. His partner Jebediah Strutt could hardly have provided a greater contrast.

Jebediah Strutt was apprenticed as a wheelwright in his youth, but appears to have been a highly literate wheelwright. During his apprenticeship, he stayed with the Woollett family and soon began to pay attention to Elizabeth Woollett. His correspondence with the young lady was as flowery as the most romantic heart could desire, even if he took rather a long time to come to the point:

> 'Ye Findern groves & bowers, who haunts your shades now I'm away or hears your warblers sing! Who treads your peaceful walks, or tastes your cooling springs, or counts your silent hours! O my dear Betty, can you, can I repeat these, a thousand other happy circumstances, and not remember it was the charms of good company that rendered them so delightful, and that only that gives so much sweetness to the remembrance of them once having been and such Bitterness to think they will no more. ... '

When the point was reached, it was so well wrapped as to be almost lost from sight, as when he claimed to detect a glance of love from Elizabeth:

> '... if so that one generous instance of truth and constancy has made a greater and more lasting impression on my mind than all the united claims of beauty, wit and fortune of your sex so far as I have had opportunity of conversing, were ever able to make, therefore it is upon this foundation I promise to tell you that from a wandering inconstant and roving swain I am become entirely yours.'

Strutt's convoluted proposal was accepted by Elizabeth, but, in spite of any evidence to the contrary, he complained in later life that he frequently felt the lack of a good education. He wrote to his son in August 1774: 'If I would I could describe the awkward figure one makes ... for the want of not knowing how to behave and the want of assurance to put what one does know into practice.' One could not imagine his partner, Arkwright, ever complaining of a lack of assurance. The difference in the two men is pointed by an entry in the letters of Maria Edgeworth, who visited the Strutts in 1813: 'This house is indeed ... a palace; and it is plain that the convenience of the inhabitants has everywhere been consulted; the ostentation of wealth nowhere appears.' The Strutts were quiet, nonconformist, firmly middle class.

Strutt's invention of the ribbing machine helped to establish a good business as a hosier before the partnership with Arkwright began, and this established position helped him to take a more relaxed view of developments in the cotton trade. As we have seen, relationships between the partners soon became strained and the break came in 1781. Arkwright settled in Cromford and Strutt established his base in Belper. The Strutts soon dominated Belper much as Arkwright dominated his little township. Unlike Cromford, however, Belper had an industrial history of its own as a centre for the nail-making industry. This can be traced back to the fourteenth century, and a number of nailers' workshops can still be found in the town. Nevertheless, Strutt soon established himself as the town's major employer, and built houses for his workers of a quality at least equal to that of the Cromford houses. The best known of Strutt's houses are the two terraces of stone, three-storey buildings in Long Row (plate VI). The styling is rather more refined than in the houses of North Row, Cromford, with more sophisticated treatment of features such as door and windows. The street is wide, and the houses have small front gardens. Nearby, foreshadowing the 'back-to-backs' of the later cotton towns, are houses built in square blocks of four, and aptly named 'The Clusters'. A mark of Strutt's paternalistic approach towards his employees can be seen at the end of the bridge across the Derwent, where Mrs Strutt ran the cottage hospital. At the other end of the bridge, however, the footbridge across the road has gun embrasures – a reminder that even paternalistic employers were not necessarily immune from the violence of the age.

Paternalistic he might be, but Strutt extracted the same hard work and paid the same comparatively low wages as other employers. Frances Collier in *The Family Economy of the Working Classes in the Cotton Industry 1784–1833* (1965), quotes figures for family earnings at Belper for the years 1801–5. These showed, at one end of the scale, a family with two adults and five children at work receiving an average of slightly over £2 a week, while other families, of similar size, sometimes only managed half that amount. The earnings, though, are very much in line with those of other textile-workers, and are considerably better than those for some workers in other parts of the country. Sir Frederick Eden in his Report on *The State of the Poor* (1797), for example, gives the wages for an agricultural worker in Devon as a shilling a day, and adds:

> 'No labourer can, at present, maintain himself, wife and two children, on his earnings: they have all relief from the parish, either in money, or in corn at a reduced price. Before the present war, wheaten bread, and cheese, and about twice a week, meat, were their usual food; it is now barley bread, and no meat: they have, however, of late, made great use of potatoes. . . . Labourers' children, here, are often bound out apprentices, at 8 years of age. . . . A very few years ago, labourers thought themselves disgraced by receiving aid from the parish; but this sense of shame is now totally extinguished.'

The housing at Belper is itself indicative of a far better standard of living than that of the Devon labourer.

The main interest in Belper is to be found in the mill buildings themselves, and North mill which shows us how a mill of this period was organized is a building of great historical significance. The first Belper mill was built in 1778, the second, North mill, was added in 1786, and West mill was built in 1795. All these buildings were constructed using timber as the main framework, and in an industry that used crude machinery, which frequently overheated, to work a highly inflammable raw material, the fire risks were high. This fate overtook North mill, which went up in flames early in the morning of 12 January 1803, taking with it a lot of valuable machinery, none of which was insured. Strutt immediately began a new building, but this time he intended it to be fireproof. He had already built a fireproof mill at Derby, but in the rebuilding of North mill he went much further in the use of new construction techniques.

Seen from the outside, North mill is a typical industrial building of its period. The main range runs parallel to the river, six storeys high and fifteen bays long, with a six-bay wing projecting at right angles, both ranges being quite narrow. It is built of stone up to first floor level and brick above that to the slate roof. The windows are the usual wooden-framed segmented arched pattern. It is attractive but unremarkable. Inside, however, the interest soon quickens. The building is constructed on a series of very low-rise brick arches which spring from iron beams supported on iron pillars A brick floor is laid on these arches, and the pillars are held together by iron ties to resist the thrust of the arches (plate 26). In this way Strutt achieved a very rigid, fireproof framework, although it looks surprisingly delicate when seen on the upper floors. Going down to ground floor and semi-basement level, however, the appearance of the structure changes dramatically. Ramps lead down from the street outside and up again to the main body of the mill, and at this lowest level everything is dark and massive, more like the vaults of a medieval abbey than part of any industrial building. The base of the whole elaborate structure of pillars and arches can now be seen to rest on huge stone pyramids, from which thick pillars protrude (plate 27). The main power source for the mill was situated down here as well, and though the water wheel has gone, the circular markings in the wheel pit indicate its size. Again, the size is impressive, for the wheel was eighteen foot diameter and twenty-three foot long, and the pit is spanned by a single great stone arch. From the wheel, a main shaft led to the upper floors, and this in turn was geared to a number of overhead horizontal shafts from which belts were taken to drive the individual machines. According to Rees' *Cyclopædia* (1812), there were thirty-four spinning frames with a total of 4,236 spindles, as well as carding engines and other machines. One last point to look at at this lowest level of the mill is a space under the stairs which once housed a stove from which air rose through flues to all the upper floors – not just a fireproof building, but centrally heated too.

There are a number of other features of special interest at North mill. For example, the attic was used as a Sunday school room for the factory children (plate 26). Inside the eaves are curious internal gutters – lead-lined troughs which eventually carry the water away down to pipes that emerge half-way down the building. The idea, presumably, was to save on maintenance costs, as they can be repaired without the expense of erecting scaffolding. Unfortunately, someone miscalculated, and in heavy rain they overflow.

The machinery has all gone from North mill, leaving the bare workrooms, with the counting houses at the ends. But even disused it is possible to gauge the great strides made by the cotton industry in the thirty years that passed between the establishment of the first mill and this building at Belper. In 1770 the spinning of cotton was still a job for the domestic worker, or at its most elaborate was carried out using jennies in small workshops. The Cromford mill was large, but was built by traditional methods. Yet here we have a specially designed building based on an iron framework, and of such a quality that it has hardly deteriorated after almost two centuries of use. More importantly, we have a building which represents a very high capital outlay by its owner, and its rows of clattering machines required the constant attendance of the operatives, working at the same time and in the same way, if the owner was to get the return he expected from his investment. We have, in fact, all the different features that we look for in a society that has passed into an industrial phase.

5
Connecting Links

By the middle of the eighteenth century there were already sufficient signs of an unprecedented growth in trade for the lack of an appropriate transport system to be felt as a severe handicap. The bad state of the roads was mentioned in chapter 1, and their truly atrocious condition, particularly in Northern England and Scotland, was emphasized by the English army's struggle to move northward to deal with the Jacobite rebellion of 1745. Road improvements became a prime concern, particularly among the rising class of industrialists.

The old system of public highways and road works being made the responsibility of local parishes was collapsing under the double weights of apathy and ineptitude, and in its place the new system of turnpike roads was growing. The essence of the turnpikes was that a private company or trust applied to Parliament for permission to construct a specific road. After a certain amount of wrangling between interested parties, an Act was usually approved, and permission given to the trust to begin the business of raising the cash and building the road. The first thing one notices is that road-building involved raising quite considerable funds, which, in theory, were recouped from the tolls levied on the road's users, though many industrialists supported the trusts more because they needed the roads than because they hoped to gain revenue. Some roads were little more than improvements on existing routes, but in the new industrial areas major road-building programmes were often undertaken, and were considered to be of the greatest importance. An example of just how important the industrialists thought them to be can be found by studying the changes in the cloth-making area round Stroud in Gloucestershire. Paul Hawkins Fisher in *Notes and Recollections of Stroud* (1891) describes the old routes as following along the sides of the valleys, only occasionally cutting across along the lines of narrow tributary streams. This made journeys both long and complicated, so that even a journey such as that from Stroud to Chalford, only four miles apart, took a full day for a team of horses pulling a loaded waggon. An Act for turnpiking the road was not obtained until 1814, and even then there was so much local opposition, that the commissioners assembled their gangs of labourers by night and set to work levelling hedges even before the purchase contracts for the land had been agreed.

The turnpikes represented a great improvement, but by no means a complete answer to transport problems. Repairs for sections within parish boundaries were still the responsibility of the parish – a system that worked no better under the new dispensation than under the old. The new routes too often showed, in their general line, the necessity for appeasing local interests. John Scott in his *Digests of the General Highway and Turnpike Laws* (1778) puts the matter clearly:

'A Road, in my Neighbourhood, was made Turnpike about Twenty Years ago: It was proposed, in one Place, to leave the old Track (which was a hollow winding Washway), and to cross some Fields in a direct line ... unluckily there were Six or Seven little Trees, that would scarcely measure as Timber, at the further End of the Line: These belonged to a Gentleman whose *Fac Totum* was a Farmer, and an active Trustee of the Road: It was worse than sacrilege to touch these *fine young thrifty Sticks*. ... Indeed, on these and many other Occasions, with regard to Roads, Interest writes a very legible Hand ... he may read as clearly as if it were wrote on a Board by the Way Side, "The Land here belongs to some *little Great Man*, or to his particular Acquaintance; it will not be given, and dare not be taken." '

Scott lists many faults found on the turnpikes – dangerous fords still in use to save the expense of bridge-building, narrow roads, roads badly built and badly maintained. The main problem, as he saw it, lay in the practice of 'farming out' tolls, whereby the trustees handed over responsibility for the road to the highest bidder:

> 'The Trustees, when once a Road is *farmed*, have nothing to do, but meet once a year to eat Venison, and pay the *Farmer* his Annuity: the *Farmer* has nothing to do, but to do as little work, and pocket as much Money as he possibly can; he has other *Fish to fry*, other Matters to mind, than *Road-mending*: Incroachment after Incroachment takes place, the Hedges and the Trees grow till they meet overhead, the Landholders are excused from their Statute-duty, and the Water and the narrow-wheeled Waggons complete the Business. At length, perhaps, the universal Complaint of Travellers, or Menaces of Indictment, rouse the Trustees for a Moment; a Meeting is called, the Farmer sent for and reprimanded, and a few Loads of Gravel buried among the Mud, serve to keep the Way barely passable.'

The government attempted to ensure better roads by passing legislation to limit the use of the narrow-wheeled vehicles that created most of the damage – but the laws were half-hearted and their enforcement unenthusiastically pursued. Real improvement in roads had to wait for improved methods of surveying and construction to be introduced by men prepared to devote time to the problems of road-building.

Three individuals stand out for their contributions to road improvement. The first of these was a remarkable man, Jack Metcalfe, who in spite of total blindness was responsible for road construction throughout the West Riding of Yorkshire in the 1750s and 1760s, and who stressed the importance of selecting the right line and ensuring good drainage. The surveying instruments that he used are preserved in the castle of his native Knaresborough.

The second of the trio was the great Scottish engineer, Thomas Telford. In his early life he worked as a stone mason, but gradually moved on to become an architect, and began a career in road-building and bridge construction when he was appointed county surveyor for Shropshire in 1786. That was the beginning of a splendid career, during which he built roads throughout the Scottish Highlands and was employed as chief engineer for the immense London to Holyhead road project of the 1820s. The latter project, which involved the construction of the famous Conway suspension bridge and the equally famous bridge over the Menai Straits, represents the pinnacle of his achievement as a road-builder. It also gave him an opportunity to exercise his architectural talents – a chance that Telford rarely let slip by – and the results can be seen in the toll-houses he built along the road. But Telford's most important contribution was the new technique for road-surfacing that he developed. His roads were built up from carefully graded stones, starting with a solid foundation and ending with gravel or stone chips. Care over detail and professionalism were the hallmarks of Telford's road work. He stressed the point himself in his Report to the Holyhead Road Commissioners in 1820:

'The making and maintaining of roads should be considered as a separate and very important business. Workmen should be bred, and induced constantly to apply themselves to this work only, in like manner to any other distinct trade. They would then become acquainted with the quality of materials, and the proper method of using them; and contractors, by attending to roads only, would acquire experience and have better profits from low prices. Hitherto road-making and repairing have not had sufficient importance attached to them.'

We can admire Telford's skill in surveying the London–Holyhead road, particularly in the sections where it passes through the mountains of North Wales. We can also still see many examples of the bridges he built, both here and in Scotland. Rather than illustrate his work by the better-known Welsh bridges, a Scottish bridge has been selected. Tongland Bridge crosses the river Dee in Kirkcudbrightshire (plate 29). It was built to Telford's design, between 1804 and 1808, with a main span of 110 feet and with three narrow pointed arches on either side. The main arch is accentuated by heavy stones, and the appropriate Scottish baronial effect is achieved by building a projecting course on prominent dentils just below the crenellated parapet. Simulated turrets at the ends complete the effect. This is a good bridge, built in a style appropriate to its setting. To see the structure of the roads themselves is more difficult, but at the Blists

Hill Open Air Museum a section of Telford road is being reconstructed next to one of the toll-houses removed from the Holyhead Road and re-erected on this site (plate 28).

Telford's roads were entirely successful, but unfortunately very expensive, and it was left to the last of the trio, John Loudon McAdam to devise a system of road-building that was both effective and reasonably cheap. He realized that dry soil was an adequate foundation for any road so long as it could be kept dry, and that that could be achieved by covering it with graded stones, which could be hammered down to form a compact, water-tight surface. The 'macadamized' road became the most popular of all road types. When the government appointed a Select Committee to look into the state of the highways and turnpikes, they reported that there were 19,725 miles of turnpike and 95,104 miles of other roads and, while they found there was still very much work to be done and many totally inadequate roads still existed, they were unanimous in their praise of McAdam, and recommended that the government should make a suitable payment in recognition of his work. The surveyor and superintendent of mail coaches stated in his evidence that 'wherever I have found any thing done under Mr McAdam's immediate direction, or by his pupils, or even in imitation of his principles, the improvement has been most decisive, and the superiority over the common method of repairing roads most evident'. McAdam himself reported that in the years up to 1814 he had travelled some thirty thousand miles in viewing and advising on road works:

'Several of the trusts which I have been called upon to visit have paid the expenses of my journies to inspect their roads; many of them have not; and in no instance have I consented to receive any remuneration for my labour, my sole object having been to promote and extend a better and more economical system of road management, in the pursuit of which, success has exceeded my most sanguine expectations. . . .

'Wherever the roads were worst, and the season most severe, there and then I considered it my duty to be posted; for it was only by accurate observations at that time of the year, that the most useful of my inquiries could avail, as showing at the breaking up of the frosts, the effects produced on the various materials, and differently formed roads of Great Britain.'

Today, the turnpikes have been absorbed into the general road system, though it is still often easy enough to see the hand of Scott's 'little Great Man' in the bends and twists that appear without any obvious rational explanation. Some of the distinctive features of the turnpikes remain, of which the toll-houses are the most notable. They are very clearly recognizable by the way in which they jut out into the roadway to enable the collector to gather the fees from the travellers, also by the windows giving views both up and down the road, so that the collector could ensure that no one sneaked past without his noticing, and, lastly, by the space, usually left blank now, where the board once hung that informed the road's users of the tolls they were expected to pay. One of the best-known examples in the London area is the toll-house opposite the *Spaniards Inn* on Hampstead Heath, but there are many others to be seen all over the country. Another, and often attractive, reminder of the turnpike age is the milestone. These stones were made compulsory in 1773, although they were already in use on some roads at an earlier date. As each turnpike trust was responsible for the milestones along its own road, we can see the change in ownership of a road as the style of the milestones changes. There is still a quite amazing variety of different styles to be found by the roadsides, as can be seen from the small selection shown in plate 30.

But, in spite of the efforts of the road engineers, the turnpike system was better suited to the traveller in a hurry than to the needs of the industrialist looking for a way to move heavy goods in bulk. When it came to shifting commodities such as coal, land transport did not begin to compare for efficiency with transport by water. It was the need to reduce the cost of moving coal that led directly to the beginning of the great civil engineering achievement of the industrial revolution – the construction of almost three thousand miles of canal that formed a watery network linking the main industrial centres to each other and to the ports.

The canal age began when a young nobleman, frustrated by his inability to come to terms with the old river navigation companies over the business of shifting coals from his mines, took the bold step of constructing his own waterway. Francis Egerton, third Duke of Bridgewater, owned mines at Worsley in Lancashire, and the waterway that he planned was to take the coals direct from the mines into the centre of Manchester. With his agent, John Gilbert, and a millwright who was already gaining something of a reputation as an engineer, James Brindley, he proposed building a broad canal, which was to have two features that put it in a quite different class from any of the previous navigations: first, it was to take a line that was entirely independent of any natural waterway, and secondly, it was to cross the river Irwell on an aqueduct. Apart from the engineering difficulties involved, the construction of the canal was to involve the protagonist in many struggles. Before work could begin, a private Act of Parliament had to be obtained in the face of bitter opposition from the old river navigation interests. Next, the cash had to be found: the Duke had sufficient faith in the enterprise to undertake the whole of the financing from his own funds, but as the work progressed the funds often reached a perilously low state. The Duke borrowed heavily, mortgaged his estates and reached the nadir when he literally had to hide from his creditors. But, somehow, the money was found. The engineer Brindley was a stubborn and single-minded man, and needed to be; for while the duke had to cope with creditors, the engineer had to face the ridicule of other members of his profession. The idea of taking a canal across a river came in for the most criticism, and there is a story that an 'expert' was called in to give his considered view of the matter. As no one had ever attempted to build a canal in Britain of this type, let alone an aqueduct, there was in truth no such animal as a canal expert. Nevertheless, the gentleman came, viewed the proposed site at Barton and remarked, caustically, that he had often heard of castles in the air, but this was the first time he had been to see where one was to be built. The 'expert' was confounded, the aqueduct was built and the canal was opened in 1761, proving an immediate success. The Duke of Bridgewater was able to halve the price of the coal he could offer for sale in Manchester, and the amazed spectators were treated to the sight of barges sailing peacefully along, high above the Irwell. As John Phillips wrote in his *General History of Inland Navigation* (1792):

'The difference in favour of canal navigation was never more exemplified, nor appeared to more full and striking advantage than at Barton-bridge, in Lancashire, where one may see, at the same time, seven or eight stout fellows labouring like slaves to drag a boat slowly up the Irwell, and one horse or mule, or sometimes two men at most, drawing five or six of the duke's barges, linked together, at a great rate upon the canal.'

The Barton aqueduct has been demolished, but the Bridgewater canal remains. At Worsley Delph, the canal emerges from its beginnings in the Duke's mines deep in the hillside, where coal was loaded directly into the waiting boats. Because it is fed by water from the mine, the canal at this point is tinted by the dissolved minerals, so that it looks like nothing so much as tinned tomato soup (plate VII). Although later canals have involved structures even more dramatic than the Barton aqueduct, so that it is not quite the tourist attraction that it was two hundred years ago, the Bridgewater canal remains a fine broad waterway and an industrial monument of the greatest importance.

The success of the Bridgewater canal in cutting costs and making profits for its owner opened the way to the canal age. The Duke began to refill his depleted coffers and plan an extension to the Mersey at Runcorn, and James Brindley suddenly found himself in great demand as the country's one and only experienced canal engineer. He rushed around the country from London to Scotland, advising and planning – he was chief engineer for many canal projects, advised on more, made a fortune and ruined his health. But James Brindley has left his own distinctive mark on the face of the country – canals such as the Oxford, the Trent and Mersey, the Staffordshire and Worcester and many others are as clearly the work of Brindley as if he had signed them. For James Brindley had firm views of how canals should be built. He was the main exponent of the technique known as 'contour cutting', that is, keeping to one contour level for as long as possible, so that there are long uninterrupted stretches of canal, winding their way round every hump and hollow that the British countryside has to offer. The Brindley canals that delight the pleasure-boaters of today must have often infuriated the working boatmen of an earlier age: there used to be a saying among the boatmen plying their trade on the northern section of the Oxford canal that you could travel all day within earshot of the clock at Brinklow, and at Wormleighton, farther south, the canal practically encircles the hill.

Brindley was responsible for at least one other major canal engineering achievement after the Barton aqueduct, the tunnel that took the Trent and Mersey canal through the hill at Harecastle. The tunnel is 2,897 yards long, and when it was planned, doubters again appeared. But Brindley, having proved the sceptics wrong once, was quite ready to prove them wrong again. The potter, Josiah Wedgwood, who was one of the main promoters of the Trent and Mersey, reported in a letter of 12 March 1767 of a meeting of the Canal Committee:

'Mr Brindley was there & assured the Gentn. that he could complete the whole in five years from Xmas next, & there being a Gentn. present (not one of the Committee) who doubted of the possibility of its being completed in so short a time & seem'd inclin'd to lay a wager upon it, Mr B. told him, that it was a challenge he never refused upon anything which he seriously asserted & offer'd them to article in a Wager of £200 that he perform'd what he said.'

Brindley's confidence was, for once, misplaced. The five years passed and the workers struggled with rock, quicksand and water that could only be kept out of the workings by keeping an atmospheric engine working night and day. Brindley died in 1772 with the work still unfinished. It was eventually completed in 1777, and became almost as great a wonder as the Barton aqueduct had been.

Perhaps the most important decision Brindley ever took was on the occasion that he decided on the dimensions of the first lock he ever built, on the Staffordshire and Worcestershire, near to the junction with the Severn. In a country such as Britain, any artificial waterway must undergo many changes of level, and this is normally accomplished by the lock – a chamber, usually built of masonry, with gates at each end, in which the level of water can be changed by letting it into and out of the lock through sluices controlled by paddle gears. The significance of Brindley's decision was that having selected a size, and then having used the same size for every canal that he built, he established the standard pattern for the whole system. The lock he built was long and narrow, and its shape determined the shape of the boats that were to use the canal – the famous narrow boats, seventy foot long, with a 6 ft 10 in. beam.

The importance of Brindley's contribution to the canal network and the importance of the early canals to the country as a whole can be seen from the buildings, wharfs and warehouses and even towns that developed on their banks. Stourport, on the Severn, is a town which entirely owes its existence to the coming of the canals. When Brindley was looking for a suitable site for the junction between his Staffordshire and Worcestershire canal and the river, his first thoughts were to bring the canal to Bewdley, which was already established as an important trading centre, where as many as four hundred pack horses could be stabled at one time. The citizens of Bewdley, however, were quite satisfied with the *status quo* and wanted nothing to do with either the engineer or his 'stinking ditch'.The offended Brindley stomped away until he reached an inn, where, one assumes, he received a rather more friendly reception, for it was at that spot that he chose to make his junction, and it was there that the town of Stourport was born. Canal basins, maintenance yards and warehouses were built. Stables, offices, hotels for visiting tradesmen, and houses for the new citizens were also constructed. The whole area based on this junction is a perfect example of a busy Georgian trading centre. The architectural elegance of buildings such as the Tontine Hotel (plate v III) is matched by that of the purely functional buildings, such as the warehouse and maintenance buildings bordering the main basin, or even the tiny toll-house just outside the main dock area (plates 31 and 32).

A new generation of engineers carried on the work after Brindley's death, and the fascination which so many find in the present canal system derives in no small part from the individual character given to different waterways by their different engineers. John Rennie's canals are notable for their beautiful classical aqueducts, the Avoncliff and Dundas on the Kennet and Avon, and the incomparable Lune aqueduct on the Lancaster canal at Lancaster (plate 33).

28 A Telford toll house reconstructed at Blists Hill beside a section of road built to the Telford formula of graded stones and good drainage

Above left Telford's stylish road bridge crosses the River Dee
ongland. The centre arch has a 110 foot span

30 Below left and this page A selection of milestones

Stourport: 31 *Above left* Part of the Georgian town that grew up at the junction of river and canal; 32 *Below left* Toll cottage at the beginning of the Staffordshire and Worcester canal

33 *Right* John Rennie's masterpiece – the classical aqueduct that carries the canal over the River Lune

34 *Above* A rock cutting at the foot of Tyrley locks on the Shropshire Union canal. The rock still carries the scars of pick and drill

35 *Left* The great aqueduct at Pont Cysyllte carries the Ellesmere canal over a hundred feet above the De valley

Gloucester docks: 36 *Above* The towering
warehouses that tell of days of prosperity; 37
Left The 'pillar warehouse' at the entrance to the
docks

A common canal problem – to take the towpath across the water in such a way that there is no need to unharness the horse from the boat: 38 *Left* At Congleton on the Macclesfield canal, the problem finds a uniquely elegant solution; 39 *Below* The other side of the bridge with a pair of narrow boats passing through, but no longer horse-drawn 40 *Above right* Another problem solved by canal engineers – how to build a bridge on the skew. This example is on the Glasson arm of the Lancaster canal 41 *Below right* Wharf, wharf manager's house and warehouse, where the tramway meets the Brecon and Abervagenny canal at Llanfoist

Blaenavon iron works: 42 *Above* A
general view showing, on the right, the
line of blast furnaces set against the hill.
At the bottom are the remains of the
engine house and one casting house;
43 *Right* Like a medieval castle – the
crumbling core of a furnace with the
balance tower behind

Right Blaenavon's casting house and engine stack
Below Workers' houses, literally in the shadow of the works

Iron workers' houses in South Wales: 46 *Left* Ynysfach, Merthyr Tydfil; 47 *Below left* The Triangle, Pentrebach

Above A bizarre sight in an empty landscape – the chunky
pyramids of the blast furnaces of the Morley Park ironworks

Right All that remains of the Muirkirk ironworks

Wortley Top forge: 50 *Above* A general view, showing the great wooden cranes used to move the railway axles that were the main product of the forge in later years; 51 *Left* One of the two belly helve hammers, showing the water wheel used for power, the wooden 'spring', and the shaped anvil

Abbeydale scythe works: 52 *Left* The tilt hammers; 53 *Below* The courtyard and its surrounding buildings; the oblong chimney marks the crucible furnace shop, the tilt hammer shop is in the foreground

54 A placid exterior hiding a lethal interior – Redditch
forge mill, where needles were manufactured

William Jessop was not much given to dramatic flourishes in his work, but was a superb planner and surveyor, which makes it more difficult to appreciate the value of his work, except by travelling one of his routes. His greatest achievement was the Grand Junction, now part of the Grand Union canal, with its double locks and long wide tunnels providing a new ease of movement. Then there was Thomas Telford, whose authorship of the great aqueduct that carries the Ellesmere canal over the river Dee at Pont Cysyllte is in doubt, but who was responsible for the deep cuttings and high embankments that enabled him to take a direct line through the landscape, as in his Birmingham and Liverpool Junction canal, now part of the Shropshire Union (plate 34).

The great boom in canal-building came in the 1790s, when canal-financing moved from being the concern of local industrialists, as interested in improving the means to transport their goods as in the possible profits, to being the hunting ground of speculators. Early canals such as the Trent and Mersey and the Birmingham were soon showing their value as trading routes, and as the receipts began to pour in, so the price of the company shares rose. Birmingham shares, for example, which had cost £140 in 1767, rose to £370 in 1782 and then rocketed to £1,170 by 1792. In the undignified scramble to get a share in each and every new canal venture, the combatants rarely paused to assess the value of the schemes they were so eager to help promote. The speculators neither cared whether a proposed route was feasible, nor whether there would ever be any traffic to use it – as far as they were concerned every canal was going to be another Birmingham or Bridgewater. The proverbial pot of gold had moved from the end of the rainbow to the end of the canal, and proved equally elusive. Inevitably, although some companies were formed which got sensibly on with the job of filling a gap in the expanding system, many were formed which had little more to show at the end of the day than a bundle of papers and a mile or two of cut starting at nowhere in particular and ending in a very similar position. Others managed to complete the canals, only to find that they were not really needed, and the expected revenue never materialized. The years following the speculative mania saw many of the companies in difficulty, faced with problems no less familiar today –

trade recession leading to shortage of cash, the shortage of cash accompanied by steadily rising costs. The story of many a canal construction was one of frustrating delays while work was held up for lack of funds. Of the canals that were finally completed, the most successful were those which had obeyed the Duke of Bridgewater's dictum, that a good canal should always have 'coal at the heel of it'.

Inevitably, the rapid spread of canals led to an equally rapid development in canal technology. A feature which greatly helped in later developments was the growth of a specialized work force from the original *ad hoc* collection of local labourers. The canal-workers took their name from the earlier routes, and became known as 'navigators', soon shortened to the more familiar 'navvy'. The canal navvy developed two reputations – one for a remarkable capacity for hard physical work, the other for an equally remarkable capacity for drunkenness and rioting. It is difficult to say in which he took the greater pride. With this skilled work force at his disposal, the canal engineer was able to take a more adventurous line. Where the old canals had meandered over the countryside, the new generation pushed their way straight through it. Tunnels were made longer and wide enough for boats to pass each other, hills were overcome by building spectacular flights of locks, such as the group of thirty at Tardebigge on the Worcester and Birmingham canal, or the very impressive flight of twenty-nine on the Kennet and Avon at Caen Hill; occasionally locks were run together to form 'staircases', in which the top gate of one lock formed the bottom of the next, as at Bingley where the five-lock staircase lifts the Leeds and Liverpool canal over sixty feet. More important, if less spectacular, was the development of the technique of 'cut and fill'. This consisted of digging a deep cutting through high ground – a laborious technique, involving the use of barrow runs by which men wheeled barrow loads of excavated dirt up the slippery planks laid along the muddy slopes of the cut – and then carting the excavated material away to the valley to build up an embankment. But of all the techniques used to overcome the difficulties of getting an essentially flat canal across an inconveniently bumpy landscape, none is so impressive as the aqueduct, and no aqueduct is as impressive as the Pont Cysyllte on the Ellesmere canal (plate 35).

Spectacular features have undoubtedly helped to make canals popular with twentieth-century holiday-makers, but it is as well to remember they were built as engineering solutions to specific problems of geography, and when assessing the value of canals it was the balance sheet that received the careful scrutiny not the aqueducts. The canal system grew because it provided good cheap transport, and if we want to assess what it meant to the industrial development of Britain it is to the great mesh of canals that centred on Birmingham that we should turn. It was Birmingham, which finished the age with more miles of canals than Venice, that typifies the commercial value of the system.

The final stage of the canal age came with the construction of ship canals. Judged as a piece of engineering, the most important of these is Telford's Caledonian canal, built to enable boats to avoid the long and hazardous passage round the north coast of Scotland. It was an engineering triumph, but a commercial failure. More successful if more modest, was the Gloucester and Berkeley ship canal, built to take ships from the Severn up to Gloucester. Its importance lay in enabling large vessels to reach Gloucester, so that the city retained its position as a major inland port. The importance is underlined by the scale of dock and warehouse building to be seen at Sharpness at the junction with the Severn, and is stressed even more sharply at the terminus in the heart of Gloucester. The red brick warehouses, their regular horizontal patterns of windows only broken by the verticals of loading bays and hoists, line the canal basins, and their stark, functional bulks contrast oddly with the ornate tower of the cathedral that just manages to poke its head over the roof line (plates 36 and 37). A comparison of the illustrations of Stourport and Gloucester says more clearly than words just how far inland navigation had advanced in half a century.

The growth of canals brought into existence a new group of workers, the canal boatmen – a group whose reputation soon began to rival that of the canal navvy. They had an equal capacity for hard work, which was needed for some of the arduous tasks they were called on to perform, particularly 'legging'. Many of the early tunnels had no towpaths, so the horse was unhitched and the boat was 'legged' through the tunnel by the boatmen, who lay on their backs on boards projecting from the sides of the boats, pushing with their feet against the side of the tunnel to move the boat along. The boatmen also shared the navvies' reputation for quarrelsomeness and bloody-mindedness. Among the many complaints about the bad behaviour of the boatmen, this by George Forest, the agent for the Glamorgan Canal Company, to the Dowlais Iron Company, is typical:

'I scarcely know one Boatman so *determinedly bad in his Conduct on the Canal*, in the present instance he on Saturday last wilfully stopped at the Canal at the Treble Locks (*where the greatest obstacle on the line already exists*) for more than an hour & a half, without any pretext whatever of misunderstanding or any thing of the kind, but because he *would* wilfully & knowingly force his Boat into the lock before his turn, and afterwards having gone with his Boat three miles higher up the Canal he then left it to the sole Care of a little Child (his Brother) who true to the example set him, when told by the lock-keeper to stop the Boat till his brother returned, only cursed him & went on in spite of all remonstrances, and it was only when I came up with him on my return from Cardiff that this embryo Villain would stop.'

Even more lurid tales appeared in the pages of a short-lived magazine *The Canal Boatman*, begun by a group of evangelists whose aim – unrealized – was the reform of the working boatmen. To convince their readers that reform was necessary, they published stories of their atrocious behaviour, such as that of Mr Attlebury who was accused of maltreating his horse. The police attempted to arrest him, but other boatmen arrived on the scene, and in the fight that followed 'Sergeant Collins was struck a tremendous blow in the face by George, and Walters at the same time being pierced by a boat-hook through the lip. They were then thrust into the canal, and the prisoners vociferating "Drown them! – Murder them!" The policemen now begged for mercy, and the prisoners proceeded with their barges.'

But whatever the faults of the boatmen, the canals answered the immediate need of the new industrial age for cheap and convenient transport for bulk goods. This announcement from *The Times* of 11 April 1807 says it perfectly:

'It is with considerable pleasure we announce to the public, the progress of the Worcester and Birmingham canal, which, on Monday the 30th March, was opened from Hopwood to Tardebig, an extension of nearly five miles. On that day a number of vessels arrived at the wharf at Tardebig, laden with upwards of 300 tons of coals, most part of which was immediately sold on such terms as to insure a continued supply of that indispensable article. This must prove of vast importance to the Owners of Coal Mines communicating with that Canal. We now contemplate with pleasure the conclusion of this important work ... which renders the conveyance between the port of Bristol and Birmingham certain, cheap, and expeditious.'

Much of the great system of waterways built up in those years has become derelict, and the life of the working boats is almost at an end. Yet approximately two-thirds does remain, and has found a new use by the thousands who take to the water for pleasure rather than business. The canals have a unique distinction in being virtually the only modern transport system that has enhanced rather than ruined the countryside through which it was built, and this is because its construction has been so closely governed by the nature of the countryside itself. The plain canal-side buildings and the hundreds of simple bridges were almost invariably built from the most appropriate local material – clay dug in the excavation work was burned for bricks to use in the Caen Hill flight, and where a canal passed through stone country, as does the Leeds and Liverpool, then stone was the material used. The line of the canal is also a function of the physical characteristics of the landscape, so much so that when on the Oxford canal the route joins for a few miles with the natural waters of the river Cherwell, the change from artificial cut to natural waterway hardly registers. It is this blending in with the landscape that makes what was once the major transport route of the early industrial age, the escape route for thousands trying to get away from a later industrial age.

The canal age was short lived, and even before the end of the eighteenth century the system that was to supplant it was well established. The tramway was developed from the old wooden railways that were built on the Tyneside coal field. The major step forward was the replacement of wooden by iron rails, and the tramway soon became an important part of the transport system, linking coal fields, iron-works and other industrial sites to each other and to the canal network. The name predominating in the history of tramway construction is that of Benjamin Outram. He was also a canal engineer, responsible for, among others, the Peak Forest canal with its fine flight of locks and handsome stone aqueduct at Marple in Cheshire, but it is for his tramways that he became famous. One area, in particular, made extensive use of tramway systems and Outram's expertise, and that was the valleys of South Wales. The narrow valleys might have been suitable for canal construction along a north–south axis, but the high, bordering hills made construction of connecting routes between the valleys virtually impossible. The tramway was the obvious solution to the problem. One such canal-tramway interchange can be seen at Llanfoist on the Brecon and Abergavenny canal.

The tramway was constructed of iron rails resting on stone blocks. The trucks from the local Garnddyrys iron-works were drawn by horses to the top of the hillside overlooking the canal. The horses were unhitched, and the trucks winched down the track to run across a bridge over the canal or be diverted to run up to the canal-side warehouse. The warehouse itself is a two-storey building, with the ground floor open to the canal and the upper floor supported by wooden beams carried on solid stone pillars (plate 41). It is built against a slight slope so that goods could be brought direct to the covered first floor of the warehouse and then lowered through trap-doors for loading into the barges. In some canal-tramway inter-sections, the body of the truck could be lifted from its bogie and fitted into place in the waiting barge – eighteenth-century container-ization. This was not the case here. In the plate, a truck of the type once used at Llanfoist can be seen standing outside the warehouse – this particular one having been recovered from an old abandoned drift mine. The wharf manager's house can also be seen in the back-ground, and an interesting point to note here is that a small tunnel leads under the canal by the house – a necessary piece of work to provide access to the house that didn't involve crossing the tramway bridge in the face of the rapidly descending trucks. Traces of the tramway itself can be found by following the track up the wooded hillside, where a number of the original stone blocks with the characteristic bolt holes can still be seen, and, in places, lengths of rail have been recently spiked in place by enthusiastic school parties (plate ix).

It was on the tramways of South Wales that Trevithick conducted his successful experiments with steam locomotives and began the process that ended the canal age, thus, incidentally bearing out another of the Duke of Bridgewater's dicta, who claimed that canals would do well enough if they could keep clear of 'those damned tramroads'. But, in their day, the tramroads played an important part in the build-up of the industrial life of South Wales. The iron railways not only helped make the growth of the iron industry in the area a possibility, but they were also themselves symptomatic of the increased demand for the metal. The iron industry may have been slow to take up the lead of the Darbys, but in the second half of the eighteenth century, it more than made up for its earlier inactivity.

6
Growth of the Iron Industry

The main difficulty that stood in the way of widespread use of the coke-smelting process in iron production was the continuing difficulty of producing malleable iron that could be squeezed out between rollers to make rods and bars, or that could be slit and drawn into wires. Abraham Darby II had some success in producing iron for the forges, but a simple, economical and reliable method was not yet found. The solution to the problems of coke-smelting came from a remote wooded valley in Shropshire, the solution to the problem of producing iron for the forges came from another area far from traditional industrial regions – Fareham in Hampshire.

Henry Cort arrived in the iron-making industry almost by accident. He had loaned money to a Mr Morgan, who owned the Fintley iron mill, and when Morgan was unable either to make the mill profitable or to repay his debts, Cort took over the concern in 1775. It was an old-fashioned business, that was failing mainly because there was insufficient water to keep the machinery working, and Cort's first task was to set about improving the water supply. In 1780 he received an important contract for supplying iron hoops for masts for the Portsmouth dockyard. This acted as an incentive to Cort to make even more strenuous efforts to improve the water situation, and also to investigate ways in which he could improve the techniques of production. His first success led to a patent in 1783 for a method of producing circular rods of iron by passing heated bars of the metal between grooved rollers, turned by water power – the rolling mill. The following year he applied for a far more important patent, for his new technique of making wrought iron by 'puddling'.

Cort's process was very simple to work. The iron from the furnaces is reheated in a reverbatory furnace – that is one in which the heat is not applied directly, but by hot gases passing over the metal. The gases are produced by heating coke at one end of the furnace, and are then allowed to pass through a constricted space between the surface of the metal and the roof of the furnace, before passing out through a chimney. While this is going on, the molten metal is stirred with iron bars passed through holes in the brickwork of the furnace. The molten metal begins to form clods – 'comes into nature' – and is, after hammering, then ready for the rollers. Not much remains of the site where this simple, but effective, process was invented, though part of a reverbatory furnace with the holes for the puddlers' stirring rods can still be seen.*

Cort's invention removed the last obstacle to the move away from the traditional iron-making areas and the dependence on charcoal. The new areas to be developed were those where the main raw materials were most conveniently grouped together – iron ore, coal, and stone for building and for use as a flux to aid the melting of the metals in the furnaces. South Wales met all the criteria, and development soon began as the English iron-masters came to set up business in the wild valleys. Thomas Hill, of Stafford, for example, with his associates Thomas Hopkins and Benjamin Pratt, obtained a lease from the Earl of Abergavenny in 1789 for the establishment of an iron-works at Blaenavon. William Coxe visited the site in 1798 and described what he saw in his *Historical Tour Through Monmouthshire* (1801):

'At some distance, the works have the appearance of a small town, surrounded with heaps of ore, coal and limestone, and enlivened with all the bustle and activity of an opulent and increasing establishment. The view of the buildings, which are constructed in the excavations of the rocks, is extremely picturesque, and heightened by the volumes of black smoke emitted by the furnaces. . . .

*The site was fully described in two articles in *Industrial Archaeology*, February 1971.

Although these works were only finished in 1789, three hundred and fifty men are employed.'

The site now looks less like a small town and more like the remains of an old fortress as the bustle and activity have all gone, leaving a landscape dominated by the crumbling towers of the furnaces (plate 42). The furnaces themselves are typical of the type to be found in a late eighteenth-century iron-works. Most of their outer cladding of masonry has fallen away, revealing the circular brick furnace strengthened by iron bands (plate 43). The row of five furnaces is, as usual, built against the hillside to make for easier loading, and originally a charge house stood at the top of the furnace bank to hold the charge, which was then wheeled across the bridges to the top of the furnaces. This arrangement can be seen in plate 42. The furnaces were tapped at the bottom, and the molten metal allowed to run into moulds set in the sand of the casting-house floor. Where bar metal was required, the moulds were in the form of a single central channel with side channels radiating off from it – the similarity to a sow and its litter produced the name 'pig iron'. The gable ends and walls of two of the casting houses still stand (plate 44). It is interesting to compare these remains with the illustration that accompanied Coxe's description of the works – the blast furnaces look very different from the square towers shown in the Coxe engraving, but the casting houses and other details are much the same. Beyond the casting houses is the stack that marks the site of the engine house for the blowing engine for the furnaces.

The most impressive single structure at Blaenavon is the huge masonry tower, topped by iron pillars of a classical style that seems rather out of place in this rough landscape (plate 43). This splendid pile of masonry represents the remains of a water balance tower. The main transport for Blaenavon was provided by the tramway that linked the works to other iron-working sites and ultimately to the canal at Llanfoist. Movement within the site was more of a problem, for although the steep hillside was ideal for charging the furnaces, it made the shifting of heavy material between the upper and lower levels very difficult. So this device, which used the weight of water to move the goods up and down, was constructed. Two balanced containers were used – add water to one and it would descend while the other rose, pump the water out again, and the process would be reversed.

A major difficulty facing the iron-masters when they first came to Blaenavon was the housing of the work force. They found a quiet little hamlet, occupied by a few farmers; as can be seen in the plates, it is surrounded by bleak and inhospitable moorland. When Coxe visited the works, they had only been in operation for ten years, but already, as he mentions, they were employing three hundred and and fifty workers: the housing shortage was acute, and extraordinary measures had been taken to deal with it. The tramway, from the ore and coal mines, at one point passed over a ten-arched viaduct, and the owners hit on the bright idea of putting a pitched roof over the whole structure and filling in the arches to provide living space. Coxe describes the scene at the viaduct: 'Numerous workmen continually pass and repass, and low cars, laden with coal or iron ore, roll along with their broad and grooved wheels.' It is, he adds 'a singular and animated picture'. He does not, alas, record the comments of the families forced to live beneath this scene of animation. This kind of *ad hoc* housing was not unique to Blaenavon. At the Dowlais works, in nearby Merthyr Tydfil, an even more unlikely piece of in-filling went on, a family actually being housed under the furnace bridge, with tragic results, as recorded in a document of June 1793:

> 'Old Edward Maddy . . . his wife, and another old Man, found dead in their House under the Bridge House in the Old Furnace, Suffocated as is supposed (and without doubt it is so) by the Damp coming thro' the Air Holes of the Furnace into their House.'

The skilled workmen who had to be enticed to come to Blaenavon obviously expected something better than a bricked-up railway arch for themselves and their families. A group of houses was built across from the furnace bank, and as the works extended from the three furnaces operating in 1796 to the five furnaces now on the site, so the housing was extended. The oldest surviving houses face each other across the open square at the foot of the balance tower (plate 45). They are not large – the floor area inside is an average of nineteen foot by fourteen foot – but they are strongly built of rough sandstone rubble with flagstone paving on the ground floor. Evidence that the builders came with the other workers from England can be seen in the construction, where the brick arches over the windows are typical of English rather than local Welsh practice. A map of 1819, when all five furnaces were at work, shows the square much as it is today (plate 45), but with one of the houses being used as a shop. More houses were added at Blaenavon between 1812 and 1832 – terraces of mainly three-roomed houses, such as Upper New Rank in Blaen-avon.

The closeness of the early houses to the works was more than a physical closeness, for it emphasized the complete dependence of the workers on their employers: workers who had been tempted to come from as far away as Northumberland or even Scotland could not easily look for another job, particularly when their only home was owned by the company. As the Welsh industry grew, more men came into the area, and more new houses had to be built. The main centre was at Merthyr Tydfil where, for example, the Ynysfach works were established in 1801 by the Crawshay family as an extension of their Cyfarthfa works. The blast for the new furnaces was supplied by steam engine, and the Ynysfach engine house, behind the College of Further Education, is a fine example of the high quality of local masonry work. The use of contrasting stone for the prominent quoins and the main walls reflects a very popular Welsh vernacular tradition, to be seen in hundreds of chapels in South Wales (plate x). The workers' houses were built in terraces near the works, and many of these are very similar both in size and design to those of Blaenavon, though some are even smaller, and again show the influence of continuing local traditions in building (plate 46). The best example of a group of specially built houses is to be found in the triangle at Pentrebach to the south of Merthyr (plate 47).

The characteristic that at once strikes one about these early houses is their closeness to the works, which in the case of the iron industry meant living within the sight and sound of the furnaces with their heat, dirt and twenty-four-hour working pattern. Life cannot have been very comfortable in such surroundings, and many of the cottages were very cramped for living space – look, for example, at the tiny first-floor windows right under the eaves of the Ynysfach cottages. Against that must be set the fact that these are very solidly constructed cottages – that they have survived is evidence in itself – and they are buildings which still inspire affection from their occupants. Visiting the cottages, notebook and pencil in hand, I was taken at once for 'the man from the council', and it is a sad reflection of attitudes towards the council that the next assumption made was that the destruction rather than improvement of the cottages was the object of the visit. It was made very clear indeed that the families who lived in these terraces had no wish whatsoever to be moved elsewhere. Like many communities based on a particular industry, places like Ynysfach or Blaenavon build up into something greater than the stones of their houses. Conditions today, however, are very different from those found when the iron-works first came to this area, and to elaborate on the evidence from the buildings we can add the documentary evidence from the surviving papers of one of the most famous of the Merthyr companies, the Dowlais Iron Company.

The Dowlais Company was formed in 1759, and soon began recruiting workers from all over Britain. By the end of the century, the great expansion in the South Wales iron-works had led to a shortage of skilled workmen, and the iron-masters were not above attempting a little poaching from other nearby concerns. The offended party usually expressed the greatest indignation, as Joseph Priest shows in a letter to Joseph Guest of Dowlais: 'I conceive thou canst not be aware that someone from your works has been down here twice enticing our men away by offers of high wages.' But if the iron-masters were prepared to argue with each other and offer out lures to workmen, they soon closed ranks if the men themselves tried to move elsewhere in the hunt for better pay. William Wood of the Penydarren works wrote this letter in 1803:

'In consequence of a disagreement with some of our Pudlers we are apprehensive that the following Men or some of them may leave the place and in that case probably apply to you for work. Should they make this application we hope and request that you will not employ them, the dispute being such as materially concerns every iron-master in the Country.'

Richard Crawshay put the matter even more strongly in a letter of May 1797. He had been trying for some time to change from the piece-work system of payment, under which the men were getting 'such excessive Wages as are Scandalous to pay', to payment of a standard weekly wage. But the men turned his proposals down, saying that they could earn 15s a week with house and fuel provided, by working as cinder-wheelers at Dowlais. Crawshay wrote off in horror, protesting that 'if when any of our Men or yours insist upon Wages incompatible the other will Countenance them by immediate employ, we shall injure all our Works and make resistance to all reasonable remonstrances with the Workmen in vain'.

The iron-masters believed it was their right, and their duty, to fix prices. At 'a Meeting of Iron-masters concerned in the Casting Trade' in January 1811, they all agreed on minimum prices for all categories of tramway rails – and, as we have just seen, they also believed in getting together to fix wages. The attempts of the workers to follow their example by forming their own unions – 'those drunken Combinations', the masters called them – were met with fierce opposition. Nowhere in Britain was the movement of workers to combine resisted more fiercely than in the iron-works of South Wales. The 'imported' workers were usually employed under contract, rather like the workers brought to Cromford, and similarly they could be hauled up before the magistrate for speaking out. In 1799, the Dowlais workmen protested about a rise in coal prices, and the unfortunate spokesman found himself in the Bridewell, from where he wrote 'I ham sorry that I abueses your Honor in taking so much Upon me to Speek for Others', and pleaded to be set free.

Confrontations between masters and men almost invariably ended in victory for the former. Early in 1799 the Dowlais employers decided to discontinue the practice of handing out a guinea when the output from a furnace passed a particular level. Increased production they argued was due to their 'having expended £3,000 to improve our Blast' rather than increased exertions on the part of the men. So, without making any announcement of their decision, they abruptly discontinued the payments. The results are told in a letter from one of the protesting workmen, who had lost both job and home by his protest:

'About 18 months back I agreed to Come to Dowlais to be keeper at No. 3. So when I went to set to work I found the furnace in very bad Condition for the hearth would not hold the iron of 3 hours blowing and Mr Onnions tould Me Several times that they Could do no good with her from the first blowing in to that time I came to her, but however I got the furnace in good Condition Enough in about the Space of 9 days or a fortnight and Sir I refer you to the truth of what I write to Mr Onnions who I make no doubt will Sertify the same: I did not Expect no reward, but I must confess I thought I should have been placed a little more in the Confidence of my Employers than if the furnace had done well before, all this I submit to your Consideration: and Now Sir another thing I have to Lay before you is: we made at No. 3 Something above 51 tons of iron about 3 weeks back and the other two furnaces had made something above 40 tons each. So Dick Davis hapened to go to the office first and the guenea was refused to him as was Costomary, so he Came and told the Rest of the keepers and me how it was. Then they all declared that they would not work Except they should have it. So we went all together to the office, and because Dick Davis and me Could Speak English they deseired us to taugh for them as well as our selves. So Consiquently there was Some dispute but there Was nothing spoke that was vexatious. But however we insisted on having the gueneas that was then due, and we did not Look at it to be just to stop this money without any previous Notice; and then we where Willing to work, for the same as they did in other iron-works, or we would Come to aney other agreement that Was reasonable; and now Sir, I am informed by Mr Onnions that I am to be discharged and Dick Davis likewise because we spoke and the rest did not, when at the same time they was all there and spoke the words in the Welsh tongue to us as we spoke to the masters. . . .'

Unhappy relations between masters and men continued on into the nineteenth century, with the former doing all in their power to prevent the formation of unions. Thomas Guest found scriptural evidence of the evil of unionism, and sternly pointed out exactly why it was unchristian to ask for higher wages: 'In providing for your own house you are not to infringe on the providential order of God, by invading the rights of others, by attempting to force upon those whom God has set over you, the adoption of such regulations and the payment of such wages as would be beneficial to yourselves.'

Although many of the South Wales iron-works have disappeared, leaving no more trace than the slag from the furnaces, in many others there are still remains that speak of the age of their prosperity. The scale of the works constructed at the end of the eighteenth century tells a clear tale of expanding business and high capital investment. At Hirwaun, for example, the scale of work necessary to provide for the transport of ore and coal to the furnace banks is hinted at by the high causeway across the river valley, which still has its twin lines of stone sleepers marking the line of the old tramway. Work on this scale was not undertaken unless the builders felt that it was worth the trouble – and trouble it must have been, judging by the spattering of iron tie beams all over the structure. Even here, where the furnaces and surface buildings have all but disappeared, the extent of the works can still be traced, and the size of the town, with its many examples of houses of the period, shows again the effect that the iron industry had on this area of Britain.

It was not only in South Wales and Shropshire that the iron-making industry flourished. The Black Country was a scene of great activity, and rivalry between the different areas was often intense. The older iron-makers took rather a dim view of what they regarded as an upstart and inferior branch of their trade. A letter from Shropshire in 1819 looks at the doings in the Midlands with a very jaundiced eye:

'In Staffordshire landed property is very much divided; and, naturally, all the proprietors desirous of turning their coal and iron mines to *immediate* account. Hence there is a colliery in almost every field. As there is not sale for such an immense quantity of coal and ironstone, several of those little proprietors unite together and build furnaces; clerks from the neighbouring manufactories are taken in as partners to direct the concerns; the tradesmen of the towns in the vicinity who can raise a hundred or two hundred pounds, form part of the firm; and it is in this way that the iron-works have been multiplied in that county. The proprietors embark all their property, and *all that they can borrow* in these establishments. This slippery foundation is rendered still more so by an inferiority in the quality of their iron when compared with that of South Wales and Shropshire. From this latter circumstance, whenever the make of iron exceeds the demand Staffordshire is the first in feeling the deficiency in the orders, and as the trade of that county cannot (for want of capital) bear stock, they immediately reduce the prices to obtain new customers. ... In short that county is "a millstone round the neck of the iron trade" and from which it cannot extricate itself.'

Or to put it another way, the Staffordshire iron-works were under-pricing the Welsh, and, from the many complaints found in the Dowlais records, the iron from those works was not always up to standard, either. The iron industry was, in any case, entering a period of great expansion, as the tramways developed into railways. An interesting sidelight on the beginning of the railway age is a letter written to the Dowlais Company, asking for an opinion on the value of different types of railway. The writer, a subscriber to the proposed Stockton and Darlington railway, writes with an earthiness seldom found in official documents: 'It is astonishing the number of different opinions we have received upon this Subject, one Person says, "I am of opinion there is as much difference between a Rail and a Tram Road as there is on a dark Night between the best part of a Black and White Woman."'

There was much activity outside these main areas of iron-making, though in many parts the industry has simply died, leaving behind bizarre monuments in unlikely places. The Morley Park iron-works near Heage in Derbyshire, for example, once employed four hundred men, but now the area has gone back to the farmers, leaving two stone furnaces standing in the middle of the fields. The furnaces are over thirty feet high, yet they seem almost insignificant as you approach them – it is only when you are close that the dwarfing effect of the wide, open landscape disappears and they can be seen for the massive structures that they are (plate 48). They are built of sandstone with the harder gritstone reinforcing arches and quoins; the older of the two dates from 1780, the second from 1818.

The Scottish industry was slower to change to the new methods, although the famous and very progressive Carron Company was founded as early as 1759. Little of the early works remains, but Carron has established a special place in British industrial history through the notable skill of its armament manufacturers who developed the 'Carronade', a short large-bore cannon that was used at Waterloo and at Trafalgar. More peaceably, it was here that the inventor James Watt received early help and encouragement. B. Faujas de Saint-Fond visited Carron, and although he was not allowed to see the secret boring process for the carronades, he did see a great deal of the iron-making, which he described in his *Travels in England, Scotland and the Hebrides* (1799). His description is typical of that of an educated man of his time, mixing careful observation of technology with high-flown romanticism and classical allusion. His first description, of the methods used for coking the coal, is straightforward enough:

> 'A quantity of coal is placed on the ground, in a round heap, of from twelve to fifteen feet in diameter, and about two feet in height. As many as possible of the large pieces are set on end, to form passages for the air; above them are thrown the smaller pieces, and coal dust, and in the midst of this circular heap is left a vacancy of a foot wide, where a few faggots are placed to kindle it. Four or five apertures of this kind are formed round the ring, particularly on the side exposed to the wind. . . . As the fire spreads, the mass increases in bulk, becomes spongy and light, cakes into one body, and at length loses its bitumen, and emits no more smoke. It then acquires a red, uniform colour, inclining a little to white; in which state it begins to break into gaps and chinks, and to assume the appearance of the underside of a mushroom. At this moment the heap must be quickly covered with ashes . . . to deprive it of air.'

Having described this rather primitive coking technique, Saint-Fond gets notably more excited when he is taken to see the furnaces themselves. At that time there were four at Carron, each being forty-five feet high, with a blast supplied by water bellows. They were tapped every six hours.

'Each furnace is supplied by four air pumps, of a great width; where the air compressed into cylinders, uniting into one tunnel and directed towards the flame, produces a sharp rustling noise, and so violent a tremor, that one not previously informed of it, would find it difficult to avoid a sensation of terror. . . . When one observes, at a little distance, so many masses of burning coal on one side, and so many volumes of flame, darting to a great height above the high furnace, on the other – and at the same time hears the noise of weighty hammers striking upon resounding anvils, mingled with the loud roaring of bellows – one doubts whether he is at the foot of a volcano in actual eruption, or whether he has been transported by some magical effect to the brink of the cavern, where Vulcan and his Cyclops are occupied in preparing thunderbolts.'

In the half century following the foundation of the Carron works, very few other iron-works were started, and of those that were, many have subsequently closed. The village of Glenbuck was the site of a brief venture by English iron-makers, who started a furnace in 1795 and went bankrupt in 1813. The furnace remains standing in what is now an almost deserted village, as a somewhat forlorn reminder of a once-busy industry. At nearby Muirkirk the industry survived for a considerably longer time – from 1787 to 1921. Muirkirk was a much larger concern and John Butt in *Industrial Archaeology of Scotland* (1967) describes the scene as he found it: 'The remains of furnaces, the blowing-engine house and the furnace bank are spectacular.' How quickly industrial remains can disappear from the landscape – plate 49 shows the same scene, photographed in 1973. Foundations can still be traced, the company canal, no longer in water, is still to be seen, but soon even these traces will disappear under spreading undergrowth.

The use of iron did not, of course, begin with the industrial revolution, and mention has already been made of the domestic industry of nail-making at Belper. Nailers' cottages and workshops can also be found in many parts of Scotland – at St Ninians, on the edge of Stirling, for example, there was a mixed community of nailers and weavers, and in many of the tiny villages that cluster round Stirling – Torbex, Chattershall and others – the same style of Scottish vernacular cottage housed both sets of worker (plate 50). The figure most commonly associated with the use of iron is the village blacksmith, hammering at the heated metal on his anvil. The process of industrialization could be said to begin when the strong arm of the blacksmith was replaced by the stronger power of the water wheel.

The siting of early forges depended on the availability of the iron and an adequate water supply, and as the earliest forges used iron from the charcoal furnaces, it is in those regions they were found. Many have, not surprisingly, disappeared with the disappearance of the charcoal furnaces, but some have managed to maintain an extraordinarily long life. One of the best examples is to be found in a beautiful wooded valley, north of Sheffield at Wortley Top. Wrought iron has been worked here for nearly three centuries, beginning in 1640.

Forges such as Wortley Top were needed to convert the iron from the furnaces into malleable wrought iron, by reheating the metal in a furnace and then, while still hot, hammering out the excess carbon. The present buildings mostly date from the modernization of 1713, recorded on a date stone near the entrance. The arrangement of water wheels, furnaces and hammers shows the processes that the iron passed through.

The water supply for the wheels that worked all the machinery was the river Don, where a weir was built and water diverted to fill the forge pool. Water could be released from the pool by opening sluice gates, operated by a lever inside the forge, and allowing it to fall on to the succession of wheels. The first of these wheels was needed to power the bellows that blew air into the small furnaces where the iron was reheated. The next pair of wheels powered the two great hammers (plate 51). The hammers at Wortley are of a type known as belly helve hammers – that is the head was raised by projections on a turning wheel, powered directly by the water wheel, and situated half-way down the length of the hammer. As the projection cleared the hammer, the head fell on to the anvil under its own weight. The large wooden beam on top of the hammer acted as a spring, providing extra force to the blow. The immense impetus of these helve hammers can be seen from the size and strength of the beams needed to form the supporting frame. Arthur Young, in his *Six Months Tour Through the North of England* (2nd ed. 1770) made a point of recommending visitors to the Sheffield area not to miss a visit to the 'tilting mills' to see the hammers at work: 'The force of this mechanism is so prodigious: so great, that you cannot lay your hands upon a gate at three perches distance, without feeling a strong trembling motion.'

Although at first sight Wortley Top forge seems a rather primitive industrial site, with its sides open to the elements, it was in fact remarkably prosperous and enterprising. It was among the first to use the new methods of puddling and rolling introduced by Henry Cort and, because of the high standard of workmanship, was able to continue long after it should, on any reasonable estimate, have been declared obsolete. Wortley Top managed to retain a good trade right through the nineteenth century, forging railway axles and chains. The grooved anvils indicate where the axles were forged, and the sturdy cranes, used to lift the metal between furnace and anvil, provide added evidence of the great power of the forge (plate 50).

The workers at forges such as Wortley Top were craftsmen, and already, by the time Arthur Young visited the area, Sheffield had an established reputation as a centre for the craftsmen of the cutlery and hard-edged tools industries. It is not difficult to see why Sheffield developed in this way, for it had all the right ingredients – iron was available from the furnaces of the district, there was millstone grit in plenty in the surrounding hills for the grinding stones, coal for the furnaces was available from local collieries, and the Pennine rivers and streams were there to provide the power. We are fortunate that in Abbeydale scythe works on the river Sheaf in the south of Sheffield we have a superb example of a late eighteenth-century edge-tool works, preserved virtually as it existed in its working days.

Edged tools depended on the use of the third variety of iron: steel, which like wrought iron is a commercially pure form of the metal but has quite different physical properties and is much harder. The steel used at Abbeydale was manufactured by the crucible process invented by Benjamin Huntsman in the 1740s. Before that time, most steel had been produced by the 'cementation' furnace, a process which involved heating iron and carbon together for several days, but which was a rather hit-and-miss affair, resulting in steel of very variable quality. The great advantage of Huntsman's process was that quality could be controlled, and it was this ability to control quality that helped give Sheffield its reputation. At Abbeydale, the continuous process can be traced from the manufacture of the steel to the final carting away of the completed scythe blades.

The process begins at the crucible steel furnace, a building immediately recognizable by the odd rectangular chimney stack, typical of this type of furnace (plate 53). Before steel-making could begin, however, the crucibles themselves had to be made. In the pot shop, bare-footed men stomped up and down on the wet clay, kneading the different ingredients together, before shaping the long narrow crucibles. When they had dried out, the pots were taken to the charge room where they were filled with carefully weighed amounts of iron and charcoal. When all the pots were ready they were lowered through holes in the floor, two crucibles to a hole, into the heart of the furnace itself. It took four to five hours heating to complete the transformation into steel, and after that time the crucibles were removed and the molten metal poured into ingots. Outside the furnace is a water trough – not put there to provide a quick drink for a passing horse, but used by the furnacemen, who soaked sacking in the water and then wrapped the damp sacks round their legs to give them at least some protection from the fierce heat of the furnace.

From the furnace, the ingots were taken to be reheated for shaping under the hammers of the forge – a process very similar to that carried out at Wortley Top. The reheating furnace is coupled to a blowing engine, powered by the water wheel. This is a curiously satisfying little machine to see at work. An eccentric cam is rotated by a shaft driven from the water wheel, and a small wheel runs over it, moving up and down with the irregularities of the cam. The wheel is attached to a piston, which in turn moves up and down inside a cylinder, providing the blast of air. This is not only fascinating to watch, but is also a delight to listen to, producing a whole range of sounds from the squeak of metal on metal to a succession of grunts, hisses and wheezes. The water wheel was also used to power two tilt hammers, similar to the Wortley hammers, except that the projections on the rotating wheel pick up the end instead of the centre of the hammers (plate 52). The metal from the furnaces was placed on the anvils and roughly shaped by the hammers, and in order to help them absorb the shock of the blows, the workers had to sit in special swinging chairs suspended from the roof.

The rough scythe blades were next straightened out and hardened by more hammering in individual forges, virtually identical to the ordinary village smithy. The blade was now ready for the final stages of processing. It was sent to the boring shop, where holes were bored so that the blade could be fitted to its wooden handle, and then finally reached the workshop or grinding hull, where the blades were sharpened on the rows of whirling grindstones, powered by another of Abbeydale's water wheels. It was this part of the process that represented a genuine threat to the safety of the workmen. Arthur Young noted that grinders were very highly paid, from 18s to 20s a week in the 1770s, 'but this height of wages is owing in a great measure to the danger of the employment; for the grindstones turn with such amazing velocity, that by the mere force of motion they now and then fly in pieces, and kill the men at work on them'. Young does not mention, and was probably not even aware of, an even greater danger to the men's lives – silicosis, caused by the fine metal particles and stone dust spraying from the wheels into the faces of the grinders. In fact, the Abbeydale workers were comparatively fortunate, for they were wet-grinders, using wheels running in water which helped to keep down the dust.

Doctor G. Calvert Holland, who was one of the first to investigate what was then known as 'grinders' disease', published his findings in 1843 in a book called *Diseases of the Lungs from Mechanical Causes*. He noted that the scythe workers were doubly fortunate, for the works along the river Sheaf were set 'in the midst of scenery exquisitely picturesque and beautiful', so that the men had the opportunity to escape into a clean healthy atmosphere, and they all worked as wet-grinders, which was a comparatively harmless branch of the trade: 'They are a fine healthy class of men, and have abundant means of securing the rational enjoyment of life ... all the workmen and apprentices can both read and write.' This confirms one's impressions of Abbeydale as a place with more in common with an older system based on master craftsmen and journeymen than with later factory development. Looking, for example, at the workers' houses and the manager's house that all form part of the same enclosed group of buildings as the workshops, one finds that the eighteenth-century terraced cottages and the detached house are all similar sturdy, no-nonsense stone buildings – the homes of independent craftsmen. Although in some ways Abbeydale scythe works looks backwards, in every other respect it is a well organized, complete work unit, with process following process in ordered succession. A final point of interest at the last stop on the scythe blades' journey round Abbeydale – the warehouse where blades were stored to await transport has an upper storey supported on pillars, which on the Yorkshireman's favourite 'waste not, want not' principle, are constructed entirely from disused grindstones.

Unfortunately, conditions at Abbeydale were not repeated in other parts of Sheffield. In the finer grinding business the work was done dry, with terrible results for the workers. Dr Holland wrote:

'There is, perhaps, no town in the united empire in which thoracic diseases prevail to so great an extent, among a large class of artisans, as in Sheffield. Grinding the various articles of cutlery and hardware, as we shall shortly explain, is an occupation peculiarly destructive to human life. The instances of suffering are not few and occasional, but numerous and constantly produced by the unmitigated evil of the occupation. Every practitioner here is more or less familiar with the disease induced; it is brought almost daily under his consideration.'

The life expectancy of a grinder was frighteningly low. Holland quotes statistics to show that, in the country as a whole, sixteen per cent of working men died between the ages of twenty and thirty: in the case of fork-grinders the proportion rose to 47·5 per cent. Dr Holland campaigned hard for the provision of such necessities as proper ventilation at the works, but twenty years later Dr J. C. Hall found no improvement and wrote, in 1865: 'A fork-grinder told me some years ago, "I shall be thirty-six next month, and you know that is getting an old man at our trade" ... I found the average age of the men only twenty-eight.'

Among the worst affected of the different grinders were the needle-makers. Holland quotes facts gathered from Heathersage in Derbyshire: 'The new hands are young men from seventeen to twenty years of age, rough and uncultivated from the plough: and in those manufactories where ventilation is not secured, they are dead before the age of thirty, perhaps after two or three years of suffering.' This in spite of regulations that have 'always existed' limiting work to six hours a day, and in spite of the fact that the youngest grinders are seventeen. Once he started in the trade, a needle-grinder had a life expectancy of ten years. Small wonder that they had a reputation for stopping away from work whenever possible to set out on lengthy bouts of drinking that often ended in riot.

The centre of the needle-making industry became established at Redditch in Warwickshire where, at the Forge Mill needle factory, one can still see all too clearly the working conditions that killed generations of young men. There is nothing on the outside to suggest any lethal occupation – on the contrary, what we see is a mill pond, a water wheel and two charming red-brick buildings, a scene to attract the eye of one of Jane Austen's young ladies looking for a suitably picturesque subject for a water colour (plate 54). The calm exterior gives no hint of the mass of machinery that fills the inside of the mills.

The starting point for needle-making is rough, heavily scaled, steel wire, and most of the machinery is concerned with smoothing and polishing. First the wire is packed, with abrasive stones, into large wooden boxes, which are rocked violently backwards and forwards, using the water wheel for power (plate XII). Further polishing takes place in wooden barrels (plate XIII). The wire is then cut to the right length, and taken to the second building, the grinding hull, for pointing and sharpening. Dr Hall pointed out that the original meaning of the word 'hull' was a sty, and added 'a more happy or appropriate apellation could not possibly be selected'. The grinding hull at Redditch contains a grisly memento of the danger from breaking stones, for embedded in one of the walls is a fragment of stone, and it is claimed that the initials carved upon it are those of the unfortunate grinder whose head accompanied the stone as it hurtled away from the wheel. But, more importantly, one can see here the cramped space, with no provision for special ventilation, where the grinders worked, bent low over the small wheels. When rows of these wheels were at work, one can well imagine that as Dr Holland noted 'a stranger entering the rooms at certain times, would find it difficult to breathe in them'. Perhaps no greater condemnation could be found of any social and economic system than to say that under it young men could be found willing to work in such conditions.

The independent craftsmen who, in the early years of the industrial revolution, still played a very important part in the iron industry, found themselves having to adapt to a new pattern of life. For the few who could get a living in a rural setting such as Abbeydale, there were many more who had to move into the towns and cities. Instead of the solid stone cottages, they found the speculators' terraces. Dr Holland who investigated the grinders' disease also investigated housing conditions, and in *The Vital Statistics of Sheffield* (1843) described the changes that took place in the early years of the nineteenth century. The typical town cottage of that period was three storeys high, consisting of a half-cellar day room, 12 foot square and $8\frac{1}{2}$ foot high, above which was the main bedroom, 8 foot high and above that a 7 foot high attic. The speculators, he claimed, 'never dream of the legitimate necessities of the population', and as demand increased they began to build flimsier and flimsier houses. They used tricks to give a false impression of solidity, such as sawing joists in half across the diagonal – seen from below they were two inches thick, but under the plaster they were tapering away. More importantly for the individual worker, he was steadily losing his independence in the face of an increasingly organized industrial system. The same process was to be seen in other traditional craft industries, and in its most spectacular form in the potteries, where only a few decades were to see a complete revolution in production techniques.

7
Josiah Wedgwood and the Revolution in the Potteries

The main centre for the development of the British pottery industry was and is based on the group of six small towns – Burslem, Fenton, Hanley, Longton, Tunstall and Stoke – known, collectively if unmathematically, as the 'Five Towns'. In the middle of the eighteenth century they were little more than villages in which masterpotters, helped by journeymen and apprentices, shaped the clay and fired it in small kilns or ovens. Raw materials were all close at hand – coal was plentiful and the clay lay at their feet. Celia Fiennes went to see the potteries at the end of the seventeenth century, but was unlucky: the potters having exhausted the clay at their doorstep had moved:

> 'I went to NewCastle in Staffordshire to se the makeing of ye fine tea potts. Cups and saucers of ye fine red Earth in imitation and as curious as yt wch Comes from China, but was defeated in my design, they Comeing to an End of their Clay they made use of for yt sort of ware, and therefore was remov'd to some other place where they were not settled at their work.'

At about that time, the English potters were beginning to produce more sophisticated ware, using a new technique – salt glazing. In this method, common salt was thrown into the ovens where the pots were firing, and it combined with the clay to form a hard glaze. This may have improved the pots, but did little for the environment.

Simeon Shaw in his *History of the Staffordshire Potteries* (1829) described the scene when the potters of the area 'fired-up' on a Saturday morning: the salt produced a 'dense, white cloud, which . . . so completely enveloped the whole of the interior of the town, as to cause persons often to run against each other'. Mr Shaw did not share modern preoccupations, and merely remarked 'a murky atmosphere is not regarded by the patriotic observer, who can view thro' it, an industrious population, employed for the benefit of themselves and their country, and behold vast piles of national wealth enhanced by individual industry'.

Development in the potteries was handicapped by a number of factors. First, though closer to eighteenth-century taste than the earlier rugged stoneware had been, the new salt-glazed pots could not compete with the more sophisticated continental pieces for a place at the rich man's table. The main trouble lay in the red clay referred to by Celia Fiennes, which could only be completely covered if the glaze was made heavy and clumsy. Secondly, the organization of the industry was based on the small business, usually run by a single craftsman who often had neither the capital nor the inclination for change. Lastly, the potteries were situated in the very centre of the country, far removed from convenient water transport, and surrounded by roads considered bad even in an age notorious for shocking roads. The potters themselves were not entirely blameless in the last respect, for they had an anti-social habit of making clay deficits good by digging the required amount out of the middle of the highway. So the trade depended almost entirely on the pack horse to carry raw material and finished goods. It was a trade organized to serve the needs of the country market, not the aristocrat or even the increasingly important middle classes. That this was changed was due largely to the efforts of one man, Josiah Wedgwood.

Wedgwood's claim to fame is not based on any great invention that revolutionized the technology of the potteries, although he was an innovator of no mean capabilities. But his importance lies in his reorganization of the methods of production, his lead in establishing a decent transport system for the area, and above all in his entrepreneurial skill in taking Staffordshire pottery from the country market to the tables of Europe's royal families.

Wedgwood was born in 1730, the thirteenth and youngest, but not unluckiest, child in the family. His parents were not wealthy, and at the age of nine Josiah was apprenticed out as a thrower, working for his brother Thomas. An attack of small-pox at the age of twelve weakened his right knee to such an extent that he was no longer able to work the treadle of the potter's wheel, and had to abandon throwing for other aspects of the potter's craft. He soon became interested in experimenting in ways to improve the body and glaze of the ware – but Thomas showed little interest in new-fangled methods and was glad enough to see his inquisitive young brother move on elsewhere. Wedgwood moved around the potteries, gaining experience and saving what cash he could until he had sufficient to rent the Ivy works in Burslem from two distant cousins, John and Thomas Wedgwood. He began business and prospered. His aim, from the first, was to improve the quality of the pots so that they reached an aristocratic market, and from the fact of aristocratic patronage Wedgwood was convinced he could then go on to capture the middle-class market as well. During the 1760s a number of crucial events in Wedgwood's progress occurred of which by no means the least important was an almost accidental meeting with the Liverpool merchant, Thomas Bentley. The meeting led to friendship and later partnership, and Bentley filled an important gap in Wedgwood's knowledge and experience. The merchant moved in the fashionable world and was alive to every shift of taste and style. It was Bentley who was to act as the guide to taste that enabled Wedgwood's to retain a place as the foremost potters of the day.

The search for improved ware led Wedgwood to the logical step of looking for alternatives to red clay for the body. He found what he wanted in the white clays of the West Country, and that brought him hard up against the problem of transport. He very soon became a vociferous advocate of road-building in the area, and although his agitation cost him time and money he begrudged neither. As he wrote in a letter to his brother in February 1765, after having already made one excursion to Parliament to lend support for a Turnpike Act:

'We have another Turnpike broke out amongst us here betwixt Leek & Newcastle & they have it *vi et Armis* – mounted me upon my hobby-horse again, & a prancing rouge he is at present, but hope he will not take the road of London again. . . . £2,000 is wanting for this road. My Uncles Thos & Jno. have – I am quite serious – at the first asking subscribed – I know you will not believe me, but it is a certain fact – *five hundred pounds ! ! !* – I have done the like intending 2 or 300 of it for you.'

But the mid-1760s saw an even more ambitious transport scheme calling for his energy and enthusiasm. Whatever the improved roads did for the area, they did very little to reduce the cost of carriage for bulk goods, and land transport was at least three times as expensive as transport by water. Wedgwood, inspired like many another industrialist by the example of the Duke of Bridgewater, turned canal promoter. After a period of intense political activity, against powerful opposition, an Act was granted for the construction of a canal to join the Trent to the Mersey, a route of such importance that it was also known as the Grand Trunk canal. At the passing of the Act in January 1766 the whole neighbourhood joined Wedgwood in celebrating the start of the new direct link between the potteries and the port of Liverpool.

Not all Wedgwood's energies were devoted to canal promotion. At the same time he was busy perfecting his cream ware, based on the use of the white clays, and his first ambition was realized early in 1765 when he received an order from the Court for a service of his creamy white earthenware with the lead glaze. That year a service was ordered for the Queen, and Wedgwood was quick to exploit the royal patronage to the full. He wrote to Bentley in March 1767:

'The demand for this sd. *Creamcolour*, Alias *Queen's Ware*, Alias, *Ivory*, still increases. It is really amazing how rapidly the use of it has spread allmost over the whole Globe, & how universally it is liked. – How much of this general use, & estimation, is owing to the mode of its introduction – & how much to its real utility & beauty? are questions in which we may be a good deal interested, for the governmt of our future Conduct. The reasons are too obvious to be longer dwelt upon. For instance, if a Royal, or Noble introduction be as necessary to the sale of an Article of

VII *Above* The beginnings of the Canal Age – the Bridgewater canal at Worsley Delph, stained by the ore from the mine to the colour of tomato soup

VIII *Below* The Georgian elegance of Stourport's Tontine hotel and the canal that brought it into being

IX Stone blocks and iron rail on the line of the old tramway, Llanfoist

x Masonry work of the highest order distinguishes this
engine house at the Ynysfach Iron Works, Merthyr Tydfil

xi Gears in the wheel pit at Abbeydale scythe works, Sheffield

Redditch Forge mill: XII *Above* The scouring beds that seem to fill every inch of space; XIII *Below* The barrel shop

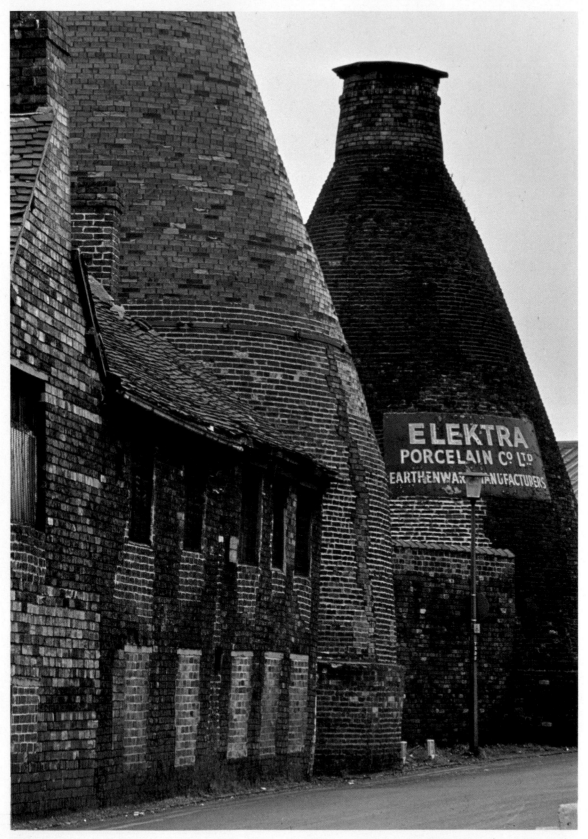

XIV The beauty of the potteries: kilns at Elektra
porcelain, Longton

XV The country cotton mill: Gibson mill on Hebden
Water, Hebden Bridge

xvi Samuel Greg's Quarry Bank cotton mill at Styal

Luxury, as real Elegance & beauty, then the Manufacturer, if he consults his own intert, will bestow as much pains, & expense too, if necessary, in gaining the former of these advantages, as he wod in bestowing the latter.'

The voice of the realist! Wedgwood's next move was to investigate the new interest in the classical style. In December 1768 he wrote: 'I have been turning two or three sorts of faithfull copys from Etruscan Vases & am quite surpris'd both at the beauty of their forms, & the difficulty of making them.' From these beginnings came all those developments in jasper, the urns, the vases and the cameos with which the name Wedgwood will always be associated. The new ware was sent to all parts of Europe and even Paris, the citadel of fashion, seemed ready to fall to Wedgwood's enthusiastic assault. 'And do you really think', he wrote, 'that we may make a *complete conquest* of France? Conquer France in Burslem? – My blood moves quicker, I feel my strength increase for the contest.'

The expansion of trade could no longer be contained within the limits of the old Burslem works, and Wedgwood began the task of building a new pottery to his own requirements. From the beginning, he had concentrated on a reorganization of working methods in his pottery, changing from the old system of the master-potter responsible for all stages of production, helped out by journeymen and apprentices, to a new system where each man carried out just one special part of the production process. His search for a more efficient use of the available manpower reached its culmination in the building of the new works, which he named 'Etruria' in honour of the new styles he was developing. He took an interest in every detail of the new building, and the care he took in the planning is shown in many letters, of which this example of April 1769 is typical:

'I have alter'd my opinion about the turning room, & unless you think of any objection shall fix the Lathes in the lower corner room under that we before proposed. Here the lights are high enough & a ground floor is much better for Lathes than a Chamber story, the latter are so apt to shake with the motion of the Lathe, & as we shall want so very often to be steping into the Lathe room, for there an *outline* is given, it will be more convenient, especially for me, to have it without any steps to it.* I have thought of another alteration to the Lathes too. . . . The alteration I propose, is to set the Lathe so that the turner shall have an *end light* instead of a *front one* which they now have . . . I have try'd the experimt upon Abrams Lathe & it answered to my wishes.'

The factory, built on the banks of the Trent and Mersey canal, was opened in 1769. But Etruria was more than just the factory: across the canal, Wedgwood built a new and very grand house for himself and his family (plate 60), and around the works he provided new houses for his workers. The scene, when everything had been completed and had been in use for some years, was described in Warner's *Tour Through the Northern Counties of England* (1802):

'A long, uniform, and neat village, inhabited entirely by the workmen of Mr Wedgwood, introduced us to the manufactory, which is as picturesque as a building of this kind can well be; the Staffordshire canal here resembling a river, rolling its waters between it and the elegant mansion of Mr W, the banks shaded with trees, and rising beautifully on each side. Here upwards of two hundred people are employed.'

Sadly, little of this remains today, and what does remain presents a very different scene from the view of 1802. Etruria Hall is dirty and dilapidated, surrounded by spoil heaps; the Etruria works have almost all been demolished, leaving only the little round modelling shop, of all the buildings which can be seen in old prints of the works (plate 59). Some of the houses still stand: by the bridge is a row of cottages built for the Wedgwood workers, and the end two provide at least one pleasing association with the past. In the middle of the nineteenth century they were converted into a pub by a boatman who had decided to give up his life on the Trent and Mersey and settle behind the bar instead.

But if little remains of the Burslem and Etruria of Josiah Wedgwood, his influence can be seen throughout the potteries. One of the most immediately striking examples is to be seen in the façades of

*The recurring trouble with his knee had eventually led to the amputation of his leg.

the major eighteenth- and nineteenth-century potteries. Here, the classical style established at Etruria has developed into the standard for the whole district. The style persisted right through into the middle of the nineteenth century, as can be seen at the Aynsley China Company in Sutherland Road, Longton, which shows all the characteristic features (plate 62). The first point to note is the wide single entrance in the middle of the façade that led into the main courtyard, around which all the buildings of the works were grouped. Over the entrance is a Venetian window, and above that is a triangular pediment. The façade was sometimes given extra classical embellishments in the forms of urns or garlanded flowers, but here the decoration is kept to the deep cornice and the ornamental use of contrasting brick and stone. An earlier, plainer variation on this theme can be seen at the nearby Crown Pottery in the Strand.

Another legacy left by Wedgwood is the canal he promoted, and there is no better introduction to the development of the potteries than to journey through the towns by boat or on the towpath. The importance of the route is at once emphasized by the scale and variety of canal-side developments, ranging from the large works such as Doulton's, which once had extensive loading bays let into the walls that fall sheer to the water, to the smaller works, such as the pottery with the distinctive bottle kilns at the end of Newport Lane, Burslem.

But the main influence of Wedgwood is seen behind the façades, in the way in which the work was organized to provide a logical flow from the arrival of the raw material to the dispatch of the finished pots. It was only very recently that the potters of Stoke realized that their past was rapidly disappearing under the developers' bulldozers, and banded together with the Stoke Council to acquire one of these old potteries. They decided to ignore the 'big names', and settled instead for a typical middle-sized pottery of the early nineteenth century, the Gladstone Pottery, Uttoxeter Road, Longton.

There is not a lot of documented evidence to go with this site, but it is known to have existed, in its present form, in 1850, and kilns were standing on this site a considerable time before that. From the evidence of the buildings themselves, parts at least of the present works date back to the late eighteenth century.

The buildings are grouped around a closed courtyard with only one entrance, so that control could be maintained over all movements into and out of the works. From Uttoxeter Road, access is by a tunnel under the main offices – the manager had his office here so that he could keep an eye on all the activities in and around the courtyard. The courtyard itself is the starting place for the manufacturing process: the raw materials were brought here, stacked and left to weather, before beginning their journey through the different processes. Although the first impression is of a chaotic jumble of buildings and kilns (plate 55), everything is, in fact, built to a pattern conforming to the sequence of processes.

The first building the materials were taken to was the sliphouse, which stands directly opposite the tunnel entrance. Here the clay and other materials were measured and mixed wet before eventually dropping into settling tanks below the building. The mixing was done by horizontal propellers, driven by a small beam engine, which was used by means of a rope drive as a power source for all the machinery.

After mixing and settling, the clay was divided: part was kept wet and was used for casting, the rest was dried and used for throwing or turning on the lathe. The pots which were formed – cups and handles might be cast, bowls thrown on the wheel, plates pressed – reunited in the building holding the saggers, the fireproof containers in which the ware was stacked for the ovens. The sagger-maker's shop is immediately behind this building. The unglazed pots – or biscuit ware – were packed into the saggers and put into the adjoining oven. Some pots had more processes to go through later – they went to the dipping house, where they were dipped in lead glaze before firing in the glost kiln, and a few special pieces which were to have gold decoration were fired in the elegantly slender enamel kilns. All these workshops and ovens concerned in the main line of production are situated at ground-floor level (plate 56); above them are other workshops – the mould-making shop where moulds for castings were prepared (plate 58), the modelling shop, the printing shop where designs were added. On the top floor of the main block was a large room with sky-lights to give as good and even a light as possible for the workers who sat here performing the delicate task of on-glaze decorating – painting directly on to the finished pots.

The final stage was reached when the goods were packed away in the warehouse block, ready for despatch. There was also a room set aside for display near the main entrance.

If the organization of the factory is modern, its appearance is quite the opposite – the constantly changing lines and angles of buildings, the different styles of detailing at doors and windows are all in marked contrast to the uniformity of the modern factory. Also, in a modern factory, there is far more likely to be a number of different processes continuing under the same roof, whereas here each section of the production process has its own enclosed space or separate building. This makes for a visually satisfying group. Perhaps aesthetics could be said to have no place in factory design, but a pottery is necessarily concerned with aesthetics, and there is something particularly appropriate in the buildings sharing the quality. Because we have been conditioned to associate industry with ugliness – often, admittedly, with cause – we can easily overlook the beauty that can sometimes be found. There are few more attractive buildings put up by man than the traditional bottle kiln of the potteries: the graceful, curved line of the exterior is one aspect we know well, but seen from inside they have an almost mystical quality. This is, perhaps, an over-romantic reaction, but to see the interior, lit by the single shaft of light from the top of the kiln, is to see that romanticism is well justified (plate 57).

There are variations on this general theme to be found in the potteries: for example, in nearby Lawley Street, the clay was loaded directly into the works from packhorse or cart through a hole in the wall. The siting of kilns differs between different potteries – at some they were built into the square workshops so that only the very tops are visible, in others, as at the Elektra Porcelain Company works in Edensor Street, Longton, the whole curve of the kiln wall can be seen projecting into the street (plate XIV). But these are small variations, and the pattern of orderly progress and specialization, begun by Wedgwood, is the distinctive feature of the eighteenth- and nineteenth-century potteries.

The obvious question to ask next is what sort of working life did the men, women and children who came to Etruria or Gladstone lead? Wedgwood's treatment of his work force was very similar to that of other of the more benign eighteenth-century industrialists: that is, he was a paternalist, affable when things went well but not prepared to stand for any nonsense from 'the family'. He was a man of humane impulses – he was, for example, a leading member of the anti-slavery movement – but, like so many of his fellows, he did not take kindly to even a hint of opposition from any of his workers. The paternalist too easily became the patronizer, and it is clearly spelled out in a letter to Bentley of June 1768 that although he regarded the workers in a favourable light, they were and should remain slightly inferior beings:

> 'Mr P. has much of the Bashaw in his treatmt of workmen, & does not seem to consider their havg any feelings at all. I have seen a great many instances of it, & may perhaps sometime or other find out a mode of conveying a lecture to him upon a proper treatmt of our inferiors, & to prove that, our *humble friends* as somebody beautifully calls them, have like passions wth ourselves, & are capable of feelg pain, or pleasure, nearly in the same manner as their Masters.'

It is that 'nearly' that grates so terribly. Wedgwood could also show a less benign face when the humble friends made demands on their own behalf. In 1773 he recommended sacking a whole group of workers who had the temerity to ask for a rise, though he blamed himself for mentioning in their presence that there was a boom in the trade and thus a steadily increasing demand for ware. Wedgwood the individual was a man of great compassion and humanity; Wedgwood the employer was very much a man of his time. In 1783 a grain shortage led to bread riots throughout the country, including Staffordshire, and Wedgwood sent out an address to the young of the area, telling them not to follow the evil example of their parents. Part of this address is virtually identical to the address sent out from the Dowlais iron works (p. 112):

> 'It is admitted that provisions are dear: but before any censure and abuse is on this account offered to people who may be as innocent as ourselves, we ought first to enquire if the hand of

providence is not visible, to all who see it, in this dispensation; and surely that consideration may be sufficient to stop the most daring man, and to induce him to bear with becoming patience his share of the public calamity, and submit quietly to the will of heaven.'

It would be unjust to give the impression that Wedgwood was a bad employer – on the contrary, in comparison with his contemporaries he paid well and provided working conditions far better than in most factories. He showed concern for the health of the workers – though he was unable to remove the threat of disease that hung over the workers responsible for lead-glazing. Like all employers of the period, he made extensive use of child labour, and the hours they were forced to work were long. On the other hand, there were few of the very young children to be found in other industries. After Wedgwood's death, evidence was given to the Peel Committee of 1816 on the working conditions of the children at Etruria. At that time there were only thirteen children employed who were under ten years of age, and 103 who were between ten and eighteen. Hours in the factory were 6.30 a.m. to 6 p.m. in the summer with half an hour for breakfast and an hour for dinner, but shorter hours were worked in winter. On the other hand, the evidence stated that working extra hours, working 'half nights' or 'out of time', was common in the industry, and the children, who were employed directly by the men, had to stay the same hours. The young Josiah Wedgwood readily agreed that the children would be better off playing or at school 'but that is a condition, if I may be allowed to say so, unattainable'. The children did, however, have a day school and there was also a Methodist Sunday school – standards of literacy among the children at the Wedgwood works, and in the potteries in general, were far higher than in most manufacturing districts.

Away from the beneficial eye of a Wedgwood, conditions for children in the potteries were at least as bad as in any other industry of the period. The working life of a child in a small nineteenth-century pottery, such as the Gladstone works, is vividly described in C. Shaw's *When I was a Child*. He began his working life as a handle-maker in a pottery owned by a county magistrate.

'This old employer showed in many ways that his trade connection was rather irksome, so the business was left to others to manage, whose responsibility was leavened with freedom. But the employer did not disdain to accept the profit out of seventy to eighty hours' labour per week for a child nine years of age, while the child got one-and-six or two shillings. Probably his carriage horses would eat as much food at one meal as such sums would buy. But they were "carriage" horses, and I and others were only work children. Anyone can see the difference.'

The boys in the works were entirely at the mercy of the workmen they assisted, and if the men took time off that had to be made up later, then the boys were beaten and cajoled into keeping pace with them. Shaw spent a great deal of his time at the pottery as apprentice to a 'muffin-maker', and the following extract tells something of the life he led:

'It is necessary to explain that a "muffin-maker" was one who made small plates less than seven inches in diameter. Such a workman needed a "mould-runner". These moulds were a cast of plaster on which the clay was laid in something like the shape of a pancake. The clay was pressed by the wet right hand of the maker upon the plaster mould which was being spun round upon the clay, and by this gave the outer surface the required shape. By this tool, the foot-ring of the plate was formed on which it stands when used. When the plate had gone through those processes, the plaster cast on which it had been made had to be quickly carried away by the boy-help into a hot stove close by. Hence the term "mould-runner". This stove was a room four to five yards square, shelved all round at regular intervals, on which the plaster moulds were placed by the boy so that the soft clay plate just made could be dried to a certain extent. In the middle of this so-called stove-room was placed an iron stove full of fire, with a sheet-iron pipe carried into the chimney. It was no unusual thing for this stove and the chimney pipe to be red with the intense heat of the fire. Frequently there was no light in this stove-room but such as came from the glare of the fire. It was the mould-runner's business to place the plaster moulds on the shelves on their edge, slightly leaning against the wall, so as to get full surface heat, and to avoid damage to the soft plates on the moulds.

'To enable the boy to reach the higher shelves in this stove-room, a small pair of wooden steps was used. Up these he had to run for all the higher shelves, say one-fifth of the whole number. He had to run to his "master" with an empty mould, and return with a full one to the stove-room. This was properly called "mould-running", for nothing less than running would do. A boy would be kept going for twenty minutes or half an hour at a time, the perspiration coursing down his face and back, making channels on both, as if some curious system of irrigation were going on upon the surface of this small piece of humanity. . . . I should say there were regular intervals of change in the work when a "set" of plates had been made, and this interval was filled up by the plate-maker and the boy "wedging clay" or making "battings". This "wedging clay" was nominally the work of the boy, sometimes assisted by the plate-maker, and the latter made the battings, that is, from balls of wedged or refined clay, he made the pancake-like shapes of clay which he had to use in making the next "set" of plates. Wedging clay, for a boy, was as common as it was cruel. What is now done by hydraulic pressure was then done by the bone and muscle of, perhaps, a half-fed boy. He had to take a lump of raw clay upon a plaster block, cut it in two with a piece of wire, lift one half above his head, and then bring it down upon the lower half, to mix them, with whatever force he could command. This had to be repeated till the clay was brought to the consistency of something like putty. Doing such work as this was "rest" from the mould-running. Imagine a mere boy, running in and out of this stove-room, winter and summer, with its blazing iron stove, his speed determined by his master's speed at his work, coarse oaths, and threats, and brutal blows in many cases following any failure to be at the bench at the required moment. Thank God there is no mould-running or wedging now.'

The houses where Shaw and his friends would have lived are rapidly disappearing in the redevelopment of the potteries. The area round Gladstone Pottery that was once thick with the terraced cottages of the workers has now been largely cleared. A few of the houses do remain, looking strange in their unaccustomed isolation, as for example at Warren Terrace (plate 61). This is a row of plain cottages, built to a two-up two-down pattern. What one does notice is the close intermixing of works and houses – even today, if you stand with your back to the end of Warren Terrace you have eight bottle kilns in view. The same mixture can be seen at Burslem, where the kilns can be seen poking up behind the buildings of the main squares.

Development in the pottery industry was by no means limited to Staffordshire. The first British porcelain was manufactured at Bow, and famous potteries flourished, for example, at Chelsea, Worcester, and Derby. Individual potteries also appeared on isolated sites, such as the Coalport Pottery (plate 71) on the Severn near Ironbridge, which had a brief but glorious flowering in the nineteenth century, and then declined again. But the main impetus came from Staffordshire and the Five Towns, and it was here that the important changes in organization took place. The increase in pottery production, and the changed production techniques, also had their effects in other parts of the country. In Cornwall the china clay industry soon developed into a major factor in the life of the county, and has certainly had a weird effect on the landscape – as in the great white heaps of spoil known locally as the Cornish Alps in the area round St Austell. The development of the industry also created demands for improved transport, and major works such as Charlestown harbour were put in hand. The harbour was designed by John Smeaton, and still has the wooden chutes in place, down which the clay is dropped to the waiting boats. Another important ingredient in pottery manufacture was powdered flint, which was used to whiten the body of the pot, and the mills in which the flints were ground played an important part in the industry.

Cheddleton flint mill, by the side of the Caldon branch of the Trent and Mersey, is a particularly good example to study. The canal was laid out by James Brindley, who was still making use of his original training as a millwright, and it seems almost certain that the machinery at this mill was his work. More importantly, the mill has been very carefully preserved, so that it has the appearance of a working site that could be put to use at any time, rather than an over-elaborate museum.

The process begins at the wharf, where the flints were unloaded and stacked ready to be fed into the kilns for calcining – that is heating to make them more brittle and thus easier to grind. Mill-stones were also unloaded here, and were lowered by crane to a short tramway where trucks took them to the mill buildings. The wharf area is very well planned and the kilns were built into the structure of the wharf itself, with openings for charging at the canal level (plates 63 and 64). A neat detail can be seen in the way in which some of the stone slabs of the side wall have been extended outwards to form a set of open steps.

The tramway crosses the leat from the river Churnet which provides the power to drive the two water wheels, one on each of the mill buildings (plates 65 and 66). North mill, the one farthest from the canal, was altered sometime in the 1780s, as part of a process of modernization. Evidence of the adaptation can be seen in the change of the size of bricks between ground and first floor – the larger bricks were sneaked into buildings to try to reduce the effect of the brick tax, which was later repealed in 1783.

Inside the building, the gearing from the water wheel can be seen: the vertical pit wheel, worked directly from the water wheel, engages with a horizontal wheel, the wallower, to turn the vertical shaft that goes up to the first floor – the same arrangement that can be found in any grinding mill (plate 67). The flint grinding pan itself is on the first floor – a circular iron trough lined with paving stones on which the flints are placed. The vertical shaft passes up through the pan and carries four sweep arms, from which are hung the heavy, hard stones that crush the flints (plate 68). Water is added to the pan by means of a pump, which is also powered by the water wheel. As the flints are ground smaller and smaller, the mixture in the pan turns into a sort of milky slurry, which is eventually allowed to run away into a wash tub. There the slurry is mixed with more water, so that heavier particles drop to the bottom, and the properly ground flints, or 'fines', remain in suspension. These fines are then passed into a tank known as the settling ark, where they are allowed to settle and the water is run off. Finally the flints are taken for drying, a job originally done in sun pans – not a satisfactory arrangement in this unsunny climate – and later in a drying kiln.

The South mill shows evidence of many generations of building, starting at one end with the original stone structure, continuing to eighteenth-century brickwork, and ending with modern brick additions. This is the oldest part of the mill buildings and, from the method of construction to be seen in the queen post roof, could go back to the seventeenth century or even earlier. The machinery is basically the same as in the North mill, though there are some interesting variations. The pump used to provide water for the pan is a very ingenious beam pump, in which the pivotal point of the beam can be shifted to alter the length of the pump stroke. The hoist here, used to lift the flint or mill stones from the trucks up to the pan, is also interesting and unusual in being built entirely of wood.

There is not much in the way of documentation to go with the mill buildings, but we can work out a good deal of its history from the physical structure. There is little doubt that the old corn mill that stood here has been incorporated into the South mill. Equally, it seems certain that the North mill was at first used for dry-grinding flints. This was a murderous occupation, which led to the inevitable grinder's disease of silicosis. The extra storey marks the change from dry- to wet-grinding – the extra height being needed to provide sufficient head of water to wash away the slurry from the pans. These developments at the end of the eighteenth century mark more than a change of techniques, they are the mark of what at that time was a complete rethinking of the processes to transform Cheddleton into a very advanced plant. Because we tend to associate devices such as the water wheel with adjectives like 'quaint' or 'old-fashioned', it is sometimes easy to lose sight of the fact that some of the installations powered by these versatile power units could be remarkably sophisticated. Just simple details, such as laying a plate railway to bring trucks right into the mill under the hoist, show the careful planning that went into this site. The canal itself was of course the most important innovation at Cheddleton. The site here is at a junction where the new turnpike met the canal, so it is not surprising to find that a busy little community developed. For as well as the flint mill, there were also a silk mill, houses for the workers, a brewery, an inn with stabling and, beyond the bridge, a dry dock and impressive lime kilns – altogether a striking example of the importance of improved transport to the growth of industry.

The main changes in the pottery industry were social rather than technological in the sense of depending on new inventions. The changes came gradually rather than with any great dramatic rush; the same could not be said of the changes that were simultaneously taking place as the cotton industry spread through Derbyshire and the north-western counties.

8

The Cotton Boom

The spinning jenny, the water frame and the flying shuttle made possible a dramatic increase in the production of cotton yarn and cotton cloth and, once they had been shown to work, they made such an increase inevitable. For a short while, Arkwright, his various partners and other manufacturers working under licence, led the way in cotton-spinning, safe behind the protection of the patents. But, once these were overthrown in 1783, the way was open for anyone and everyone – provided they had a little capital to invest – to try for a fortune in the cotton industry. The development that followed was by no means a smooth progress of ever-increasing production. Being heavily reliant on overseas trade, events, particularly the American War of Independence and the Napoleonic Wars, produced periods of deep, if temporary, depressions during which many speculative millowners ended in bankruptcy.

At first, the cotton trade was concerned with the production of rather coarse cloth, but as soon as it became possible to spin a fine and regular yarn, then a whole new range of markets opened up. Now the manufacturers could meet the demand for cheap, light but strong cloth for America, and could also produce fine and *cleanable* clothing to satisfy the dictates of the fastidious Beau Brummell. The new invention that made the production of fine yarn possible was Samuel Crompton's spinning mule.

In essence, the machine was a hybrid of the water frame and the spinning jenny, though it is most unlikely that Crompton knew much about the latter. The mule used rollers, as in Arkwright's machine, to draw out the threads which then passed to rows of spindles mounted on a carriage. As the yarn wound off the rollers the carriage was pulled backwards and the yarn further stretched – but as thick yarn is less resilient than thin the process also resulted in the production of a more even thread. Once the carriage had reached its fullest extent, the tension in the yarn was removed by use of a simple lever, the carriage was returned to wind on the yarn, and the whole process was repeated. Eventually, the process was improved by making the movement of the carriage, and the tightening and slackening of the yarn, automatic, and the self-acting mule became the mainstay of the industry. Its inventor, however, was no Arkwright. He never took out a patent for his spindle carriage, and instead agreed to give the secret to a group of Lancashire cotton-spinners in exchange for an unspecified sum of money to be raised by subscription. The agreement, drawn up in Bolton on 20 November 1780, was couched in the vaguest of terms:

> 'Several of the principal tradesmen in Manchester, Bolton &c., having seen his new machine, approve of it, and are of opinion it would be of the greatest public utility to make it generally known, to which end a contribution is desired from every well-wisher of the trade.'

The 'well-wishers' raised a paltry £60 and Crompton died an embittered man, made doubly so by having the example of the wealthy Arkwright so often in front of him. In Gilbert French's biography of Crompton (1859), one of Crompton's letters is quoted in which the inventor bemoans, all too accurately, the fact that 'I found to my sorrow I was not calculated to contend with men of the world'.

The Turner family of Helmshore, whose fulling mill was discussed in chapter 1, were among the many who profited by Crompton's invention. They branched out from wool into cotton, and installed mules (plate 72). Part of the mill is still at work, and although the machines in use are rather more modern, spinning is still carried out using self-acting mules, which have not changed in principle from the original.

Crompton's mule completed the armoury of the early cotton-spinners, and a formidable array it turned out to be. The earliest developments came in different forms – either in small mills, built in or near existing textile communities, or in 'company towns' like Arkwright's Cromford where the mill was built and a work force imported. On a smaller scale still, some domestic workers managed to scrape enough cash together to fit up a mule or jenny in an outhouse or small workshop.

Many of the small mills were built along the courses of the hill streams of Pennine Yorkshire and Lancashire. Water was the main requirement for a new mill, and it seems amazing that so little water could often support so many mills. John Byng spent one happy day viewing the rural delights of Aysgarth and ruminated on the possibilities of rebuilding Nappa House where 'retired from the world, a man might here enjoy fly-fishing and grouse shooting in the highest perfection'. But, alas, on turning a bend of the river, he was greeted with the sight of a new cotton mill which 'completed the destruction of every rural thought'. The sight led him into even deeper gloom, as his thoughts moved from shooting and fishing to a contemplation of the rise of a new class and the decline of the old: 'If men can thus start into riches; or if riches from trade are too easily procured, woe to us men of middling income, and settled revenue.' Byng was right – a new class was growing in importance – but he might have taken consolation from the thought that mills such as Aysgarth which so affronted him have now largely disappeared, often leaving little more than the outline of the foundations beside a hill stream. In some cases an empty shell remains, as at the site of the old cotton mill above Littleborough in Lancashire (plate 73). A winding track follows the course of the stream, where remains of dams and sluices indicate the use of water wheels, to an old two-storey mill built on a wooden frame, and now crumbling and decayed. Behind the mill the weavers' cottages stand isolated on the edge of the moor. Sometimes decay has turned a once busy industrial site into a purely romantic landscape that even John Byng might have enjoyed. The streams that drained southwards from Cowpe Moss in Lancashire once supported a whole succession of mills. Some have disappeared, and the remains have to be looked for among the moorland bracken.

Cheesden Lumb mill has not quite vanished. One wall stands, arched out over the river which drops through the stonework in a man-made waterfall, completing the transformation from industrial back to pastoral scene. For the more prosaically minded it is a three-storey stone mill, and the main shaft of the water wheel can still be seen in the wheel pit.

An example of a Pennine country mill, but in a rather better state of preservation, is Gibson's mill on Hebden Water, the small river that runs down to Hebden Bridge on the Yorkshire–Lancashire border. The river valley is deep and heavily wooded, overlooked by the high rocks of Harecastle Crags. It has become popular as a local beauty spot, but a walk along the riverside soon reveals the valley's history. Starting at the end of the road from Hebden Bridge, and following the line of the river, dams and weirs soon become evident. A flat grassy area makes an ideal picnic spot beside the water, and the dammed river provides a perfect paddling pool – the flat space marks the foundations of New Bridge mills, and the dam was built to control the water for the mill. Continuing along the course of the river, more dams and remains appear until Gibson's mill itself is reached – a three-storey stone mill built beside a small bridge (plate xv). It was first used in about 1800 and, from the reports of the factory commissioners, even in its busy days it never employed more than some twenty or so workers. Mills such as this have never been attached to towns or surrounded by housing, and the work force had a long trudge from their homes in the morning and what must have seemed a far longer trudge back in the evening. Their one consolation was that they were at least able to work among beautiful countryside, even if they had little enough time to appreciate it.

The development of mills on sites far from towns, villages or any form of housing, and in areas which often had no previous connection with the cotton trade, was symptomatic of the rush to use the new profitable techniques. The rush was not limited to the cotton-spinners – weavers too saw the possibilities of a new prosperity in the expanding trade. William Radcliffe was born in 1761 into a family that earned a living in the traditional way by working a smallholding and supplementing its income with the loom and the spinning wheel. In his book *Origins of Power Loom Weaving* (1828) he describes the changes in the cotton industry as he remembers them. In 1770, cottage rents 'with convenient loom-shop and a small garden attached' were one and a half to two guineas a year. 'The father of a family would earn from eight shillings to half a guinea at his loom, and his sons if he had one . . . six or eight shillings each per week; but the great sheet anchor of all cottages and small farms, was the labour attached to the hand-wheel.' Between 1770 and the early 1780s 'cotton, cotton, cotton was become the almost universal material for employment'. Then, when mule-twist joined water-twist and all the cotton for the looms could come from the new machines, the effects on the district were dramatic:

'These families, up to the time I have been speaking of, whether as cottagers or small farmers, had supported themselves by the different occupations I have mentioned in spinning and manufacturing, as their progenitors from the earliest institutions of society had done before them. But the mule-twist now coming into vogue, for the warp, as well as weft, added to the water-twist and common jenny yarns, with an increasing demand for every fabric the loom could produce, put all hands in request of every age and description. The fabrics made from wool or linen vanished, while the old loom-shops being insufficient, every lumber-room, even old barns, cart-houses, and outbuildings of any description were repaired, windows broke through the old blank walls, and all fitted up for loom-shops. This source of making room being at length exhausted, new weavers' cottages with loom-shops rose up in every direction.'

The upsurge of prosperity was brief, for the weavers were the storm signals for the industry – the first to feel the effect of any slight shift in the trade winds. Spinners could stockpile, merchants could dump – but when the market was overstocked, weavers could only starve. Nevertheless, in the period described by Radcliffe, there was a great increase in building activity all over the manufacturing districts of the north-west. The development can be traced in villages such as Wardle in Lancashire. New mill buildings appeared in the village, such as Wardle mill, and the new weavers' cottages were built in the village centre and developments spread out to the surrounding countryside, with more mill-building and weavers' cottages and loom sheds attached to every farm and smallholding. Mostly these country mills were small concerns, employing few workers. But, because their owners worked to very small margins, the temptation to push the work force beyond all reasonable limits was great and too seldom resisted. The large mills and factories attracted the attention of travellers and reformers, partly because of their novelty, yet it was often in these small and handsome buildings that the worst excesses occurred. The small owners found great difficulty in remaining solvent during trade depressions – a story told by Charlotte Brontë in her novel *Shirley*. This novel, incidentally, contains a passage in which the heroine puts perfectly the view of even the best-intentioned owners when faced by a work force roused to action: 'At present I am no patrician, nor do I regard the poor around me as plebeians; but if once they violently wrong me or mine, and then presume to dictate to us, I shall quite forget pity for their wretchedness and respect for their poverty, in scorn of their ignorance and wrath at their insolence.'

A quite different type of employer, who presided over a quite different type of community, was the large-scale manufacturer who followed after the Strutts and Arkwrights – men such as Samuel Oldknow and Samuel Greg. Both men employed hundreds of workers – Greg in his own mill village, Oldknow spreading his interests between the mills at Marple and Mellor in Cheshire and a considerable number of outworkers, as well as other concerns, including transport, quarries and limeworks, and farming.

The surviving records of Oldknow's different enterprises give fascinating insights into his many and varied activities, into the problems created by fluctuations in trade, and into the social and economic conditions of both employer and employed. Bills and accounts give a curious patchwork picture of private as well as commercial life. On the private side, Oldknow's doctor's bills make alarming reading, full of ominous prescriptions such as 'vomit' at one shilling a bottle and 'opening mixture'. The style and wealth of the man can be guessed at from items such as a personal tailor's bill of 1811 for £11 8s 10d, to which was attached 'servants and game-keepers a/c £4–18–5'. The major expenditures naturally appear in the commercial accounts, which tell of the scale of the works and the expenses involved in running them. A month's coal bill for the Marple works for 1793, for example, came to £53 10s, and a similar amount was paid out for a new spinning frame with ninety-two spindles. The most important accounts are those dealing with the supply of the materials of his trade, notably raw cotton. Dipping at random into the accounts produces bills from one of the major suppliers, Thomas Norris, who between March 1797 and March 1798 supplied Oldknow with cotton worth £3,798 3s 9d. Smaller bills appear for other raw material, including a payment to B. Hibbert in 1803 for 'Introducing 48 Boys'. Bills also show Oldknow's activities in other fields, including transport. There are regular entries for payments towards the upkeep of roads, either in cash or in supplying workers to do the job. In 1788 he employed a contractor to look after road works between Disley and Marple, at a total cost of £28 17s 5d, individual items including,

'3 men ¾ of a day sinking and regulating the road 0–4–6
206 yds sinking a road across the wood   4–3–8'

It is also clear that the various workmen required constant lubrication – the ale bill for a single month rose to as much as £13, which represents something like 130 gallons of beer. There are also expenses for canal-cutting, for Oldknow was a promoter and committee member for the Peak Forest Canal Company, and regular payments to contractors appear.

On the opposite side of the accounts are the receipts from the sale of yarn. The following consecutive extracts from the account with the largest of Oldknow's customers, Stockport Manufactory, indicate the scale of the trade:

'12 Dec. 1792 – 550 lbs – £101–16–3
29 Dec. 1792 – 450 lbs – £80– 0–6
12 Jan. 1793 – 750 lbs – £136– 8–9
16 Jan. 1793 – 500 lbs – £91– 3–6
23 Jan. 1793 – 660 lbs – £119–16–0'

The largest single purchase in this series came on 30 March, with an order for 1,440 lbs at a cost of £287 3s 9d. Taken as a whole, the accounts, though incomplete, show a variety of business interests being followed on a very large scale. The correspondence confirms this view, and also shows something of the problems that beset both master and men in their daily lives.

In many of the letters we can trace the effects of trade fluctuations. In bad years Oldknow was pressed to continue taking raw cotton, simply to keep the suppliers solvent. 'We are very sorry to find your Trade flatt, but hope for a speedy change – we shall be happy in your future favours and as you cannot do without a small consumption we shall always be happy to serve you if ever so small an order,' wrote John Cowpe, one of Oldknow's suppliers in January 1788. Oldknow had his own problems during recessions, and sometimes found it convenient to put off settling his debts for as long as possible, as this letter of August 1797 indicates (part of the letter is torn):

'[I am] sorry to be under the necessity of [writing] you so often, &, what I cannot help [but] consider as very extraordinary never yet have I rec. an answer to any one: I will beg leave to say that the balance is too much to lie out of any longer, I cannot do it; I am now losing money by what I have sold, this and this done to a Gentleman of that sensibility I always thought you posest of would be sufficient to create a particular exertion to support what ought to be particularly dear to yourself, as well as taking into consideration my interest.'

A number of letters indicate that a modern problem also affected the eighteenth-century manufacturer – the problem of keeping up with the vagaries of fashion. 'We have Opend the 6/4 check which are middling but which are all to the Old Patterns which we cannot I fear sell. We wanted corded checks.' Big checks, small checks, finer cloth, coarser cloth, 'turkey red' handkerchiefs: the demands for new lines came in a constant flow.

A good deal of the correspondence in the Oldknow papers is concerned with the outworkers – spinners and weavers. The majority of the weavers were employed through Oldknow's agent at Anderton, and the most commonly recurring problems arose from the uncertainty of the work – men held up by a shortage of cotton, correct reeds not being available, uncertainty about the prices to be paid.

'These two Weavers Jn Heys & James Woostern have been to Enquire for work – but on finding we had got the number we was to have at present they immediately determind to come to see you – if they meet with success I think you will have more of them – I sent Cart yesterday to the tol Bar & there was neither any more Reeds nor Cotton there was then near 200 Spinners waiting for it – how we shall get this day over I dont know – I desire you will let me know when we may depend on having some & also the Reeds – weavers come every Day & I cannot tel what to say to them.'

The hard-pressed agent who wrote that letter in September 1788 received his supplies the next day. The letter shows a number of important points – first, Oldknow was still employing domestic spinners as well as the spinners in his mills, and the weavers used machines provided by Oldknow. The outworkers themselves had problems and caused problems, and in the hard times occasionally resorted to dishonesty, as a letter from a spinner dated 14 June 1787 and written in a copperplate hand that suggests the use of a professional scribe, indicates:

'I am sorry to inform you that your cotton is spun & sold, & until I received your letter I did not know but my husband had delivered it to the right owner: having seen my husband since, who is exceeding sorry for what he has done being then in great need of Money humbly desires the Favour not to be put to any Expence about the recovery of the same, and in a very short time he will either pay you the Value in cash or buy and deliver to you the same Quantity of equal or better Quality either in the Wool or Yarn at your Option.'

The difficulties with the outworkers may have been a factor in the decision to limit the weaving activities to other concerns at home or abroad. The Brothers Van de Becke of Leipzig wrote in May 1795: 'We have now taken notice that you have declined the making of Piece Goods – we wish you would send us a regular Bill of Prices of all your Twist.' Not surprisingly, this brought a strong reaction from the weavers. As the practice became more general, the Association of Weavers petitioned Parliament in 1799, complaining that 'every necessary of life has increased in price, while the price of labour has undergone a continual decrease'. They asked Parliament to ban the export of yarn, so that the country should not become 'merely spinners for the rest of Europe'. Their faith in Parliament proved ill-founded, for no action was taken to help them, and as their standard of living steadily declined, so their militancy rose (see chapter 11).

Some of the most interesting documents preserved among the Oldknow papers are the shop accounts for Mellor. The workers in Oldknow's mills were paid by bills which they could cash at his shop – taking payment in cash, in goods or in a mixture of the two. It was not quite a truck system – payment in goods – but it was very close to it. The system had obvious advantages for Oldknow. Cash supply was often an acute problem in the eighteenth century, so if workers could be persuaded to take payment in goods, it helped to ease the situation. Again, Oldknow profited from the deal – as farmer he sold produce to his shop at a profit, as shopowner he sold the goods to the workers again at a profit, and as employer he profited from the workers' production as well. From the workers' point of view the system was not entirely bad – provided it was honestly administered – for they were often able to get goods cheaper in Oldknow's shop than they could elsewhere. In many cases, it is clear that the whole of the wages were spent at the shop, so that the shop accounts are uniquely valuable as a guide to the standard of living of the workers. What one notices first is the monotony of the diet of the cotton-workers. Many seem to have existed on little beyond bread and cheese, and even the higher-paid families fared little better. The Hudson family, for example, had five working in the mills – the parents and three children. Taking a typical week – in May 1793 – we find the total family income to be £2 8s 1d; two shillings was deducted for rent, and £2 0s 1d went on food, and this is what they got for their money:

'Bread	– 11s	Bacon	– 6s 6d
Meal	– 9s 9d	Flour	– 3s 10d
Cheese	– 8s 0½d	Butter	– 11½d'

That left them with six shillings which they drew as cash. The basic diet of bread and cheese with a little bacon was common for all the families employed at the mills.

Samuel Oldknow's mills have been demolished, but his other activities have left a more permanent mark on the landscape: there are, for example, the extensive lime kilns at Marple, and the transport system he developed. The turnpike roads and bridges centred on Marple were the result of Oldknow's work, but most important was the Peak Forest Canal. The features of the canal, such as the locks and aqueduct, have already been mentioned (p. 102), but there is still one even more direct link with Oldknow to be seen. Half-way down the Marple flight is the Oldknow warehouse, which is a particularly fine example of this type of building (plate 76). It is a three-storey stone building with a slate roof, but what makes it rather special is the arrangement adopted to ease the transfer of goods between road and canal. On the landward side, the warehouse has the normal arrangement of large loading bays and hoists, but the other side is built out into the canal, so that boats can be brought through the arched entrance, right under the warehouse for loading and unloading under cover. A small toll-house stands just behind the warehouse, where fees were collected for the use of the road and wharf.

Where Oldknow's interests were wide-ranging, in every sense, those of Samuel Greg were narrower. He hailed originally from Belfast, and in 1784 he came to the hamlet of Styal in Cheshire and there, on the banks of the Bollin, built the Quarry Bank mills at a cost of £16,000. The few farms and cottages provided nothing like enough accommodation to house the work force needed for such an important new factory, so Greg then set to work to build up a village. Some farm buildings were converted into cottages, but most of the housing had to be specially built by Greg. He built a shop, similar to Oldknow's, and like Oldknow acquired a farm to help supply it. As the community of Styal developed, he added a chapel in 1822, appointing a minister at a stipend of £80 per annum. The school and the Institution followed the next year. Those years also saw a steady expansion of the mill buildings. First a wing was added and an extra storey built on to the mill. Then a second water wheel was constructed – the first in that district to be built in iron. An important date in the history of the mill was 1796, when Peter Ewart joined the partnership. It was said that he 'brought no capital but extensive mechanical knowledge'. He was a member of the Manchester Literary and Philosophical Society, had worked on the theory as well as the practice of cotton machinery, and was 'profoundly learned in all that has reference to steam'. His influence soon appeared in an extensive programme of modernization. In 1800, a small steam engine was installed at the mill and new improved water frames added. In 1818 a new tunnel, wheel race and water wheel were added, the mill was further extended and still more frames introduced. Quarry Bank mill remained as a spinning mill until after Samuel Greg's death in 1834 when looms were added to the machinery. Styal is now a preserved site of the very greatest importance, for the mill and village remain much as they were in Greg's time and it is well documented – providing a fine opportunity to build a picture of life in a cotton village in the late eighteenth and early nineteenth centuries.

The most important, and largest, building at Styal is the mill itself. The main building is stately, unadorned, Georgian redbrick (plate XVI). No attempt at extra embellishment has been made, and none is needed. The crisp white of window frames and the pattern of iron tie-beam ends against a background of brickwork broken only by years of encroaching ivy are all that is necessary to complete a wholly satisfying appearance. The bell tower that tops the building is no ornament but an important factor in the working life of the mill (plate 77). At a time when few families owned clocks or watches, they relied on the factory bell to tell them when to start and finish work and, not being able to check on its accuracy, they also depended on the honesty of the official timekeeper who rang it. The ownership of the mill is proclaimed in an inscription over the mill door, which reads 'Built by Samuel Greg Esquire of Belfast Ireland Anno Domini 1784'.

In 1790 there were 183 wage-earners in the mill, mostly employed in the spinning and carding rooms at wages ranging from 1s 6d a week for a doffer – the child whose job it was to change the spindles – to fifteen shillings a week for an overlooker. Added to that number there were eighty apprentices. By 1831 there were 351 wage-earners and a hundred apprentices, but although the doffers had almost doubled their wages, the overseers still received no more than seventeen to eighteen shillings a week. These wages are considerably lower than those paid in the mills of Manchester and the other expanding cotton towns. But the work force at Styal was mainly recruited, like the Cromford workers, from the poorer parts of southern England. As the figures quoted from Eden's survey (p. 84) show, the wages at Styal represented a definite improvement for them. It is also worth remembering that, when Greg was recruiting his workers, the notorious Speenhamland system was in operation in the agricultural areas, by means of which farmers were able to pay less than a living wage, secure in the knowledge that the working population would be kept to a bare subsistence level by payments out of the Poor Rates – a system that added degradation to near starvation. Styal offered better than that in terms of wages and could offer the added inducement of a decent home.

Next to the mill is the owner's house – a fine country mansion in which he could sit and contemplate the peaceful river or the less peaceful, but more profitable, mill (plate 78). At a decent distance beyond that stands the apprentices' house. This was the home of the pauper apprentices, children bought from the poor-houses of the district, or, more frequently, from farther afield, a large number coming from the poor-houses in Chelsea and Liverpool. It was usual for the children to be sent out as apprentices by order of a local magistrate, a convenient system which relieved the local parish of the necessity of providing for them. The vicar of Congleton wrote in 1817:

> 'The thought has occurred to me that some of the younger branches of the poor of this parish might be useful to you as Apprentices in your Factory at Quarry Bank. If you are in want of any of the above, we could readily furnish you with Ten or more at from nine to twelve years of age of both sexes.'

Greg replied:

> 'I am much obliged by your attention and find we have room at present for about 12 young Girls of from 10 to 12 yrs old . . . the terms at which we take them are:

'Two guineas each will be expected from the Parish, and clothing sufficient to keep the Children clean,
Say 2 shifts
        2 Pair stockings
        2 Frocks
        2 Brats or aprons
and 2 guineas to provide them other necessaries.'

Other children were signed up on indentures at the request of the parents, usually because they were unable to keep them at home themselves. A typical indenture of the period reads:

'It is this day agreed by and between Samuel Greg, of Styal in the County of Chester, of the one Part and Sarah Irwin Daughter of John Irwin of Newcastle of the other Part, who Agrees to the Terms as follows: That the said Sarah Irwin shall serve the said Samuel Greg in his Cotton Mill, in Styal, in the County of Chester, as a just and honest Servant, Twelve hours in each of the six working days, and to be at her own liberty at all other times; the Commencement of the Hours to be fixed from Time to Time by the said Samuel Greg, for the Term of four years at the Wages of one Penny p week also Sufficient meat drink apparel lodging washing and other things necessary and fit for one in her situation.'

The treatment of apprentice children became a subject of bitter controversy in the early part of the nineteenth century. There is an immense body of documentary evidence on the conditions of children in the mills of the north-west, which has been much quoted. The phrase 'the beds of Lancashire never grew cold' passed into popular folklore, to describe the conditions of some apprentice houses, where as the day shift staggered back from their work, the night shift left for theirs. It is a harrowing story of overwork and brutality. Tired workmen beating exhausted children is a recurring theme in the pages of the famous 1833 Parliamentary Report on the condition of the factory children. This single extract from that report tells almost as much of the pathetic state of the workman giving the evidence as it does of the condition of the children he maltreated:

'They'd try a man's patience sometimes, aggravating him, and then run away home. It is not allowed to take the billy roller [a wooden baton]. I may have taken it sometimes in the heat of passion, but not to hurt them. No man as had children of his own could bear to do it. . . . I have kept them till ten or eleven, or sometimes twelve at night; happen once in a fortnight; beginning at six in the morning. Sometimes I might have taken the strap to them to waken them a little.'

In some apprentice houses the beds had to be checked every night to ensure that children had not run away or, more commonly, fallen asleep at the mill. The opponents of child labour published many such stories, in an attempt to rouse public opinion and to put pressure on Parliament to pass an Act limiting working hours to ten per day. Writers such as John Fielden MP, author of *The Curse of the Factory System* (1836), were frequently accused of exaggerating the evils of the system in order to strengthen their case. It was argued, quite correctly, that child labour was no new thing, and that the children employed in the homes of spinners or weavers worked equally long hours. This might be true, but there is at least a qualitative difference between the child helping its own parents in its home, and the child shut away in a factory for twelve hours in the day. Descriptions of children at work given by the apologists for the system, such as Andrew Ure, strike one as, to say the least, unlikely:

'They seemed to be always cheerful and alert, taking pleasure in the light play of their muscles – enjoying the mobility natural to their age. The scene of industry, so far from exciting sad emotions in my mind, was always exhilarating. It was delightful to observe the nimbleness with which they pieced the broken ends, as the mule-carriage began to recede from the fixed roller beam. . . . The work of these lively elves seemed to resemble a sport, in which habit gave them a pleasing dexterity.'

Ure was an opponent of the proposed ten-hour bill. A powerful proponent was William Cobbett and reading his scathing speech to the House of Commons, quoted in full in Fielden's book, it is hard to resist standing and cheering:

'I have only one observation to make, and I will not detain the House two minutes in doing so. We have, Sir, this night made one of the greatest discoveries ever made by a House of Commons. . . . Hitherto, we have been told that our navy was the glory of the country, and that our maritime commerce and extensive manufactures were the mainstays of the realm. We have also been told that the land had its share in our greatness, and should justly be considered as the pride and glory of England. The Bank, also, has put in its claim to share in this praise, and has stated that public credit is due to it; but now, a most surprising discovery has been made, namely, that all our greatness and prosperity, that our superiority over other nations, is owing to 300,000 little girls in Lancashire. We have made the notable discovery, that, if these little girls work two hours less in a day than they now do, it would occasion the ruin of the country; that it would enable other countries to compete with us; and thus make an end to our boasted wealth, and bring us to beggary!'

In assessing the opposing views of writers such as Fielden and Ure one needs rather more than their own bald assertions. Styal provides an opportunity to put the rival claims to the test. Both opponents and proponents were agreed that Samuel Greg represented the better class of employer, and that the apprentices' house at Styal was a model for its kind. In Andrew Ure's words:

'Here are well-fed, clothed, educated, and lodged, under kind superintendence, sixty young girls, who by their deportment at the mill . . . evince a degree of comfort most creditable to the humane and intelligent proprietors.'

From the mill records, we know that Ure underestimated the numbers of apprentices, though it is possible that he was intending to be taken literally, and was not counting the boys at the house. There appear to have usually been ninety to a hundred children in the house, under the care of a pair of resident housekeepers. The apprentice house today is a pleasant, but not unduly large, family house (plate xvii). It seems almost incredible to think that it once provided quarters for a married couple and the hundred children in their care. Yet this was a model house, run by exceptionally kindly employers. One can only guess at the conditions in the worst.

On the actual conditions at Styal we have the evidence of two apprentices who ran away, but were caught and gave a full account of their lives to the magistrates on 2 August 1806. The following is part of the evidence of Joseph Sefton:

'I am 17 yrs of age this August. My father I am informed deserted me or went for a soldier when I was about 2 yrs old. His name was John Sefton. I have been told that I was born in Clerkenwell I had been in the workhouse of the Parish of Hackney from an infant about 3½ yrs I consented before the magistrates at this office Worship St to be bound apprentice to Samuel Greg cotton spinner and manufacturer. There were 8 boys and 4 girls of us bound at the same time. We went to Styal and were employed in the cotton mills of Mr Saml Gregs which are a short distance. I was first employed to doff bobbins. . . . I used to oil the machinery every morning. In fact I was employed in the mill work. I did not spin. I liked my employment very well. I was obliged to make over time every night but I did not like this as I wanted to learn my book. We had a school every night but we used to attend about once a week (besides Sundays when we all attended). . . . I wanted to go oftener to school than twice a week including Sundays, but Richard Bamford would not let me go. . . . I have no reason to complain of my master Mr Greg nor Richard Bamford who overlooks the works there were 42 boys and more girls apprenticed. We lodged in the Prentice House near the Mill. We were under the care of Richard Sims and his wife. The boys slept on one side of the house and the girls on the other. The girls all slept in one room. The boys in three. There was a door betwixt their apartments which was locked of a night. Our rooms were very clean, the floors frequently washed, the rooms aired every day, whitewashed once a year. Our beds were good. We slept two in a bed and had clean sheets once a month. We had clean shirts every Sunday. We had new clothes for Sunday once in two years. We had working jackets new when those were worn out and when our working trousers were dirty we had them washed. Some had new

jackets last Summer but they were making new ours when I came
away.

On Sunday we went to church in the morning and to school
in the afternoon after which we had time to play.

On Sunday we had for dinner boiled Pork and potatoes. We
had also peas beans turnips and cabbages in their season.

Monday we had for dinner milk & bread and sometimes thick
porridge. We had always as much as we could eat.

Tuesday we had milk and potatoes.

Wednesday sometimes Bacon and Potatoes sometimes milk and
bread.

Thursday If we had Bacon on Wednesday we had milk and
bread.

Friday we used to have Lobs couse.

Saturday we used to dine on thick porridge.
We had only water to drink, when ill we were allowed tea.'

The other runaway, thirteen-year-old Thomas Priestley, tells a
similar story, and adds a few more details:

'Our working hours were from six o'clock morning Summer and
Winter till 7 in the evening. There were no nights worked. We
had only 10 minutes allowed us for our breakfasts which were
always brought to the Mill to us and we worked that up at night
again – 2 days in the week we had an hour allowed us for dinner,
while the machines were oiled, for doing this I was paid $\frac{1}{2}$d a time,
on other days we were allowed half an hour for dinner. When the
Boys worked over time, they were paid 1d an hour.'

Shortly before he ran away, he had one of his fingers torn off by the
machinery.

Faced with these accounts of living and working conditions in a
model mill, discussion of whether things were once worse seems
almost irrelevant. The central fact that emerges is that the children,
packed into this modest house, considered themselves fortunate in
comparison with other children at other mills. The attractive mill
and house, set in equally attractive scenery, represent the very top
end of a scale that sank considerably lower.

55 Gladstone pottery, Longton: the tunnel entrance and courtyard with the china biscuit kiln to the right

Gladstone pottery, Longton: 56 *Above* The apparent
disorder that hides a logical sequence of building;
57 *Right* The interior of the biscuit kiln; 58 *Far right*
Inside the mould-making shop

59 *Far left* The sad
dereliction that was once
Wedgwood's Etruria works
60 *Left* Etruria Hall, its
elegance submerged
61 *Below left* Pottery
workers' houses: Warren
Terrace, Longton
62 *Below right* The façade
of the potteries: Aynsley
china, Longton

Cheddleton flint mill: 63 *Above* Flints are
unloaded at the wharf built over calcining
kilns; 64 *Right* They are fed directly into the
kilns

Cheddleton flint mill: 65
Above After heating, the flints
are taken by plateway to one
of the two mills; 66 *Left*
Both mills are water-powered

Cheddleton flint mill: 67 *Above* The horizontal drive from the wheel is transmitted by the pit wheel and wallower to a vertical shaft which passes up to the first floor; 68 *Right* There the shaft turns the sweep arms in the flint pan to grind the flints, which are mixed with water. Cheddleton has other machinery; 69 *Far right, above* An edge roller used for grinding colour; 70 *Far right, below* The workshop

71 *Far left* Coalport
pottery
72 *Left* A Crompton
mule at Helmshore
73 *Below* Clough
cotton mill, Littleborough
– now a romantic ruin in a
moorland setting.
Weavers' cottages are
scattered over the hillside

74 *Left* Cotton workers' houses at Todmorden

75 *Right* The ivy-covered ruins of a cotton bobbin mill at Gatehouse-of-Fleet

76 *Below* Oldknow's warehouse on the Peak Forest canal, showing the arch through which boats passed to be loaded under cover

Styal cotton mill and village: 77 *Left*
The factory bell that summoned the
workers; 78 *Below left* The owners'
house; 79 *Above right* The workers'
houses; 80 *Below right* The village shop

81 Tenements and Owen's New Institution at New
Lanark

The village that Samuel Greg built is undeniably pleasant, and to the pauper families that came must have seemed positively luxurious. These families signed indentures very similar to the apprentices' indentures, binding them to Styal for a set number of years. Many were given loans when they first arrived to help them set up home, and repayments were made by deduction from their wages. The houses are built to the high standard that characterizes so many of the early company towns (plate 79). They are cellar houses, and were probably used in part as domestic workshops by any members of the family who did not work in the mill. Greg's shop still stands in the middle of the village (plate 80), and shop receipts show that family earnings were very similar to those of the Oldknow workers, and were spent in a very similar manner. One interesting point about the economy of the mill is that Greg worked out that although the apprentice children received virtually no pay, they were more costly than the children of the village, who worked for wages.

Visiting the mill and village at Styal, the over-riding impression is of neat cottages, set in a pleasant open countryside, and it is certainly not difficult to see how it came to be upheld as a model of benevolent development. That it still stands is itself a reflection that the village was built to a higher standard than the houses of the speculative builders of other cotton towns. There is also no question that, although wages were considerably lower than in nearby Manchester, the families who came here were better off for the move, and the apprentices would have preferred the life at Styal to the parish poor-house. A final point to note is that Greg himself became a wealthy man. In 1824 he gave the following details of his household to the tax assessors: the staff consisted of butler, footman, coachman, gardener and bailiff, he had one 'chariot', three horses for personal use and hounds, one horse for his bailiff, one exempt from tax for cavalry use, and four horses for trade. By the end of his career, Greg owned five mills, and worked 1 per cent of the cotton worked in the whole country.

The development of the cotton industry was not limited to north-west England. At the same time as Greg and Oldknow were establishing their cotton kingdoms, similar developments were under way north of the border, in Scotland. Throughout most of the eighteenth century, Scottish textiles were dominated by linen manufacture, and cotton mills were only slowly established. One of the first mills to be built was begun at Rothesay on the Isle of Bute. An island, even one close to the mainland, might seem an odd starting place, but the mill's builder, John Kenyon, had sound reasons for his choice. There were no labour shortages, and the available workers were already experienced in the linen industry; there were plentiful water supplies for power; and, most importantly, it was far enough out of the way for Kenyon cheerfully to infringe Arkwright's patent with very little risk of discovery. Kenyon even managed to do a little surreptitious enticement of Arkwright's workmen, who came to Rothesay to help with the setting-up of the machinery. In 1813 the works were taken over by two partners, William Kelly and an engineer, Robert Thom, who greatly improved the water supply to the mills. More mills were added, and Rothesay developed into a cotton town, with company houses and payment by tokens that could be cashed at the company shop – the system already familiar in England. Altogether four mills were built at Rothesay, two of which remain today. Similar mills and factory communities appeared in an apparently random manner in different parts of the country. Two examples that still stand are at the very limit of the industrialized region of Scotland, on the edge of the Highlands: Stanley mill in Perthshire, which was completed in 1790, and from the outside resembles Strutt's North mill at Belper in its method of construction, though inside it has the older style of wooden beams supported on cast iron pillars; and the sandstone, six-storey mill at Deanston, north of Stirling, built in 1785.

This random pattern of development is in marked contrast to the way in which the English industry concentrated on a comparatively small region. Occasionally, the would-be millowner was forced into a particular choice of site, against his wishes. Robert Heron, who toured Scotland in 1792, and produced the inevitable volume of reminiscences of his travels in 1799, records that Messrs Birtwhistle had just set up a cotton mill at Gatehouse-of-Fleet, Kircudbright-shire: 'It was said, that these gentlemen had previously applied to the Earl of Selkirk for a lease of grounds near Kirdcudbright, on which they might have erected their cotton-work; but that his

Lordship apprehending that an earl's mansion might be disgraced by the vicinity of an establishment of manufacturing industry, rejected their offers with earnestness.' Two mills were built here, beside the river, both making use of the same water supply. The first of the mills, farthest from the river, is the original cotton mill, now reduced to a single storey. One notices straight away that the building is remarkably crude – walls built of random rubble work, surrounds for windows and doors constructed from vast slabs of undressed stone. A launder still carries water to the mill, but now it splashes down over the crumbling walls to no purpose. The remains of the second mill are rather more impressive, if still in a very ruinous condition (plate 75). The building stands directly on the river bank, and shows the same rough and ready construction as its neighbour. It is three storeys high, twelve bays long, and timber-framed. The wheel pit is still clearly distinguishable, but the building itself is a mere shell, open to the skies and almost covered, inside and out, with creepers. These two mills employed three hundred, of whom two hundred were children, and the total weekly wage bill of £50 bears out Heron's view that one of the main reasons that the English came to Scotland to establish their mills was that 'Scotland having been, till very lately a much poorer and less improved country than England, the price of labour was, in consequence, cheaper in the former'. Heron took a fairly jaundiced view of developments at Gatehouse-of-Fleet, noting that the breakdown of the old order of things was accompanied by a fall in moral standards. The influx of new workers meant more people in the neighbourhood, and in Scotland there was no Poor Rate to help them out if they fell on hard times. At that time the system was for charity to be doled out by the Church, and if there was not enough from that source 'it has generally been thought necessary to permit the parish poor to beg from door to door': a system, Heron declares, which 'of all schemes that political wisdom, or the cares of pious charity has contrived, in order to relieve want, without encouraging vicious idleness, is perhaps the best'. The trouble with places such as Gatehouse, as Heron and other commentators saw it, was that it encouraged workers to earn more money, which in turn meant that they were able to buy luxuries, and then the road to damnation was open before them. There are, however, no signs left of unbridled luxury and vice in the small, neat, well-planned town that we see today.

It was possible to take a different view of cotton-operatives. Not everyone regarded them as a class of potential criminals only to be kept in check by being worked so hard they had no energy left for riotous behaviour, and paid such low wages that if they found the energy they would not have the means. One community based on a cotton mill became famous for a different treatment of the workers and a different philosophy of labour – New Lanark. The name is now always associated with that of Robert Owen, but the New Lanark story begins long before his arrival in the area.

As already described, the works here were begun by David Dale, who operated them under licence from Arkwright. A mill was established near the Corra Linn falls on the Clyde, and Owen described the problems of the early years in his famous book *A New View of Society* (1813):

'It was the power which could be obtained from the falls of water which induced Mr Dale to erect his mills in this situation, for in other respects it was not well chosen; the country around was uncultivated; the inhabitants were poor, and few in number; and the roads in the neighbourhood were so bad, that the Falls now so celebrated were then unknown to strangers.

It was therefore necessary to collect a new population to supply the infant establishment with labourers. This however was no light task; for all the regularly trained Scotch peasantry disdained the idea of working early and late, day after day, within cotton mills. Two modes then only remained of obtaining these labourers: the one, to procure children from the various public charities of the country; and the other, to induce families to settle around the works.

To accommodate the first, a large house was erected, which ultimately contained about five hundred children, who were procured chiefly from workhouses and charities in Edinburgh. These children were to be fed, clothed, and educated; and these duties Mr Dale performed with the unwearied benevolence which it is well known he possessed.

To obtain the second, a village was built, and the houses were let at a low rent to such families as could be induced to accept employment in the mills; but such was the general dislike to that occupation at the time, that, with a few exceptions, only persons destitute of friends, employment, and character, were found willing to try the experiment; and of these a sufficient number to supply a constant increase of the manufactory could not be obtained.'

Dale was, as Owen wrote, a benevolent employer, but the Charities who sent the children to New Lanark insisted on their being six to eight years old, and the mill's economy depended on these children. For all his benevolence, Dale found he had to work the children from six in the morning to seven at night. He supplied them with good living accommodation, proper medical supervision, decent food and education, but this was small compensation for the thirteen-hour day, at the end of which such young children could hardly be expected to take much interest in food, let alone books. Dale also set about recruiting adult workers, and one important group literally arrived by accident. They were Highlanders setting out from the Clyde for America, who became stormbound, took shelter at New Lanark and stayed. The bell hanging in the bellcote at New Lanark was intended for the church they planned to build in the New World.

As Dale grew older, he was able to take less of an active interest in the business. In 1798, Robert Owen arrived to help run the works and a year later became a partner. He arrived at New Lanark from Manchester with a reputation as a highly efficient mill manager rather than a reformer, but he had already formed his own ideas on how a factory community should be managed. No doubt in his writings he exaggerated the appalling nature of the conditions he found and the efficacy of his own improvement. But, even allowing for possible exaggeration, the community was certainly badly in need of improvement:

'At this period they possessed almost all the vices and very few of the virtues of a social community. Theft and the receipt of stolen goods was their trade, idleness and drunkenness their habit, falsehood and deception their garb, dissentions civil and religious their daily practice: they united only in a zealous systematic opposition to their employers.'

Over the following years, Owen embarked on a series of experiments at New Lanark that made himself and the community world-famous, and brought thousands and thousands of visitors to Scotland to see the new system at work. Part of Owen's fame rests on his later proposals for 'Villages of Co-operation' – but there was none of this in the organization of New Lanark society. There Owen played the despot – a uniquely benevolent despot, but a despot nonetheless. He enforced his views on the organization of every detail of life in the town, without any form of consultation with his work force. He was as paternalist as the Gregs, the Strutts or the Wedgwoods – only differing from them in his views of the best way to treat the workers.

His first actions had to be to put a stop to the theft, drunkenness and filth that characterized the community. He ignored the popular remedy for theft – swingeing punishment – and settled instead for prevention – 'not one legal punishment was inflicted, not one individual imprisoned even for an hour'. Drunkenness was dealt with on the same principle, by gradually closing down the pot-houses and pubs. Cleanliness was vigorously enforced by Owen himself taking regular tours of inspection of the homes of the town, which no doubt improved the hygiene but could hardly have endeared him to the housewife. But Owen placed his greatest emphasis on the value of education – no building in New Lanark held a greater importance for him than the New Institution (plate 81), where children and adults could obtain a decent schooling. He insisted that children between the ages of five and ten should go to school and not to work, and pre-empted modern educational theorists by emphasizing the importance of the pre-school years and the dangers of a bad home environment. An enclosed playground was built outside the school.

'Into this playground the children are to be received as soon as they can freely walk alone; to be superintended by persons instructed to take charge of them . . . as any sentiments and habits may be given to all infants, it becomes of primary importance that those alone should be given to them which can contribute to their happiness. Each child, therefore on his entrance into the play-ground is to be told in language he can understand, that "he is never to injure his play-fellows but on the contrary he is to contribute all in his power to make them happy".'

An even more revolutionary innovation was Owen's reduction of the working hours at the mill. Working young children and obtaining the maximum possible hours of labour from all workers were practically tenets of faith with most manufacturers, so it is hardly surprising to find Owen in frequent disagreement with his partners. Owen relied on practical as well as humane arguments. What is the point, he argued, in pushing workers to the limits of exhaustion? The end result is mistakes and bad workmanship. Give workers decent hours, show that you care for their well-being, and they will reward you with better workmanship. They will even do more work in the short working day than in the long day, which they start tired and end exhausted.

Results proved Owen's theories to be right, but they continued to baffle other industrialists, much as they baffled the members of Peel's 1816 committee. The committee interrogated Owen, asking the same questions and getting the same answers again and again with obvious incredulity: Owen explained his system, and the resulting higher productivity. 'Is the committee to understand,' they asked, 'that since the first of January the machinery has been quickened? If it has not been quickened, how is it possible to state that a larger proportionable quantity has been produced?' Owen explained. Could Owen's machines, they then asked, produce more yarn 'from any other cause whatever but the quickening of the motion of the machine?' It could, replied Owen. The committee again asked how, and Owen again told them. At the end of this explanation, the committee reiterated the same questions. 'If, therefore, the velocity of the machine has not been increased, how do you account for the produce per spindle being anything different from the proportion that would arise from the difference of the hours of labour?' Owen explained yet again, adding with understandable impatience: 'It is far from my wish to deceive the committee in any respect.' At that point, the committee apparently gave up the attempt to understand.

At the time of the Peel Committee, the population of New Lanark had risen to two thousand, of whom some three-quarters worked in the mill. To the people of the town, Robert Owen was a kind of industrial squire, and like many another squire was given to odd quirks that the people accepted, more or less with a good grace. Some of his obsessions, such as his great faith in the benevolent effects of music and dance, must have proved rather irksome, and it is doubtful if busy cotton operatives felt much inclination for hopping up and down to the fiddle or fife in the middle of the day. However, many modern Japanese industrialists seem to find value in putting their workers through much the same routine, so perhaps Owen had a point. In any case, the dancing display was an inevitable part of the programme for any visiting notables at New Lanark. Robert Southey described a visit he made with his great friend, Thomas Telford, in his *Journal of a Tour of Scotland in 1819*. His first impressions were favourable. He found the streets of the town to be cleaner than most, though 'not quite so clean as they ought to be'. They were then given the customary dancing display, which Southey enjoyed not at all. Some two hundred children took part: 'They turned to the right or left, faced about, fell forwards and backwards, and stamped at command, performing manoeuvres the object of which was not very clear, with perfect regularity. . . . I could not but think that these puppet-like motions might, with a little ingenuity, have been produced by the great water-wheel.' Still, he admitted, the children seemed to enjoy it, and when he came to the infants' playground, Southey found things more to his liking. The infants 'made a glorious noise, worth all the concerts of New Lanark, and of London to boot. It was really delightful to see how the little creatures crowded about Owen to make their bows and their curtsies, looking up and smiling in his face; and the genuine benignity and pleasure with which he noticed them.' Southey also noted the village stores, run by the millowner, where each worker was allowed sixteen shillings a week credit, 'but may deal elsewhere if they chuse'.

Some aspects of Owen's management seem less acceptable today – the system of hanging wooden blocks over the workers, each block painted a different colour to show how well the operative was behaving, would certainly be one example. However, New Lanark represented a standard of care for the work force that few other factory communities aspired to, let alone reached. It deserves its place in history. How sad, then, to see New Lanark today. The village is all but deserted, the mill buildings surrounded by heaps of scrap. The windows of the New Institution are boarded up, as some protection against vandalism, and although parts are still lived in and cared for, the general air is one of decay. The romantic setting of the river, with its rocky falls and wooded hillside facing the town, is unchanged, but now it requires more of an act of imagination to see the busy town of Owen's time.

In spite of this, there is still much to see to help give a clearer picture of the community. The broad streets and the walks among the gardens laid out by Owen are still there to remind us of his concern with the quality of life. The housing at New Lanark is mainly in the form of tenement blocks (plate 81), built in four storeys, as in Rosedale Street, or with four storeys at the front and with two at the back where they are built up against the hillside. In spite of the neglect, the buildings still seem remarkably sound – the solid granite walls, at least, look as if they could stand for ever. Inside, the uninhabited tenements are in very bad condition, and there seems a real danger that unless action is taken distinctive features such as the wall beds will be lost. Strength and spaciousness seem to be the keynotes of New Lanark, and appropriately it is the New Institution that dominates the whole town.

The mill buildings are closest to the river – which means that the houses have the best of the view, out over the mill roofs to the open countryside. These buildings are a mixture of dilapidation and modern building, but perhaps they are in some ways the least important of the New Lanark buildings. True, it was the mills that created New Lanark, but it is for its unique social experiment that it will be remembered, and the town of New Lanark, in spite of its present condition, is as powerful an illustration of Owen's doctrines as any words that he wrote.

Long before Owen's reign at New Lanark had ended, the day of the factory village was already closing. New inventions again changed the geography of the industry and the communities associated with it. Just as the invention of the water-powered spinning machine moved the base of cotton-spinning, so the use of the steam engine was to move it again. The new engines also had an effect on other industries, and the improvements it made possible in mining techniques helped the development of the larger industrial towns.

9
The Separate Condenser

A separate condenser sounds neither particularly exciting nor particularly important, yet it was James Watt's invention of this comparatively simple device which was mainly responsible for changing the course of the industrial revolution: it ensured the replacement of the water wheel by the steam engine as the main source of power. The steam engine was not new when James Watt began his working life, but it was so inefficient and consumed so much coal that coal mines, where feeding the monster presented no great problem, were almost the only places where such engines could be used. In areas which did not have a ready supply of coal on the doorstep, the existing engines were all but useless. In Cornwall, for example, where new and more powerful pumping engines were urgently needed, the cost of transporting coal meant that the old Newcomen engines simply did not pay their way.

The problem lay in the fundamental design of the Newcomen engine. Steam was condensed in the cylinder by the cold water spray, and then the whole cylinder had to be reheated, and that process consumed a vast amount of energy that was not being converted into useful work. Watt's solution seems with hindsight to be simple and obvious – if the vessel containing the steam can always be kept separate from the vessel in which the steam condenses, then the former, the cylinder, can be kept permanently hot, and the latter, the condenser, permanently cold. Something of the excitement generated by Watt's realization of the possibilities of a separate condenser can be gauged from an account written by Professor Robison of Glasgow University, where Watt began his researches on the steam engine. Robison, who had his own ideas on ways of improving the steam engine, went to see Watt one day in 1765, but found him in a somewhat secretive if irritatingly smug mood. Robison's ideas were dismissed: 'You need not fash yourself any more about that Man, I have now made an Engine that shall not waste a particle of Steam.' The next day the whole secret was out. Robison described how it reached him:

'I was very anxious to learn what Mr Watt had contrived but was obliged to go to the Country in the Evening. A Gentleman who was going to the same house said that he would give me a place in his Carriage, and desired me to wait for him on the Walk by the River side. I went thither, and found Mr Alexander Brown, a very intimate Acquaintance of Mr Watt, walking with another Gentleman (Mr Craig Architect). Mr Brown immediately accosted me with Well have you seen Jamy Watt? Yes. He'll be in high spirits now with his Engine, isn't he. Yes said I very fine spirits. Gad says Mr Brown the Condenser's the thing keep it but cold enough and you may have a perfect vacuum whatever the heat of the Cylinder. The instant he said this the whole flashed on my mind at once. I did all I could to encourage the Conversation but was much embarrassed. I durst not appear ignorant of the apparatus, lest Mr Brown should find that he had communicated more than he ought to have done. I could only learn that there was a Vessel called a Condenser which communicated with the Cylinder, and that this Condenser was immersed in cold water and had a Pump to clear it of the Water which was formed in it. I also learned that the great difficulty was to make the piston tight, and that leather and felt had been tried and found quite unable to stand the heat. I saw the whole would be perfectly dry, and that Mr Watt had used Steam instead of Air to press up his Piston which I thought by Mr Brown's Conversation was inverted – We parted and I went home a very Silent Companion.'

The moment of discovery of the principle of the separate condenser was by no means enough to enable Watt to make a satisfactory working steam engine. Years of effort still lay ahead, during which he worked to perfect the different parts of his invention, but the main outline was already clear. Instead of using air pressure to force down his piston, Watt was able to use the expansive power of steam by completely enclosing his cylinder and surrounding it by insulation to keep it hot. Thus, his engine was a genuine steam engine as opposed to the atmospheric engine of Newcomen. Watt made many other improvements to his engine, but the turning point in his career came when he went into partnership with Matthew Boulton of the Soho works, Birmingham. Boulton provided the manufacturing facilities to match Watt's inventiveness, and also added the commercial expertise which helped ensure that James Watt did not go the way of so many other eighteenth-century inventors. This is necessarily an over-simplification of the relationship, but it is true to say that the sum of Boulton and Watt was something a good deal greater than a simple addition of its individual parts.

Watt established a patent for the separate condenser in 1769, and an Act of Parliament of 1775 – Watt's Fire Engine Act – gave Boulton and Watt a virtual monopoly of steam engine construction for the rest of the century. Their success in establishing their own claim and in beating off rivals lay in good measure in Matthew Boulton's ability to cultivate the 'right' people, and establish appropriate support in Parliament. It has frequently been argued that the 1775 Act effectively stifled improvements in the steam engine for a quarter of a century, since other engineers could find no way round the monopoly. This is true, but on the other hand, the Boulton and Watt partnership proved highly successful in both establishing and improving their engines, and it could be argued that without the protection of the Act, they might have been far less eager to indulge in expensive experiments. They made a good deal of money while the Act was in force, and quite a bit of it was ploughed back into research and development. The argument has still not been resolved; at the time of writing there is a considerable furore over an international drug manufacturer being accused of making too much profit on the one hand, while on the other hand they claim they need the cash to finance further research – Boulton and Watt all over again. Ironically, the partners were prevented from developing one particularly useful line by a rival patent. The simple crank, which can change linear action into a rotary action, was a device that had been known and used for a very long time, but a patent existed covering its use for steam engines – a patent bitterly denounced by Watt, who claimed in any case to have suggested its use for the steam engine himself. The result was that Watt was forced to find other devices, of which the best known is his 'sun and planet' gear, in which a cogged wheel joined to the end of the engine's beam by a rigid sweep arm meshes with a second cogged wheel, which is thus made to rotate.

The first Boulton and Watt engines were used, as were the first Newcomen engines, for pumping, but because of their greatly increased efficiency they were not limited to sites on or near the coal fields. Among the early customers for the new engines were the canal companies. John Rennie may have been an outstandingly successful builder of aqueducts, but he was rather less successful when it came to supplying sufficient water for his canals. The Kennet and Avon, in particular, has always been plagued by water shortages, so a Boulton and Watt engine was installed at Crofton in 1809 to pump water from a small lake, which acts as a natural reservoir, up into the summit level of the canal. A second Boulton and Watt engine was added in 1812, and both engines were improved in the 1840s before the older of the two was replaced by a Cornish engine. The 1812 engine, however, still exists and is the oldest steam engine in the world still able to work at the job it was built to do.

There have been a lot of changes over the years at Crofton. New boilers were put in in the 1840s when the engines were modified, and in more recent times the top of the chimney stack has been lopped off – an action that Crofton boilermen have been cursing ever since. Nevertheless there is nowhere that the power and performance of a Boulton and Watt engine can be more appreciated than at Crofton. The engines are now in the care of the Crofton Engine Society, a branch of the Kennet and Avon Trust, who arrange steaming weekends when the boilers are fired, and the public can see the engines under steam back at their original job. Our generation has become used to engines that start at the press of a button or the flick of a key, and it is a revelation to see these ponderous giants lumber into life. The twenty-nine-foot iron beams slowly begin to rock, and as the lighter of the two weighs six tons, that in itself is some measure of the power of steam. Once pumping begins, the rush of water from the pumps provides an even more dramatic illustration. The two engines, working together, are capable of shifting six and a half million gallons of water in a twenty-four-hour period, during which they use up a ton and a quarter of coal. And these are comparatively small engines. But if power is the main impression created by Crofton, it is not the only one. 'Elegance' is perhaps an odd word to apply to a beam engine, but just as mathematicians speak of elegant solutions to problems, so James Watt found elegant solutions to problems of engine design. One difficulty facing the engineer was that of keeping the piston moving vertically in the cylinder, the problem being that the piston is attached to the end of a beam which moves in the arc of a circle. In the early engines this was overcome by using flexible chains for the connection, and this remained the answer until Watt came up with his parallel linkage (plate 87). In this arrangement, the piston is no longer suspended directly from the end of the beam, but from one corner of a parallelogram of movable linkages, which keeps it to an almost completely vertical path. This has the great advantage that the rigid piston can be applied to both up and down strokes. Watching this device at work, even the most prosaic engineers have been moved to rhapsodies. As a Gwennap school-master wrote in a poem (quoted at length in D. B. Barton's *The Cornish Beam Engine*, 1969) describing the building of an engine:

> 'But here we perceive the true triumph of mind
> In the parallel motion so wiscly design'd.'

The elegance of Crofton does not end with the parallel motion; it is seen again in the beautiful system of levers and rods used to operate the different valves (plate XVIII). But if Crofton is the best place to see a Boulton and Watt engine, it was not on the canals that it found its most important role but in the deep mines, most especially in Cornwall where the lack of cheap coal was most keenly felt. It was Cornwall that was to see the greatest development of the beam engine, and it was here too that there was the greatest opposition to the Boulton and Watt monopoly, or tyranny as the Cornishmen preferred to call it.

The problem of getting coal to the many tin and copper mines of Cornwall was a great one. The major part of the coal was shipped in from South Wales, but it still had to be brought from the ports to the mines themselves. W. G. Morton, a traveller through Cornwall in the 1790s, described the primitive transport system he found. 'The coal is conveyed to its place of destination on horses' backs. A prodigious number of these animals therefore travel together in this part of the country, which from its rocks and mountainous nature is not easy to be traversed by carts or waggons.'

To understand the importance of coal and the steam engine, it is necessary first to look at the condition of tin- and copper-mining at the end of the eighteenth century. Tin-mining, which had been the major industry of the area, was in a very depressed condition. The change from pewter to earthenware for everyday use had meant a sharp drop in demand, and thus a sharp drop in price. A measure of relief came in the 1790s when the East India Company contracted for regular supplies to sell in China, but before that serious rioting had broken out among the tin-workers faced with rising prices and falling wages. However, the decline in demand for tin was accompanied by a rise in the demand for copper. In theory, all should have been well in the Duchy, and would have been had someone not discovered a mountain of copper – quite literally – in Anglesey in 1768. The Welsh copper was of a poorer quality than Cornish, but being above ground and far easier to obtain, it was considerably cheaper. The Cornish mines were in a condition of crisis, for which the only solution appeared to be the working of the rich, but deep, veins of the minerals. Deep working meant steam-powered pumps, but by the 1770s over half of the forty atmospheric engines erected in the area were idle. William Pryce writing in 1778 described the situation:

'It is a known fact, that every fire engine of magnitude consumes to the amount of three thousand pounds worth of coal in every year. This heavy tax upon mining, in some respects, amounts to a prohibition. No wonder then, that we should be more desirous to lessen the expense of maintenance in those devouring automatons, than frugal in their erection.'

This was the situation when Boulton and Watt brought their new engines to the area.

By no stretch of the imagination could the reign of Boulton and Watt in Cornwall be described as untroubled. The Cornish mine-owners bitterly resented the royalty they had to pay to the midlands engineers, which was equal to one-third of the saving in fuel costs between the new engine and a Newcomen engine of equal power. Cornish engineers went vigorously to work in designing their own engines, only to run up against the apparently impregnable defences of Watt's Act. Among the more important of the competitors was Jonathan Hornblower, who invented an engine with two cylinders, which the steam entered alternately. The inevitable war of angry words ensued, but Boulton and Watt reserved their actual legal battle for Edward Bull. Bull had built an engine which had the cylinder inverted over the mine shaft, and which therefore dispensed with the rocking beam. This was the test case for Boulton and Watt and the Cornish engineers, and Bull lost it. The Cornishmen had no choice but to sit and wait as patiently as possible for the end of the Act's protection in 1800.

By the end of the century, Boulton and Watt had erected over fifty engines in Cornwall. During that time, Watt perfected his sun and planet gear, so that engines could be used both for pumping and turning machinery. The rotative engines were mainly used as whim engines, turning drums which wound cables lifting men and ore up and down the shaft. Some were also used to operate the ore-crushing stamps. The beam engines that stood beside the mine shafts required special engine houses of their own, and it is these buildings which have become as typical of Cornwall as pasties and piskies.

The end of Boulton and Watt's period of protection was a signal for jubilation in Cornwall, and a great flurry of activity as Cornish engineers set to work improving the engines. In 1810 the *Engine Reporter* began publication, which gave details of the 'duty' performed by different engines. Duty is a measure of an engine's efficiency, and is defined as the number of pounds of water raised one foot by a bushel of coal. Regular reporting meant that everyone could now see how one engineer's machine compared with another's, and led to the duty race, in which the competitors strove to gain the prestige of heading the list. The competition undoubtedly helped to speed the improvement of the beam engine, and engineers such as Arthur Woolf and Richard Trevithick, with manufacturers such as Harveys of Hayle and the Perran foundry, made Cornish engines and engineering world famous. An estimate of the advances made in engine-building can be obtained by a study of the duty figures: the first Newcomen engines had a duty rating of just over four million, the first Watt engines were rated at about thirty million, and at the height of the duty race, in the 1830s, engines were being recorded with duties of over ninety million.

The development of the Cornish engine is the main factor in the development of Cornish mining throughout the eighteenth and nineteenth centuries. The tin trade fluctuated over the years but followed a generally downward path. The copper trade, on the other hand, boomed. The Anglesey deposit began to dwindle, while the demand continued to rise. The district around Camborne was the main centre of the mining industry and St Day, which now appears little more than an average mining village, was once known as the capital of Cornwall. Today, if one stands by the church at St Day and looks out over Gwennap Downs, one still sees a landscape entirely dominated by the spoil heaps and bristling stacks of the engine houses. Richard Thomas's *Survey of the Mining District of Cornwall from Chacewater to Camborne* (1819) shows the importance of this area. He lists twenty-three mining concerns which raised, on average, a total of 4,660 tons of copper ore per month with a value of approximately £35,000. In all, the mines employed some eight thousand workers, and ranged in size from Wheal Jewel and Wheal Quick, which mustered a work force of ten each, to Dolcoath employing sixteen hundred. Dolcoath was also the deepest mine, reaching down to 227 fathoms, 200 fathoms of which was below the level of the draining adit.

The organization of a Cornish mine was unique to that area. The system for beginning the mine was conventional enough. The 'adventurers' who intended to work the mine first agreed terms with the landowner, who received a due, or proportion of the ore raised. The adventurers were usually quite a small group of men, each contributing a proportion of the cost and each receiving an appropriate proportion of the ore. The actual work was under the control of mine 'captains' – an underground captain, an ore-dressing captain and so on. It was when it came to the organization of the work force that the distinctive character of the Cornish system appears. The main work was divided into 'tutwork' and 'tribute'. The former was work done by measure, men being paid an agreed rate per fathom to sink shafts or drive adits and levels. In tribute work, on the other hand, the miner was paid by the value of the ore he extracted. In this unique system, each tributer worked a specified section of mine, and his payment depended on the price the adventurers received for the ore from that section. So the tributer's earning power depended on his ability to assess the value of the ore in his section and to work it in the most economical way possible. If he was fortunate, and the vein turned out to be richer than he expected, then the tributer finished the period a wealthier man. If, on the other hand, the vein petered out, then not only might he be poorer than he expected, but he might even end up in debt since, before he received any payment, money was deducted for materials supplied by the adventurers and for the cost of dressing the ore. L. L. Price in his *West Barbary* (1891) quotes the following figures for two months' work by tributers at the Devon Great Consols mine.

'We find that the men are credited with . . .   £   s   d

                                       68   5   9

which is the amount due to them at 7s 6d in the £ on £182 2s 2d realized by the ore.

They are debited on the other hand with –

	£	s	d
Candles (108 lbs)	3	12	0
Powder (195 lbs)	6	10	0
Safety fuses	1	9	0
Hilts	0	1	9
Cans	0	2	6
Saws	0	6	0
Locks	0	1	6
Smith's costs	3	19	6
Drawing	3	0	11
Dressing	6	10	8
Use of grinder	0	8	10
Sampling and weighing	0	17	6
Subsist or money drawn	36	18	0
	63	18	2

And therefore they have to receive a balance only of £4 7 7.'

The term 'subsist' refers to the cash advanced during the working period to enable the men to keep going until the final payment.

The systems had certain obvious advantages for the adventurers. In the first place they ensured that they got work at the lowest possible price by auctioning out the tutwork and tributework. This was described by one of Cornwall's leading mine engineers, John Taylor, in an article published in the *Transactions of the Geological Society* (1814).

'The act of contracting with the men is called a *setting*, and this in general takes place at the end of every two months, the auction is denominated a *survey*, and is held in the open air before the counting house of the mine, which is generally provided with an elevated stage for the captains to stand on. . . .

About the middle of the day the men are summoned and assemble in considerable numbers, as not only those who worked in the mine the former two months, but all such as are in want of employ attend on these occasions, which indeed is the cause of the competition so often observed.

The business begins by reading over what is called a *general article*, or set of rules and conditions subject to which every contract is made, and which article prescribes fines for fraud or neglect in the performance of the work.

When this is read the managing captain generally begins with the tutwork, and puts up a shaft or level, declaring the number of men required, and sometimes limiting the extent of the bargain to a certain depth or length. The men who worked it last usually put it up, asking frequently double what they mean to take; this they do, not so much in the expectation that it will influence the agents, as with the view of deterring other men from opposing them. Offers are then made at lower prices, which go on until no one is inclined to bid less, when the captain throws up a small stone, and declares who is the last offerer. It seldom happens that the price bid is so low as the agents deem equivalent, therefore it is understood that the last man is only entitled to the option of closing the contract upon the terms to be named by the captain; these are therefore immediately proposed, and if refused, are tendered to the others in the order of their offers.

This plan reserves the power to the agents of withholding, in case of combination, while the men, though they may not in the first instance bid down to the price they mean to work for, seldom risk a refusal when the captain's offer is made, if they think it near the mark, lest others should instantly accept it.

The tribute pitches are set in the same way, the place intended to be worked being described, with a stated number of men, and the offer being made at so much in the pound, that is, a certain sum out of every twenty shillings worth of ore raised and sold. The tribute may vary from threepence in the pound to fourteen or fifteen shillings.'

The main advantage of tribute work for the adventurers was that they only paid out for work which showed a profit. For the men, it was a gamble – they had to decide whether to settle for the comparative safety of tutwork, or take the chance that they would strike an unusually rich vein. The system depended on the honesty of the men who administered it, and while some might have attempted to cheat the tributers, the workers themselves were not above trying to influence the course of events. According to William Pryce in *Mineralogia Cornubiensis* (1778):

'Takers . . . invite the captains to drink with them, upon free cost at publick houses; which leads to a further progress in deceit and corruption, till the incautious captains are seduced from their integrity by the presents of the Takers, whom they suffer to mix and manage the Ores in such manner as will most conduce to their own advantage; and to measure the ground which is wrought by the fathom, to the loss and injury of the adventurers.'

Whatever the advantages and disadvantages of the system, it remained in force throughout the period we are discussing and well beyond it, and no doubt helped to give the Cornish miner his reputation for exceptional skill and good judgement. The surface work of dressing and sorting the ore was mainly performed by women and children, and that too was let out at auction.

The adventurers had their own problems when the ore was raised, for the prices they received were fixed by the smelters of South Wales. Much as the independent Cornishmen resented the reliance on foreigners, such as Boulton and Watt of Birmingham, so they resented the smelters across the Bristol Channel. Numerous attempts were made to smelt the ore in Cornwall, notably at Hayle, but they failed because of the power of the Welsh smelters, and because the economics of the business were against them. Smelting used coal – freely and cheaply available in Wales, scarce and expensive in Cornwall.

The scale of Cornish mining is apparent to anyone travelling the area, from the many spoil heaps and, most obviously, from the hundreds of distinctive engine houses. One of the most interesting of these is at Wheal Busy ('wheal' is the Cornish name for mine), also known as the Chacewater mine. A Newcomen engine was built here in 1725, and was replaced by a second, built by John Smeaton in 1775. Two years later, James Watt came to Cornwall and built the first of his new engines as a trial. A year later he came back and rebuilt the Smeaton engine. A succession of engines followed at Wheal Busy until the tenth and last was finally broken up for scrap in 1946. So the site has historical importance for its long connections with the steam engine, but it is also interesting in having the most complete set of buildings associated with any large Cornish mine engine. The present group dates from a rebuilding in the mid-nineteenth century, but is also typical of the earlier period (plate 82). The engine house itself is three storeys high, built of granite. Beside it is the stack, which is also granite as high as the top of the house, but it then continued up in brick to lighten the load of the structure. Engine houses had to be made immensely strong, not to withstand the Cornish gales, but because they also had to act as frames for the engines themselves, and the constant rocking of the giant beams would soon have shaken any weaker structure to bits. It was this need to build strong which has ensured that so many engine houses have survived long after they have been abandoned. The boiler houses, on the other hand, were simply there to provide cover and have almost all collapsed – and it is the presence of the boiler house that makes the group at Wheal Busy so especially interesting.

The 'bob wall', which carried the main weight of the engine's beam, had to be made particularly strong. The photograph (plate 83) was taken inside the upper engine house at United Hills, Porthtowan, looking towards the bob wall, and the top of the shaft beyond it. It shows the great thickness of the wall, and also how large, carefully dressed granite blocks were used for this, the most important part of the structure, in comparison with the cruder blocks used for the other walls. The dark streaks on the inside of the arch were caused by the grease from the beam's bearings running down the wall.

United Hills, and the other mines round Porthtowan, exemplify many of the difficulties facing the Cornish miners. These mines were worked among wild, moorland country entirely removed from any decent transport. Plate 84 shows a general view of the Porthtowan valley with the engine house of Wheal Ellen in the foreground, and United Hills high on the moor behind it. The sides of the valley are marked by tongues of spoil, spreading out from earlier workings. The scene is beautiful and romantic and the engine houses, built from local stone, have weathered and worn to harmonize with the landscape. There is even a touch of the medieval in the castellated top to the stack at Wheal Ellen. It was considerably less romantic, though, for the men who had to climb the hillside each day to start work, or for the adventurers who had to move the ore from the shafts by strings of pack horses, threading their way along the narrow moorland tracks. Unfortunately for the miners, they could not choose for themselves where the mineral was to be found.

The most dramatic examples of having to work the ore where you find it are in the mines that line the Cornish coast, and nowhere more so than at Botallack on the cliffs above Cape Cornwall, where two engine houses perch in apparently impossible positions. The earlier of the two engines was built in the first part of the nineteenth century to hold a comparatively small pumping engine, with a cylinder of only thirty-inch diameter. What is extraordinary is that anything at all could be built on such a small ledge, half way down a cliff (plate 85). All the materials, including the huge granite blocks and, of course, the engine itself had to be lowered down the cliff and then built up. The space is so limited that the stack had to be built inside the engine house to save space, and also to supply extra structural support to help ward off the gales blowing from the Atlantic – and the photograph, taken on a rough February morning, gives some idea of just how strong the winds can blow. The upper engine house was built later when a new shaft was sunk to house a whim engine, and the stack was built on the top of the cliffs. The engine houses represent a remarkable achievement of building under the most difficult conditions. The underground workings are no less remarkable, for they stretch out from the cliffs far under the sea bed.

Not surprisingly, Botallack became a famous object of curiosity, and among those who went to view was the novelist Wilkie Collins, who wrote a very full account of his experience in *Rambles Beyond Railways* (1851). There is little in the way of technological detail, but it conveys perfectly the atmosphere of these strange submarine workings. Dressed in miner's clothing, Collins and his companion were taken to the shaft: 'Here, the miner pulled up a trapdoor, and disclosed a perpendicular ladder leading down to a black hole, like the opening of a chimney.' They stuck candles in their hats and began the descent:

'The process of getting down the ladders was not very pleasant. They were all quite perpendicular, the rounds were placed at irregular distances, were many of them much worn away, and were slippery with water and copper-ooze. Add to this, the narrowness of the shaft, the dripping wet rock shutting you in, as it were, all round your back and sides against the ladder – the fathomless-looking darkness beneath – the light flaring immediately above you, as if your head was on fire – the voice of the miner below, rumbling away in dull echoes lower and lower into the bowels of the earth – the consciousness that if the rounds of the ladder broke, you might fall down a thousand feet or so of narrow tunnel in a moment – imagine all this, and you may easily realize what are the first impressions produced by a descent into a Cornish mine.'

Collins descended to the seventy-fathom level, then travelled along a gallery.

'Rough stones of all sizes, holes here, and eminences there, impeded us at every yard. Sometimes we could walk in a stooping position – sometimes, we were obliged to crawl on our hands and knees. Occasionally, greater difficulties than these presented themselves. Certain parts of the gallery dipped into black, ugly-looking pits, crossed by thin planks over which we walked dizzily.'

Eventually the guide called a halt, and told the visitors that they were then four hundred yards out from the base of the cliff and a hundred and twenty feet below the sea bed, and that there were more and deeper galleries below them. Collins listened to the sea: 'That is *felt* on the ear as well as *heard* by it – a sound unlike anything that is heard on the upper ground.' They decided to turn back: 'There is a hot, moist, sickly vapour floating about us, which becomes more oppressive every moment; we are already perspiring at every pore . . . and our hands, faces, jackets, and trousers are covered with a mixture of mud, tallow, and iron-drippings, which we can feel and smell more acutely than is exactly desirable.' Collins was only a visitor – for the miners this was the scene of their everyday working lives, a fact not lost on Collins who summed up his views of the Cornish miners in these terms: 'As a body of men, they are industrious and intelligent; sober and orderly; neither soured by hard work, nor easily depressed by harder privations.'

A little way along the coast is the famous Levant mine, where one of Cornwall's few remaining engines is preserved (plate 86). This is a small whim engine, with a twenty-four-inch cylinder, built in Hayle, probably by Harveys, in 1840. It is unusual in having the whole of the beam and the fly wheel inside the engine house, only the drums for the cables that led down the shaft being outside. It still has an air of use about it, so that it is not too difficult to imagine the engine-man at the controls, sitting on his little bench, which can be seen at the right of the photograph, or going up the short flight of steps to look after the maintenance and greasing of the beam. The square opening through which the shaft passes connecting with the drum can be seen on the left of the picture. The surface remains at Levant show evidence of nearly two centuries of working, continuing right up to the present day. There are settlement tanks, where the ore was separated off, marked by the crumbling woodwork of old sluice gates, there are signs of the arsenic extraction plants that were introduced at a later date, when arsenic became an important by-product of the mines, and a spreading red stain in the water at the foot of the cliffs indicates current operations. Below the whim engine house, a path winds down the cliff to the end of the mine adit, which was used for a time for access to the workings. There is also the shaft which once held the main engine, used for raising and lowering the miners, which collapsed in the tragic accident of 1919 in which thirty-one miners were killed.

There are so many mining sites in Cornwall, that there is real difficulty in deciding which to describe. One group, however, does deserve special mention – the three engine houses of Wheal Peevor, near Redruth. These buildings represent the three main functions of the Cornish engines – driving pumps, winding, and powering the stamps.

Transport was always a major problem for an industry set in the farthest south-west corner of the country, scattered among hills and moorland or spread around the coast. Cornwall does, however, possess one advantage – there is nowhere very far from the sea, so that the main emphasis was first on building good harbours, and then on connecting these to the mines by road, canal, tramway, and later, railway. Hayle, on the north coast, was the most important of the ore ports. It faced out towards the smelting and tin-plate industries of South Wales and the brass works of Bristol. Such an important port became a natural centre for other activities connected with the mining industry, and it was here that the experiments in local smelting were tried, and that the great engine-building firms of Harveys and Copperhouse were situated. The disappearance of the Hayle smelting houses was certainly no loss for the poor wretches who worked in them. W. G. Morton described the smelting-house workers as he saw them on his tour of 1794–6:

'Nothing can be more shocking than the appearance which the workmen exhibit. So dreadfully deleterious are the fumes of arsenic impregnating the air of these places, and so profuse is the perspiration occasioned by the heat of the furnaces, that those who have been employed at them but a few months become most emaciated figures, and in the course of a few years are generally laid in their graves.'

One of the most enterprising transport developments took place just over the county border, on the Devon bank of the river Tamar. John Taylor – one of the few 'foreigners' to find success and acceptance in the south-west – began his mining career at the age of nineteen when he opened up Wheal Friendship, near Tavistock, in 1796. The development of rich copper mines in this area led to a proposal to build the Tavistock canal, linking the mines with the Tamar. The principal feature of the route was the mile-long tunnel (plate 88), which was built low and narrow as it had to be driven through solid granite – which explains why a comparatively short canal took thirteen years to complete. The tunnel was also intended to fulfil another purpose, as a test for possible ore deposits along its route. It was partly successful, and led to the opening up of the Crebor mines.

From the southern end of the tunnel, the canal follows a short route along the shoulder of a hill, before ending high above the banks of the Tamar. From here, ore was taken down to the river on an inclined plane. The Incline Cottage marks the top of this route, and nearby can still be seen the pit that once held the water wheel used to control the movement of the trucks on the incline. A few of the distinctive stone sleeper blocks can still be seen on the track near the bottom, where the route ends at the quays of the once important port of Morwellham. Most of these quays have been filled in, leaving a surreal landscape of granite bollards apparently standing in the middle of fields. There are still many signs of the busy working days in Morwellham's lime kilns, ore-crushers and warehouses. In its day, Morwellham flourished along with the nearby Devon Great Consol mines – with the closing of the mines, the harbour died too, but recent years have seen it resurrected as an industrial museum.

The tin and copper mines can be found in many different parts of Cornwall, from the Tamar to Land's End – some are isolated, others are clustered together in the more heavily worked areas, where mining communities have grown up around them. Mining villages such as St Day and St Just are very similar to mining villages in other parts of the country – the same terraces of workers' houses with the larger houses for the mine captains and adventurers. In St Agnes, the intermingling of mines and houses is so close that one resident now has an engine house in his back garden. The other distinctive village buildings are the chapels, reminders that Cornwall, like South Wales, proved fertile ground for the doctrines of Wesley to take root. These villages were comparatively wealthy by eighteenth-century standards – Sir Frederick Eden reported that the miners of St Day and Gwennap were earning an average of forty shillings a month, when he visited the area in the 1790s. The miners were, he said 'better paid than most labourers in England', but their wages were not up to the level of other miners, for example the coal-miners of Tyneside whom Eden recorded as earning sixteen shillings a week. Still, St Day's inhabitants were well enough off to support eight ale houses, and there were only forty poor in the work-house.

Company housing was rare in Cornwall. Mining was a gamble for adventurers as well as for tributers, so they were most unlikely to go to the expense of putting up houses near a mine that could close down at any time. A few speculators put up rows of cottages, some of which, dating back to around 1800, can be seen in Hayle. The typical cottage of this period was a one–up, one–down affair, of the type to be seen, for example, next to the engine house at Wheal Busy. A curiosity of the area is the use of slag as a building material, as in the cottages at Gwithian, near the smelting houses of Hayle. But, in most cases, miners simply looked after their own needs, building individual cottages for themselves or getting together as a group to build short terraces. The houses of the mining areas, built in this way, were of a poor standard and entirely lacking in any decent amenities. R. Q. Couch in his *Statistical Investigation of the Mortality of Miners* (1856) gave this account of a mining community:

'The population is mixed, but the miners invariably occupy the most exposed and worst built cottages . . . surrounded by cesspools, broken roads and pools of undrained rain. The village of Amal-Voen is like a cluster of cottages huddled together on the top of a hill with scarcely space between them for access. The bedrooms are rarely more than one in each house, and open to the ceiling. This gives that appearance of space; but if the roof is slate, it produces great heat during a summer day.'

A good example of this type of housing can be seen at Botallack (plate 89). The pair of cottages, now in a semi-derelict condition, show all the marks of having been built by local miners in the style described by Couch. The construction of both cottages is crude, with walls built up of large granite blocks, very similar to the method used for the engine houses nearby. The larger of the pair has a central doorway leading into a single stone-paved room. The large fireplace has a straight flue, leading to a short chimney and open to the sky. Behind, there is a small lean-to addition. The first floor is open to the rafters and the slate-clad roof. The other cottage is similar, but single-fronted and even smaller.

The hard living conditions of the miners who occupied these cottages were matched by hard working conditions. Cornish mines were mercifully free from fire damp and the risk of explosion, but were by no means free of accidents. William Pryce described the conditions of 1778:

'Suppose, for instance, that a mine employs three hundred men. . . . Now, in the course of a year, it is three hundred to one, that the trepan, or the crooked knife, will be wanted, not only once or twice, but very often; besides the ordinary accidents of burns, wounds, contusions, luxations, or simple and compounded fractures, where the knife is spared; and the blasting one or both eyes, and the last two fingers of the left hand, by gunpowder.'

The system of dealing with injuries in Pryce's day was, to say the least, inadequate, and he recounts one instance where the doctor was called and arrived all ready to treat the miner's fractured leg only to discover that the diagnosis had gone a little awry: the man's legs were in perfect condition, but he did have a fractured skull! Pryce argues that hospitals near the mines were the only answer if lives were to be saved, but with mines scattered over a wide area, the victims of accidents continued to be carried to their own homes 'full of naked children, but destitute of all conveniences, and almost of all necessaries'.

The Cornish mines were also free of another evil that plagued the coal mines – the extensive use of women and children in the underground workings. John Lichfield in *Mines and Mining* (1855) gives the following figures for mine employees in 1827: in copper-mining, there were nearly twelve thousand males to two thousand females, and in tin-mining nearly six thousand males to a hundred and thirty females. The situation was not the result of particular benevolence on the part of the Cornish employers, but a reflection of the severity of the underground work. The miner was expected, at the end of a day's work, to climb vertical ladders for a thousand feet or more before he reached the surface. The Cornish miner might be lucky in being free of fire risks, but the effect of the climb from the deep pits and the underground work combined in what were loosely known as 'diseases of the chest'. Sir Charles Lemon gave the following figures in an article in the *Journal of the Statistical Society of London* (1838), which show the toll taken by the disease. For the three great mining parishes the deaths for males between the ages of ten and sixty were split into three categories, with these results: out of 114 deaths in Gwennap 17 were due to mine accidents, 54 to chest disease and 43 to other causes; for Redruth, the corresponding figures were 16, 101 and 62; and for Illogan, 19, 87 and 53. Taking the three parishes together, the figures give $11\frac{1}{2}$ per cent dying of mine accidents, and a horrifying $53\frac{1}{2}$ per cent dying from 'diseases of the chest'.

Yet in spite of all the privations and uncertainties of his life, the Cornish miner gained an unmatched reputation for skill, which took him, when the industry declined, to every mining centre in the world. And just as the Cornish miner travelled the world, so too did the Cornish engines, which were bought up, complete with their engine houses, and re-erected in many different countries. Even knowing this to be the case, it still comes as a surprise, when following a popular holiday route along the north coast of Spain near Bilbao, suddenly to find oneself confronted with the unmistakable outline and well-weathered granite of a Cornish engine house.

The effect of the new generation of steam engines might be seen at its clearest in Cornwall, but it was by no means limited to that area. Similar developments occurred, for example, in other major ore-mining industries, such as the lead mines of Derbyshire. The village of Sheldon, and the nearby Magpie mine, are very similar to their Cornish counterparts, and if the pumping engine house (plate 90) looks very much the same, then that is not too surprising, for the site was developed by a group of Cornish adventurers. The area round the mine is marked by spoil and the sites of disused shafts, and at the main site there are extensive surface buildings, all constructed from the same local limestone. The manager's house has been burned down, but the smithy next door is intact, and now used by the Peak District Mines Historical Society, who as well as working at the restoration of the surface remains, are carrying out a valuable exploration of the underground workings. Even a short descent of the main shaft gives a suitable feeling of awe for the men who climbed up and down the fixed ladders each day of their working lives. Apart from being exhausting, stepping out into that apparently bottomless black hole is, frankly, every bit as terrifying as one would expect from Collins' account of his descent at Botallack. But, apart from providing the researcher with sensations he might well feel he could do without, the underground workings have yielded a number of important finds, of which the most interesting to date are the abandoned trucks, which still stand on wooden rails nearly a hundred fathoms below the surface. Above ground the main buildings are the pumping-engine house and the whim-engine house, and it is interesting to compare the different building techniques needed to handle the local limestone in comparison with the much stronger granite of Cornwall.

Scotland also had an extensive lead industry, although the remains now left behind, such as those of Leadhills, mainly date from the latter part of the nineteenth century. However, Leadhills was in use long before that, and was considered quite important enough to be included in the travellers' itineraries. Here is part of Thomas Pennant's account of his visit in 1772, which manages to combine a romantic's eye view of the scenery with a nonchalant note on mortality:

'The place consists of numbers of mean houses, inhabited by about fifteen hundred souls, supported by the mines. . . . Nothing can equal the barren and gloomy appearance of the country round: neither tree, nor verdure, nor picturesque rock, appear to amuse the eye: the spectator must plunge into the bowels of these mountains for entertainment or please himself with the idea of the good that is done by the well-bestowed treasures drawn from these inexhaustible mines, that are still rich, baffling the efforts of two centuries.

The miners and smelters are subject here, as in other places, to the lead distemper, or *mill-reek*, as it is called here; which brings on palsies, and sometimes madness, terminating in death in about ten days.'

It was not only the steam engine that brought improvements to the mining districts, and the underground waggons at Sheldon are a reminder of another innovation that greatly affected the industry in the eighteenth century. It was John Curr who first introduced the four-wheeled truck or corve, running on cast-iron rails, at the bottom of the pits, which took coal from the face to the foot of the shaft. He first used the system in 1776, and some twenty years later published his book *The Coal Viewer and Engine Builder's Practical Companion* (1797), in which he gave detailed instructions on how to construct corves and plateways. The corves could be pulled along by horse

I The Apprentices' House at
al. This modest building
used the overseers and more
n a hundred children

II The satisfying simplicity
a well-designed machine: the
tem of levers that operates the
ves for Crofton's beam engines

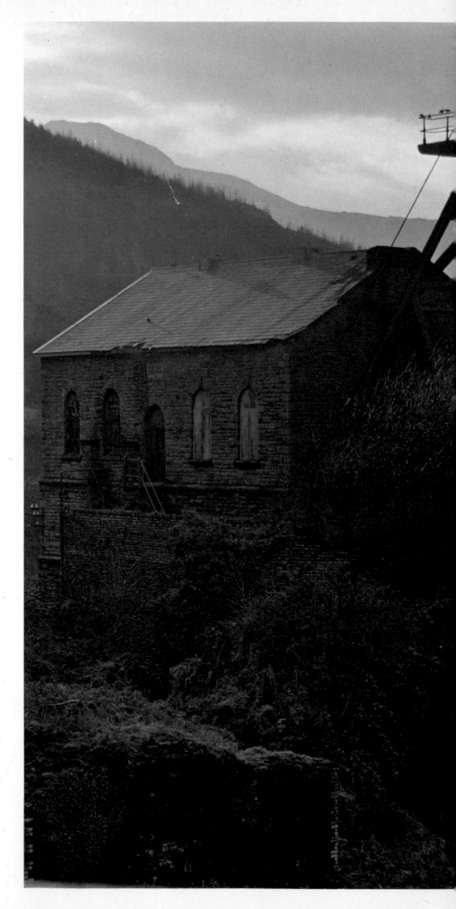

XIX The landscape of mining: engine house
and headstock gear near Pontypridd

xx Iron columns in Stanley mill, Stroud

xxi Steam power brought the mill to the town. Factories line the river at Hebden Bridge, dwarfing the old pack-horse bridge

XXII The Donisthorpe cotton factory beside
the Leicester arm of the Grand Union
canal

XXIII Swindon Railway Estate with the towers of the navvies'
lodging house beyond

whims, and he estimated that each horse could shift a train of twelve corves, each carrying $5\frac{1}{2}$ cwt of coal, for a distance of 250 yards. One horse, he reckoned, could shift 150 tons 'for a moderate days work'. The underground plateway was a great labour-saver, and the view of the putter, who had previously had the job of man-handling coal from the pit face, was expressed in appropriate Geordie verse:

'God bless the man in peace and plenty
That first invented metal plates;
Draw out his years to five times twenty,
Then slide him through the heavenly gates.

For if the human frame to spare
Frae toil an' pain ayont conceivin'
Hae aught to dae wi' gettin' there,
I'm sure he maun gan' strite to heaven.'

But the anonymous poet's praises, though justified, could certainly not be repeated throughout the mining industry, for the use of men, and women and children, to haul coal continued until the middle of the nineteenth century, when the scandal following the Report of the Select Committee on the Employment of Women and Children in Mines (1840–2), at last forced a change in methods. More than any words could have done, the drawings of women and children crawling half-naked through the pits, dragging sledges and corves behind them, brought home the reality of the barbarous degradation of the mines.

The development of the Watt engine had a far less dramatic effect in the coal fields than it had in other mining areas, as the old New-comen engines continued at work. The replacement of these engines was a gradual process, but slowly the nineteenth-century coal fields began to take on their now familiar characteristics – engine houses, the spinning wheels of headstock gear above the shafts, and the inevitable and ever-growing spoil heaps. The process of renewal has changed much, but in many areas the landscape of mining has altered little with the years. In the valleys of South Wales, for example, there are many scenes such as that in the Rhondda shown in plate XIX. There are some regional differences, however, that can be spotted. In the Durham coal field, for example, a different type of engine found favour. This was the vertical winding engine invented in 1800 by Phineas Crowther of Newcastle, in which the winding drum was placed immediately above the cylinder, so that no beam was needed. This arrangement called for a special style of tall, narrow engine house which was once common in the north-east. Now they have almost all gone, though the engine house and engine at Beamish colliery have been saved and are to be preserved (plate 92).

Surface remains of the mining industry often tell us little about important changes that might be going on underground. A major preoccupation of the developing mining industry was ventilation, and the removal of choke and fire damp. The system of using a single up-shaft and a down-shaft, with the flow of air through the galleries controlled by an elaborate system of trap-doors, was satisfactory up to a point. But as pits were sunk deeper and galleries extended farther, it became less and less satisfactory. At Walker colliery, in the north-east, for example, the air had to pass through *thirty miles* of tunnel, although the two shafts were only half a mile apart. You need never have been down a mine to imagine how fresh the air was at the end of that journey. This whole elaborate system only worked, in any case, provided the proper precautions were taken to open and close the trapdoors as men and waggons passed through the workings, and this was a job entrusted to small children who spent their days crouched in the dark passages by the doors. The problem was partially solved by the introduction of 'compound ventilation' by which more than the one current of air was passed along the galleries. Even that, however, did not solve the gravest problem of the fire damp which made mines fearful and dangerous places to work. The danger of explosion is put in its true perspective by this table, taken from Matthias Dunn's *Treatise on the Winning and Working of Collieries* (1848), giving details of accidents in the Durham and Northumberland coal fields between 1799 and 1840:

	No. of accidents	Deaths
Explosions	87	1,243
Suffocations by gases in the pit	4	18
Inundations from old workings	4	83
Falling of earth, rubbish, &c	15	33
Chains or ropes breaking	19	45
Run over by trollies or waggons	13	12
Boilers bursting	5	34
	147	1,468

Miners were aware of the danger of naked flames in fiery mines, but no one had come up with an adequate alternative. The urgent need to find a safe method of lighting for mines was tragically emphasized by explosions such as that at Felling colliery, on Tyneside.

The colliery consisted of a 204 yards deep down-shaft (the 'John Pit') which had a steam engine for drawing coal and a horse whim. The up-shaft (the 'William Pit') was 550 yards away. Felling was considered a very modern pit, with the furnace at the foot of William Pit providing the best possible ventilation. The coal was moved in wicker corves on trams, by putters and barrow men, who took it to the main wide roads where it was transferred to larger waggons which moved on a self-acting incline operated by a brake-man. The corves were winched up John Pit. The pit was worked in two shifts, the earliest being 4 am. to 11 am. The explosion that occurred at 11.30 am, 25 May 1812, just after the time for changing the shifts, was described in Rev. John Hodgson's *Funeral Sermon* (1813):

'The subterraneous fire broke forth with two heavy discharges from the John Pit, which were, almost instantaneously, followed by one from the William Pit. A slight trembling, as from an earthquake, was felt for about half a mile around the workings; and the noise of the explosion, though dull, was heard to three or four miles distance, and much resembled an unsteady fire of infantry. Immense quantities of dust and small coal accompanied these blasts, and rose high into the air, in the form of an inverted cone. The heaviest part of the ejected matter, such as corves, pieces of wood, and small coal, fell near the pits, but the dust, borne away by a strong west wind, fell in a continual shower from the pit to the distance of a mile and a half. In the village of Haworth, it caused a darkness like that of early twilight, and covered the roads so thickly, that the footsteps of passengers were strongly imprinted on it.'

Ninety-two lost their lives in the Felling disaster, and a third of these were under fifteen years of age. The fear of such appalling explosions was only reduced with the introduction of Sir Humphry Davy's safety lamp some two years later.

Mining towns and villages have always had a special quality, a sense of community, due in part at least to the shared dangers. It was this feeling of community, too, that made the Newcastle pits the centre for one of the most concerted strike actions of the early part of the nineteenth century. In 1831 the Newcastle miners, who had already formed a union, came out for higher pay, and had their demands met by the employers. This produced a good deal of head-shaking among many employers in many industries. The Dowlais papers show, for example, that the strike was closely watched in South Wales, where they began to get seriously worried about the example of the north-east being followed elsewhere. However, a second strike by the miners in 1832 found the mineowners in a distinctly sterner mood – miners were evicted from their homes, while blackleg labour was brought into the pits under military escort. These were just two episodes at the start of a long struggle between miners and mineowners.

Observers were not unduly impressed by the miners' villages and settlements, which, unlike their Cornish equivalents, were almost all owned by the employers. They were, however, impressed by the independence and individuality of the miners. Here, for example, is John Holland writing in *Fossil Fuel* (1835):

'The pitmen in the north of England, reside much less commonly in the towns or villages than in clusters of small houses adjacent to the respective collieries, and forming together little colonies, often more remarkable for the amount of the population, than the neatness or cleanness of their domestic arrangements. . . . Most of the old pitmen had a taste for expensive furniture – a taste still indulged by many; and it would be impossible for a stranger to pass in front of the lowly dwellings, three or four hundred in number, adjacent to Jarrow colliery, for example, without being struck by the succession of carved mahogany bed-posts, and tall chests of drawers, as well as chairs of the same costly material, which are presented at almost every open door. . . . These congregated dwellings are the property of the owners, or lessees of the coal, and as the occupants pay no rent – or at least, not in a direct manner, threepence a week being usually set off in the reckoning for house and coals – they are considered to be removable at pleasure: i.e. when they chose to go and work for another master.

In their dress, the pitmen, singularly enough, often affect to be gaudy, or rather they did so formerly, being fond of clothes of flaring colours. Their holiday waistcoats, called by them *posey jackets*, were frequently of very curious patterns, displaying flowers of various dyes: their stockings mostly of blue, purple, pink or mixed colours. A great part of them used to have their hair very long, which on work-days was either tied in a queue, or rolled up in curls; but when drest in their best attire, it was commonly spread over their shoulders. Some of them wore two or three narrow ribbands round their hats, placed at equal distances in which it was customary with them to insert one or more bunches of primroses or other flowers.'

Some of the housing put up by the mineowners was of well above average quality, a very fine example being at Elsecar, already mentioned for its Newcomen engine. Reform Row (plate 91) is built to the standard pattern of two-storey terraces, but nevertheless is built to a high standard, as can be seen in the photograph. There are small front gardens and backyards, with access through an arched opening to the small alley that runs behind the houses. In other parts there are variations on this pattern of housing – in some parts of Durham, and in most of the Scottish mining villages, the houses are single-storey terraces.

By the 1830s, when Reform Row was built, the revolution in the mining industry was complete in the sense that the change from shallow pits to deep pits, from machinery powered by the water wheel or horse to steam-powered machinery had been made. The use of steam power had already led to a new stage in the development in textiles, though some sections of that industry were only just beginning to join the revolution.

10

The Late Starter

While the cotton manufacturers were driving pell-mell into the new industrial age, the woollen manufacturers were travelling at a more sedate pace. Partly this was because the woollen cloth industry never received the impetus provided by outsiders, such as Richard Arkwright, forcing through changes as they set about the business of amassing fortunes; partly it was due to the resistance of the workers. As one Wiltshire clothier wrote in 1786: 'If we in this part of the kingdom attempt to introduce machinery it must be at the risk of our lives and fortunes.' Perhaps he had just received a note similar to this, sent to a Gloucestershire manufacturer, who had recently installed new machines: 'If you Dont Pull them Down in a Forght Nights Time Wee will pull them Down for you Wee will you Damd infernold Dog. And Bee four Almighty God wee will pull down all the Mills.' Where Arkwright brought in pauper families and built his mills in remote areas, the cloth manufacturers, especially those of Wiltshire and Gloucestershire, were operating in areas where thousands of families depended on domestic spinning and weaving for their livelihood. Jennies and carding engines introduced at Frome in Somerset were smashed in the spring of 1781, and as the jenny was not at first very successful at spinning wool and as the trade was, in any case, in a depressed condition, there was little incentive for manufacturers to risk a similar fate. So, until the 1790s, there was little change in the organization of the west of England cloth trade. The name 'mill' still referred to the traditional fulling mill, rather than a spinning factory.

In Gloucestershire, which manufactured a coarser cloth than Wiltshire, the finishing mill also included a gig mill, which was used for raising the nap on the cloth. Traditionally this was done by hand, using teazles, but very little ingenuity was needed to mount the teazles on a roller, which could then be turned by the same water wheel that moved the fulling stocks. An example of this type of Gloucestershire mill is Egypt mill, Nailsworth, which probably received its curious name from a seventeenth-century owner, Mr Pharaoh Webb. Although small in comparison with the familiar cotton mills of the north, this was considered quite large by the standards of eighteenth-century Gloucestershire. The ability of such a mill to survive the vagaries of trade, and still have a working life in the twentieth century, comes in part from the ease with which it could be converted from grain mill to cloth mill then back again to grain mill, its present function.

The first thing one notices about Egypt mill is that it is a most attractive building – a point which, happily, is true of the majority of mill buildings in the region (plate 93). It consists of two connected ranges of two-storey stone buildings with slate roofs, and has a small cottage attached. The western range has dormer windows and a door opening at first-floor level directly on to the roadway. Inside are two water wheels, now geared to drive the stones of a grain mill, but it is not difficult to see how a similar arrangement could be adapted for textile machinery. The age of the building is revealed in the massive wooden beams, pillars and rafters, and the two-foot thick stone wall separating the two ranges provides the comforting thought that if Egypt mill is spared the developers' bulldozers, it should be with us for a very long time to come. The clothier's house next to the mill emphasizes that even such a small concern as this could generate a good income for its owner.

It is perhaps surprising that clothiers, in general, did not attempt to follow the example of the cotton magnates, and set up factories in areas with no previous tradition in the trade. One who did, however, was Francis Hill, who left Bradford-on-Avon in 1790 and purchased a site on the banks of the Avon at Malmesbury, where he built a factory and installed spinning machinery. He must have felt rather smug the following year, when the manufacturers he had left behind attempted to install machinery at Bradford, only to see it destroyed in the riots of 1791. That Hill prospered is evident from the scale of buildings at Malmesbury – and the town was rewarded with an increase in trade and a striking addition to its architecture (plate 97). The mill is an L-shaped stone building, five storeys high and with eight bays to each wing. The sluice gates controlling the leat to the mill can be seen beside the road bridge. This is an almost perfect example of an eighteenth-century factory building – the high narrow shape is typical of buildings used to house rows of water frames, and the regular lines of segmented-arched casement windows provide quite sufficient interest in the façade to make any extra ornamentation unnecessary. Today, the building is used as an antiques showroom, but it has passed through other uses since its early days as a woollen mill. The isolation which made the site seem such an attractive proposition to Francis Hill turned into a handicap when machinery eventually spread to the other cloth-making districts, leaving Malmesbury as an uncomfortable half-way house between the centres of Wiltshire and Gloucestershire.

It was the increase in demand for cloth in the 1790s, particularly in the export markets, that led to a sudden upsurge of mill-building and the installation of new machinery, in spite of possible opposition from the workers. Many of the new developments represented little more than building small workshops to hold one or two jennies, but in other cases quite large groups of new buildings began to cluster round older sites. Trowbridge clothiers, instead of distributing hand-operated machines to the distant cottages, preferred to place their investments where they could keep an eye on them, and built workshops near their own homes. Later, these clusters formed the nuclei for factory development, and complexes such as Studley mills, beside the Town Bridge, show the evidence of the generations of building. The original clothier's house stands immediately inside the factory gates, and even though it has now suffered the indignity of conversion into offices, it remains a handsome building: a brick house, with dignified stone trimming for quoins and around doors and windows. Beyond the well-ordered house is a disordered jumble of workshops, and beyond them the factory blocks of the nineteenth century. One very interesting little building in this group is the handle house, where teazles were stored, which is built in perforated brick-work and arches across the river.

Examples of mill complexes built around old houses or fulling mills abound in Wiltshire and Gloucestershire. Longfords mill, near Nailsworth, is as good an example as any of the process of growth – eighteenth- and nineteenth-century buildings are grouped together, and individual buildings show a mixture of dates, as they were changed and adapted over the years. The present office building was begun *c.* 1700, and the 1705 date stone and attractive little window with its ogee arch probably represent part of the original, and a second date stone of 1866 marks a later set of changes. Many mill sites have records which show that cloth-working had begun perhaps as early as the sixteenth century, even though no trace of the older buildings might remain. St Mary's mill, Minchinhampton, for example, is mentioned in sixteenth-century records, but the oldest parts still standing are the house and water mill of the early nineteenth century.

The end of the eighteenth and the beginning of the nineteenth century were the great years of mill-building in the west, when the powered spinning mill, similar to the cotton mills of the north, began to appear in the area. Many grew up round the traditional areas, so that by the beginning of the nineteenth century there were more than thirty cloth factories in Bradford-on-Avon. Of these, only a few – notably Kingston mill and Greenland mill – survive. The Wiltshire clothiers were hampered by problems of water supplies, which were stretched and over-stretched. This is particularly true of the river Frome, which forms the boundary with Somerset. It is not an especially impressive river, yet tradition has it that there were once two hundred cloth mills on one six-mile stretch. A walk along the river bank suggests that the claim might not be exaggerated. There is a profusion of weirs and indications of sluice gates and leats; here and there the mills themselves survive, elsewhere only the foundations can be traced.

Perhaps the best, and certainly the most attractive example of a Frome valley mill is Shawford mill. Records show that mills have stood on this site for centuries, working both at fulling and grinding, but later being used entirely for cloth-finishing and dyeing. The present building was put up early in the nineteenth century, though part of an earlier mill was incorporated into the structure. It seems possible that it was intended also as a gig mill. Although these machines had been in use for a long time in Gloucestershire, the cloth-workers of Wiltshire and Somerset opposed their introduction – legally, by arguing that their use was forbidden under a statute of Edward vi (which was true), and illegally, by threatening violence. The clothiers won the legal battle in 1809 when the statute was repealed, but it was some time before they were prepared to face the consequences of defying the workers. However, in the boom that came at the end of the Napoleonic Wars, many clothiers found they had money to invest and were prepared, at any rate in the country districts, to take a gamble and install the machines. The new buildings at Shawford date from this period, and were clearly intended to take some form of new machinery which, on the evidence of new sluices, was water-powered.

The building is stone with typical decoration of the period, such as the prominent keystones in the door arches. The windows have stone mullions, but wooden frames, and the interior construction is all wooden. The sluices are kept in very good condition, not in order to power cloth-working machinery, but to supply water to a small wheel that is used for pumping and to drive an electrical generator. The mill must often have had to stop work because of the low level of water in the Frome during prolonged dry spells: there is evidence in records of prayers for rain, and there is evidence too in the fabric of the mill where, in the 1820s, a waiting workman passed the time carving an elegant alphabet into a window sill (plate 94). At some time the clothier must have decided that trade was a little too undignified an occupation for a gentleman, and a high wall was built between his fine house and the mill from which he and his ancestors received their income.

Of all the buildings put up to house the new machines of the industrial revolution, none can match the woollen mills of Gloucestershire for the quality and beauty of their architecture. In the river valleys that spread out from Stroud there were literally hundreds of cloth mills. Perhaps, in an odd way, the greatest compliment that has been paid to them is that so few people passing through the area are aware that they are crossing one of the great industrial centres of England. The mills are simply accepted as part of the architectural glory of the Cotswolds. Jennifer Tann's definitive work *Gloucestershire Woollen Mills* (1967) lists all the remains that can still be seen in the area. Here, we can only look at a few outstanding examples.

New Mills, near Wotton-under-Edge (plate 98), sufficiently impressed the Reverend Richard Warner for him to give a very full description in his book *Excursions from Bath* (1801):

'New Mill belongs to Messrs Austin, and employs under its roof about one hundred and ninety-five men, women and children. The construction and arrangement of this large manufactory reflect much credit both on its architect and its managers. . . . Spanish wool is alone manufactured at this work, and prepared for the weaver of broad-cloth and kerseymere. . . .

An agreeable impression arises on the contemplation of so much industrious exertion within so small a compass; nearly two hundred people busily employed under one roof; curious complicated machines above, moving with a velocity that defies the nicest vision to detect their motion; and ponderous engines below, astonishing the mind in an equal degree by their simplicity and gigantic powers. . . . The men and women work by the piece, and earn from one to two guineas per week, according to their exertions. A provision, likewise, is made for children, who at six years old are brought to the scribbling machines, and are enabled to earn one shilling and sixpence per week. Our gratification on surveying this capital manufactory is heightened by the appearance of health which the younger part of the inhabitants exhibit, and the general decency, order, and regularity, observable among the adults; circumstances which reflect particular credit on the proprietors and their agents, as this is rarely seen in similar institutions of a like extent.'

The change in the organization of the industry is exemplified here in the 'curious, complicated machines' and the 'ponderous engines'. The former were the scribbling machines, jennies and gig mills, the latter the fulling stocks – in other words, all the processes, with the exception of weaving, were carried on in the one building. At the time the description was written the New Mills were very new indeed, and it is interesting to see the reference to Austin, as he only bought the mill in 1806. Nevertheless, he must have had his eye on it from the first, and the initials 'H. A.', for Humphrey Austin, are spelled out in brickwork on the gable.

The first sight the visitor gets of the mill is across the large mill pond, fed by a half-mile-long leat. The main building is of brick, instead of the more usual stone of this area, built in a plain functional style which is attractive in itself, but given a little extra ornamentation by the addition of a clock tower ending in a shaped gable and a weather vane. There are no special points of interest about the interior, which is built of wooden joists and floors supported on cast-iron pillars. But those who remember it in its working days recall it as a comfortable building – light and airy, warm in winter and cool in summer.

Like so many sites in this area, there are still remnants of earlier industry. Behind the main mill is the old square stone count house, and next to that the circular tower of the original wool stove, which has now been converted into offices.

One of the fascinations of studying mill buildings lies in this ability to trace the pattern of growth and change over decades or even centuries of development. Dunkirk mill, Nailsworth (plate 96) provides an ideal example. At first sight the long high range of stone buildings seems all of a piece, but a closer look shows that it can be split up into different blocks, starting with an eighteenth-century building and ending with an addition from the 1820s. In spite of the changing roof line, continuity is preserved by each of the different builders following the style of the original. The ages of the different parts can be found in date stones, and can also be seen in the different pattern of weathering on the ivy-covered stonework. The two pairs of water wheels that once made this one of the most powerful installations in the area have gone, but the water that still rushes past the sluices and under the buildings at least indicates just how great that power could have been. As well as the main buildings there is also a very elegant mill house. Entrance to the mill is past a gate-house, built by the mill's most successful occupant, Peter Playne, who left his initials and the date 1829 inscribed on a keystone; and opposite that is a small red-brick warehouse and office.

The outstanding features that one looks for – and finds again and again – in the Gloucestershire mills are robust simplicity, combined with the rich texture of old weathered Cotswold stone. What one does not look for is the refined detailing of the great Georgian houses of London or Bath. Stanley mill at Stonehouse achieves the apparently impossible by combining the necessarily massive form of a large-scale cloth mill with a delicacy of detail that manages to fit into the huge frame without appearing absurd or pretentious. It was built in 1813 of red brick and stone and was a fireproof mill constructed on a cast-iron frame, using the same system of pillars and brick arches as Strutt used at his North mill at Belper. There the similarity between the two buildings ends. Strutt was quite happy to use his iron pillars for support, and leave it at that – the builders of Stanley mill took a different view. If cast-iron had to be used then they saw no reason why it should not fulfil a decorative as well as a purely functional purpose. They planned their mill and sent the details of what was required to Benjamin Gibbons at the Earl of Dudley's iron-works, where castings were prepared and shipped back on the Stroudwater canal that runs close to the site. The bulk of the iron-work consisted of the load-bearing pillars. Since the load to be carried decreases as the building gets higher, so the pillars were thicker on the lower storeys, and slender on the upper, and, although perfectly plain pillars would have provided adequate support, the pillars and connecting arches have been cast instead into traceried patterns, so that each floor has its own character and its own distinctive colonnades (plate xx). But the builders were aware that there were more ways to use iron than just for support, even if the supports were to be made rather special, so they also designed castings for other parts of the building – iron was used for the columns that stand inside the deep relieves of the Venetian windows, for fanlights and for many other features (plate 95). The careful detailing of the stonework round doors, windows and at quoins provides yet more evidence of the trouble taken over the design. If there is a dividing line between vernacular building and architecture, then

Stanley mills must be placed very firmly in the second category. Here we have far more than the simple adding of embellishments – the decorative detail is always an integral part of the whole design, as in the rows of columns that are the mill's main glory.

Conditions in the west of England mills appear, in general, to have been rather better than those in the mills to the north. The 1833 report on factory children, with its harrowing accounts of ill-treatment for adults and children, has a far milder tale to tell of conditions in this area. Nevertheless, the same story is told of children working long hours as in other industries. A Trowbridge operative, asked why he allowed his son to work such long hours, replied:

> 'I have a feeling for my children, sir, but necessity drives me, for I have a large family, and every little is of consequence; besides, he must do as the others, for I could not expect him to get away when others stayed. I don't speak this against his master, for he has a good master, but it is the custom of the mill.'

Most witnesses referred to good relations between masters and men. Donald Maclean of Macleans, Stephen and Co., who then owned Stanley mill, gave evidence. At that time, he employed between eight and nine hundred workers, he ran an infants' school, and gave preference in employment to those who had attended the school 'to encourage the parents to send the children'. He also contributed to the workers' sick fund. He seemed happy, if not particularly well-informed, about the conditions under which the work force lived. On being asked about their diets, he answered: 'I have no particular knowledge, but I can say that about one o'clock in the day the numberless fires about the factory smell like a cook-shop from the work people who bring their dinners frying their bits of bacon.'

Progress in the south-west was slow in comparison with the ever-accelerating rate of change in Lancashire – more evolution than revolution. Traditionally, the manufacturers of the fine cloths in the west rather looked down on their coarse cousins in Yorkshire. But the trade of Bradford-on-Avon, and other traditional cloth-making centres, was set for a period of decline, while the other Bradford was set for a period of unparalleled expansion.

At the end of the eighteenth century, the Yorkshire trade was still based almost entirely on the domestic system, and a merchant or manufacturer could expect to spread his interests over a wide area of countryside. Thomas Crosley of Bradford described his business at that period:

'In putting out wool to spin we sent a pack of tops at once to Skipton by the canal. A boat came on purpose for the tops of various people. . . . We had spinning done in Lancashire as far as Ormskirk; in Craven, and at Kirby Lonsdale; in Wensleydale, Swaledale, and other parts of north Yorkshire. Much difficulty was experienced with the yarn; we had to sort it, and from the same top there would be yarn as thick as sixteens and as small as twenty-fours, shewing the difference in spinners. For a pound of twenties we gave an average from ninepence to a shilling, and a good spinner from Monday morning to Saturday might earn two shillings and sixpence a week.'

The problems of spinners producing different thicknesses of yarn was as much a factor in the introduction of machinery as was the possible cost reduction. These spinners worked for very little pay, as did the weavers. Another Bradford manufacturer, writing in the middle of the nineteenth century, described the weaving side of the trade in his father's time:

'My father was a weaver of ribbed calimancoes, and was a first-rate hand. He could earn, by extraordinary exertions, ten shillings a week. I have known him weave two calimancoe pieces, but to accomplish that he had to work over hours one whole night, say Friday night. He obtained five shillings for weaving each piece. I remember an anecdote respecting wages sixty-five or seventy years since. A number of weavers were drinking at Clayton Height, and a weaver named Hartley got up and offered to bet a tankard of ale that he could say what no other person in the company could, that he had woven a five shilling piece a week, for twelve months.'

Nevertheless, there was a certain buoyancy in the trade, and a feeling of optimism among Yorkshire wool merchants. At Halifax they showed their confidence in the future by building a new and magnificent Piece Hall in 1775 to provide a suitable centre for the trade (plate 99). Entrance to the new cloth market was through a suitably imposing semi-circular arched doorway, with a pediment and bell tower above, the whole being topped by a splendid weather vane. Inside, the great open space of the courtyard was surrounded by galleries where the merchants had their small individual offices (plate 100). The galleries themselves were built in a grand style with rusticated pillars on the ground floor and Tuscan columns above. The manufacture that had begun in a tiny moorland cottage ended in rather more palatial surroundings.

The use of new machinery began gradually to creep into the West Riding. Wool-combing machines came into use in the 1790s and met immediate opposition from the hand-combers, who, as mentioned in chapter 1, already had a reputation for militancy. James in his *History of the Worsted Manufacture in England* (1857) described them as 'a turbulent ill-ordered class' who formed clubs to 'raise wages above their natural level'. The idea of a 'natural' level of wages might seem to require a little explanation. The idea was simple enough: the manufacturers' duty lay in obtaining labour at the cheapest possible price. Competition to reduce prices would ensure that no one manufacturer could offer higher wages than another and the process would continue until a level was reached below which the operative might actually begin to starve. Thus a state of affairs existed which was ruled not by decisions of individuals but by the interplay of market forces and the natural laws of nutrition. To attempt to interfere with the system was to act in an unnatural, if not downright blasphemous, manner. The carders, however, had managed to improve their lot by imposing 'unnaturally' high wages on the employers. Faced by the competition of machinery, they were forced to accept lower rates and James notes with some satisfaction: 'These proceedings humbled the wool-combers, and rendered them more tractable. When the combers accepted reasonable wages, the combing machine being an imperfect instrument, soon fell into comparative disuse, hand-combing being so much a superior process.'

It is worth noting, at this point, something of the conditions in which the combers worked as described in Thakrah's *Effects of Arts, Trades and Manufactures on Health and Longevity* (1831):

'Wool-combers work in apartments which, from the fire employed to heat the combs, are kept at the temperature of 80. The fires are made of charcoal. A light dust arises from the wool. The lungs suffer so much that many persons cannot pursue the employment. The men, however, whom we found in the rooms appeared quite healthy, and we were informed that out of one hundred individuals only two or three were absent from illness.'

Eventually combing by machine became the norm, and the combers were reduced to abject poverty before the class was eventually forced out of existence.

The early years of the nineteenth century saw the beginnings of the rapid change-over from the domestic to the factory system. Typical of the more important innovators of the woollen trade was Benjamin Gott of Leeds, whose career illustrates perfectly the transition from the old style of business to the new.

Gott came from a wealthy middle-class family and after leaving Bingley Grammar School was apprenticed in 1780 to the Leeds cloth merchants Wormald and Fountaine. This type of apprenticeship had nothing in common with that of the pauper children in the cotton mills. Young Gott was being given the opportunity to join a thriving commercial concern with a trade at that time running at some £40,000 per annum. For the privilege of learning the intricacies of such a profitable business, his father had to pay a premium of £400. At the end of the apprenticeship he joined the partnership, paying £3,660 for a one-eleventh share of the business. He joined at just the time that the new machines such as the flying shuttle and the jenny were beginning to make a real impact in the cloth industry. Companies such as Wormald and Fountaine were already part merchants part manufacturers, in the sense that they would some- times fill orders by employing workers directly to produce the cloth for their needs. At this time, they were beginning to consider the possibility of competing directly with the west of England cloth trade, by improving the quality of their own cloth. New machines seemed to offer that possibility, and they began to introduce them in spite of the inevitable opposition from the workers. In November 1791 the Leeds merchants issued a joint proclamation declaring their intention to introduce cloth-dressing machines. These, they said, would not lead to unemployment but, 'if, after all, contrary to our expectation, the introduction of machinery should for a time occasion a scarcity of work in the cloth-dressing trade, we have unanimously agreed to give a preference to such workmen as are now settled inhabitants in this parish and who give no opposition to the present scheme'. This left the workers with a perfect Hobson's choice – accept the machines and risk unemployment, oppose the machines and risk unemployment.

Gott and his partners began the move from their old functions as merchants, concerned with a little manufacture, to their new function, in which the roles were reversed, when they decided to establish a factory in Leeds – Bean Ing. It was begun with the deliberate intention of competing with the west of England in the manufacture of superfines from imported wool. Although most of the processes were still carried out on hand-operated machines, it was new in that all the different operations were concentrated in the one place. Some operations, such as scribbling, carding and fulling were carried on inside the factory itself, while jenny-spinners and weavers worked in sheds and cottages clustered around the factory walls. Almost by accident, it seems, Gott was helping to establish a new pattern for the industry. He himself said, in evidence to a House of Lords Committee in 1828: 'I was brought up as a merchant and became a manufacturer rather from possessing capital than from understanding the manufacture. I paid for the talents of others in the different branches of manufacturing.'

Gott appears to have obtained some notably adventurous talent for his money, for his works saw some of the most important innovations of the woollen industry. Bean Ing may have been only partly mechanized; nevertheless it was here that one of the first Boulton and Watt engines to be used in a textile factory was installed in 1793. The policy of concentration he adopted at Bean Ing found many imitators and led to the rapid expansion of Leeds and its trade.

The Napoleonic Wars brought distress to many manufacturing districts. Sir Frederick Eden wrote of Halifax, for example: 'The present war has affected the manufacturers of this place, and reduced the price of labour, especially of weaving and spinning: many poor women, who earned a bare subsistence by spinning, are now in a very wretched condition.' But at Bean Ing, Gott found a profitable trade providing cloth for army uniforms and blankets, and Leeds continued to grow and prosper, so that an observer, writing in 1800, could note that 'houses, nay whole streets, are building every year . . . if we may hazard from external appearances the trade and manufacture of this town seem in their effect almost equally lucrative to a Peruvian mine.'

Gott opened two more mills in the Leeds area, continued to introduce machinery and continued to meet opposition. He soon found that the Armed Association, of which he was elected commander, was of far more use in protecting machines from angry workers than in fulfilling its intended function of protecting Leeds from Napoleon and his troops. Yet Gott was not a harsh employer and ironically, always thought of himself as a traditionalist. He continued in his old role of merchant, buying cloth in the halls and markets. As late as 1828 he reckoned to buy three times as much cloth as he manufactured, and stated: 'I am as much concerned with the domestic manufacturers as I ever was in any part of my life.' Nevertheless it was Gott, and other manufacturers who followed his lead, who were responsible for the end of that system and the transformation of the West Riding of Yorkshire.

Bean Ing itself was demolished a few years ago, but Burley mills, built c. 1800 to supply blankets for the troops fighting in Europe, still stands astride a leat off the river Aire, just off Kirstall Road in Leeds. There is very little to distinguish it from many another textile mill of the period – a plain stone building on an iron frame, with a wide elliptical arch under which the leat passed to the water wheel. Much more important is the single-storey building behind the main mill that distinguished this mill from all the others previously mentioned. This was the weaving shed, and marks the fact that, for the first time, every process was being brought under the direct control of the manufacturer and into his factory. It was this process of concentration that produced the long and painful decline of the domestic industry and the beginning of a new age of factory towns.

11

An Age of Smoke and Steam

Benjamin Gott's factories were less mechanized than those of the cotton industry, but more work was concentrated within them. In the first part of the nineteenth century, mechanization came to all branches of the industry, and the change from domestic to factory system was established as complete and irreversible. The spinning wheel and the hand loom gave way to the steam factory, the mill village grew into the mill town.

The range of machinery available to the manufacturer at the beginning of the nineteenth century was formidable, and spinning machinery was almost universally adopted. Weaving, however, was a different proposition. Like so many of the textile inventions, the power loom came from a most unlikely source – Dr Edmund Cartwright, rector of Goodby Marwood, near Melton Mowbray, who decided to build a power loom for no better reason than that he heard someone say it could not be done. What is even more remarkable is that he produced his first power loom without ever having seen the ordinary hand loom. But although his new machine worked after a fashion, it was almost impossibly difficult and cumbersome to use. However, having discovered that it was possible to build such a machine, he began to set about things in a more serious and business-like manner. He went to see a hand loom in operation, and worked on improving his own invention. In 1786 he took out a patent, which led to some curiosity but little immediate activity among manufacturers. No doubt many shared the view of the correspondent who wrote to Samuel Oldknow in November 1787 on the subject, and clearly had more than a few doubts on the chances of a practical invention appearing from such an unpractical source:

'Mr Cartwright was once Professor of Poetry at Oxford, & really was a good Poet himself – But it seems he has left the Barren Mountain of Parnassus & the fountain of Helicon for other mountains and other vales & Streams in Yorkshire, & he has left them, to work on the Wild Large & Open Field of Mechanics – be it so, & may his scheme prosper, & fill his Purse with Gold ... you say not a word about the probability of success, likely to attend his weaving Invention. Can this new automaton perform the wonders in weaving so confidently & so flatteringly held out to the world? do let us have your most candid opinion & distinguish between what is Visionary & what may be practicable in this new Michaine Machine. We are far from limiting the boundary of mechanism in the arts.'

Unfortunately, no record remains of Oldknow's reply. Cartwright, meanwhile, continued to work on improving his invention, but its acceptance by the industry was a slow business. Nevertheless, the invention of the power loom did give the manufacturer the opportunity to control all aspects of textile production, and to have the whole work carried out on powered machines. The next step was as inevitable as it was obvious – to change from the water wheel as the main source of power to the steam engine. Once the problem of converting the basic up-and-down motion of the engine's beam into rotary motion had been solved, then all the old dependence on water supplies could be forgotten – no more worries about hold-ups for drought, no more need to build mills in long straggling lines, stretching along streams, away from the centres of population. To the employers and the growing middle classes, the new processes seemed to open new horizons of ever-increasing prosperity, a new Golden Age of Machines. Here is Edward Baines, writing in the *History of the Cotton Manufacture of Great Britain* (1835):

'It is by iron fingers, teeth, and wheels, moving with exhaustless energy and devouring speed, that the cotton is opened, cleaned, spread, carded, drawn, roved, spun, wound, warped, dressed, and woven. The various machines are proportional to each other in regard to their capability of work, and they are so placed in the mill as to allow the material to be carried from stage to stage with the least possible loss of time. All are moving at once – the operations chasing each other; and all derive their motion from the mighty engine, which, firmly seated in the lower part of the building, and constantly fed with water and fuel, toils through the day with the strength of perhaps a hundred horses. Men in the mean while, have merely to attend on this wonderful series of mechanism, to supply it with work, to oil its joints, and to check its slight and infrequent irregularities; each workman performing, or rather superintending, as much work as could have been done by *two or three hundred men* sixty years ago. At the approach of darkness the building is illuminated with jets of flame, whose brilliance mimics the light of day. . . . When it is remembered that all these inventions have been made within the last seventy years, it must be acknowledged that the cotton mill presents the most striking example of the dominion obtained by human science over the powers of nature, of which modern times can boast.'

The glorious effects of this revolution were not universally admired and the situation described by Baines came only after a period of struggle, which left legacies of bitterness that persisted long after the issue had been decided.

The first rotative steam engine to be installed in a textile mill was at Robinson's of Papplewick, Nottinghamshire, in 1788, but it was not until the next century that the steam mill began to establish its dominance. The effects of the change – both the advantages and disadvantages – can be seen in many parts of Yorkshire and Lancashire through the altered patterns of development. In chapter 8 the water-powered mills of Hebden Bridge were mentioned, and that is a good place to begin to see the effects of the change to steam.

The original centre of population in this district was the hill-top village of Heptonstall. Here the old stone buildings seem to turn in on each other as protection against the Pennine winter – a harsh landscape and a harsh life for the weavers who lived here, and who looked for consolation in the equally austere religion of John Wesley. From the octagonal chapel, built on the site where Wesley preached, one can look down on the 'new' town of Hebden Bridge. One important factor is at once apparent – the town had been made much more accessible by the transport improvements of the eighteenth century. From the hill one can still see the narrow winding tracks of the old pack-horse routes, but in the valley bottom, the turnpike road and the Rochdale canal run side by side next to the river Roch. In the hollow formed where the Hebden Water meets the Roch, the steam mills were built and the factory chimneys came to dominate the scene (plate XXI). Crowded round the mills are the houses, in tall, barrack-like rows.

The problem facing the house-builders was how to get as many people as possible as close to the mills as possible, while having to cope with the difficulty of building on the steep hillside. The solution they hit upon was to stack the terraces of houses on top of each other – bottom-to-top, instead of the more familiar back-to-back housing of the mill towns. What appears, on the uphill side, as a conventional terrace of two-storey houses, materializes on the downhill side as a four-storey terrace (plate 104). Seen from Heptonstall, Hebden is all tall chimneys and high terraces. The mill-workers no longer had the long trek from home to mill and back again, as they did with the water-powered mills of Hebden Water, but equally there were no longer woods and fields at the factory door, and, more importantly, they now had the factory outside their own doors.

Hebden Bridge is typical of many small mill towns, but its growth was limited by the geography of the region. The hills which brought the fast-flowing streams for water wheels were now an inconvenient barrier to expansion. Farther west, in Lancashire, the big cotton towns began their great period of growth – Rochdale, Burnley, Wigan, Blackburn, the names that still come first to mind when we think of the cotton industry. Whole new towns sprang into existence, as Wordsworth recorded, not without regret, in *The Excursion*:

'Meanwhile, at social industry's command,
How quick, how vast an increase! From the germ

Of some poor hamlet, rapidly produced
Here a huge town, continuous and compact,
Hiding the face of earth for leagues – and there,
Where not a habitation stood before,
The abodes of men irregularly mass'd
Like trees in forests, – spread through spacious tracts,
O'er which the smoke of unremitting fires
Hangs permanent, and plentiful as wreaths
Of vapour glittering in the morning sun.
And, wheresoe'er the traveller turns his step,
He sees the barren wilderness erased,
Or disappearing.'

Pre-eminent among the cotton towns was Manchester itself. As families poured in, attracted by the growing industry, the town became the scene of an increasing housing shortage. The slums of the old Manchester are, mercifully, no longer with us, but they were with the inhabitants for too long. As early as the 1790s the housing conditions of the poor were notoriously bad, with families living in single-room cellars or in lodging houses facing streets fouled by open sewers. Fever and sickness were rampant. John Ferriar, a doctor at the Infirmary, wrote a pamphlet addressed to the 'Committee for the Regulation of the Police, in the Towns of Manchester and Salford' in January 1792. In it, he offered 'a few observations, on the means of opposing the production and progress of infectious fevers, in cellars and lodging houses, where they reduce great numbers of the Industrious Poor to extreme distress, and often nearly destroy whole families'. He then listed specific examples of living conditions he had observed, of which the following are representative examples:

'(1) In some parts of the town, cellars are so damp as to be unfit for habitations. . . . I have known several industrious families lost to the community, by a short residence in damp cellars.
(3) I am persuaded, that mischief frequently arises, from a practice common in many back streets of leaving the vaults of the privies open . . . fevers prevail most, in houses exposed to the effluvia of dunghills in such situations.
(5) The lodging houses, near the extremities of the town, produce

many fevers. . . . The most fatal consequences have resulted from a nest of lodging houses in Brooks's entry . . . In those houses, a very dangerous fever constantly subsists, and has subsisted for a considerable number of years. I have known nine patients confined in fevers at the same time, in one of those houses, and crammed into three small, dirty rooms. . . . Four of these poor creatures died, absolutely from want of the common offices of humanity. . . . The horror of those houses cannot easily be described; a lodger fresh from the country often lies down in a bed, filled with infection by its last tenant, or from which the corpse of a victim to fever has only been removed a few hours before.'

Forty years later, John Fielden in his sustained tirade, *The Curse of the Factory System* (1836), found little change when he described the sudden interest shown in the slums following the cholera outbreak of 1832:

'We were panic-stricken; we knew our sins; we recollected the fevers of 1796; we knew the "squalid homes" of those who make our wealth; we knew that the malignancy would fix on them, and that this would endanger ours. It was there that we flew, not from charitable motives, but to save ourselves; we subscribed, we visited, we scoured, we whitewashed (would to God we could whitewash ourselves!), we did all that men could do – to save themselves! We instituted a SPECIAL *Board of Health* – to save our own! We found hunger, nakedness, bare earthen floors and unfurnished houses with unwhited walls: what of that! neither of these was catching. Ah! but pestilence was! We sought out pestilence where we were sure to find it; we did not carry charity where we always knew it was wanted. We were moved exactly as we were in 1796, not by the love of our neighbours, but by our fears of the visitations of God.'

It was not only in Lancashire that the growth of the cotton industry was associated with a sudden upsurge of population in the larger towns and cities. Mills were built in Nottingham and Leicester (plate XXII) to add to the already busy hosiery trade. Open land was enclosed and then built up, and the courtyards of Nottingham gained the unhappy reputation of being the worst slums in the country. This spectacular growth in the manufacturing towns brought other problems besides over-crowding and disease, and even the Pangloss of the factory system, Andrew Ure, was forced, for once, to admit their existence:

'Manufactures naturally condense a vast population within a narrow circuit; they afford every facility of secret cabal and co-operative union among the work people; they communicate intelligence and energy to the vulgar mind; they supply in their liberal wages the pecuniary sinews of contention, should a spirit of revolt become general, and the ample means of inflaming their passions and depraving their appetites by sensual indulgences of the lowest kind. Persons not trained up in moral and religious nurture, necessarily become, from the evil bent of human nature, the slaves of prejudice and vice; they can see objects only on one side, that which a sinister selfishness presents to their view; they are readily moved to outrage by crafty demagogues, and they are apt to regard their best benefactor, the enterprising and frugal capitalist who employs them, with a jealous eye.'

Nottingham and Leicester had acquired an early reputation for radicalism, and the framework-knitters had frequently shown themselves to be perfectly capable of looking after their own interests. In 1791, for example, the Oxford Blues were called in to break up a crowd of protesting workers in Nottingham, but to reach the scene had to pass down a narrow street, overlooked by the castle rock: 'The people planted themselves on the top of the rock well provided with *night soil* in vessels, from the privies, with which they plentifully supplied the troopes as they passed below.' It was from these crowded working-class districts that a more organized protest grew, which established a pattern that was to be repeated later in Lancashire. In March 1811 the framework-knitters reacted to a reduction in the price of stocking-making by a sustained outbreak of frame-smashing in the workshops of the hosiers. John Blackner described the scene in his *History of Nottingham* (1815):

'The practice of these men was to associate in parties of from six to sixty, according as circumstances required, under a supposed leader, that was stiled *General Ludd*, who had the absolute command of them, and directed their operations; placing the guards, who were armed with swords, firelocks, etc. in their proper places, while those armed with hammers, axes, &c were ordered to enter the house and demolish the frames; and when the work of mischief was completed, he called over the list of his men, who answered to a particular number, and he then gave a signal for their departure, by discharging a pistol, which implied that *all was right*.'

It is clear from the description that the Luddites were no disorganized rabble, mindlessly hitting out at new machines – the machines they attacked had been in use for over a century – but a highly-organized group of workers reacting to a reduction in pay. In the textile districts of the north, however, the violence was in part at least a final despairing rearguard action by the old independent workers of the domestic system.

No group felt the birth-pangs of the new industrial age more strongly than the hand-loom weavers. In part the growing distress of the weavers came from the gradual introduction of the power loom, with its vastly increased efficiency. Baines gives the following figures:

'A very good hand-weaver, 25 or 30 years of age, will weave two pieces of 9-8ths shirtings per week, each 24 yards long. . . .

In 1823, a steam-loom weaver, about 15 years of age, attending two looms, could weave seven similar pieces in a week.

In 1833, a steam-loom weaver, from 15 to 20 years of age, assisted by a girl about 12 years of age, attending to four looms, can weave eighteen similar pieces in a week; some can weave twenty pieces.'

The process of replacing adult workers by children, combined with the age-old problem of the weavers' sensitivity to changes in the conditions of trade, produced deep bitterness among the weavers, which showed itself in the ballads of the period.

'Come all you cotton-weavers, your looms you may pull down:
You must get employ'd in factories, in country or in town,
For our cotton-masters have found out a wonderful new scheme,
These calico goods now wove by hand they're going to weave by
steam.'

And when the end of the Napoleonic Wars brought no relief a new note of anger was added to the bitterness.

'You say that Bonyparty he's been the spoil of all,
And that we have got reason to pray for his downfall;
Now Bonyparty's dead and gone, and it is plainly shown
That we have bigger tyrants in Boneys of our own.

'*Chorus:* You tyrants of England, your race may soon be run,
You may be brought unto account for what you've
sorely done.'

The distress of the weavers, faced by a diminishing demand for their work, can be traced in the pages of the diary of William Varley, a Lancashire weaver. The following extracts have not been carefully selected to present a particularly harassing picture, but as typical of the record as a whole.

'8 January 1820. A great talk of an advance of wages which was to take place this day, but all is a mistake. Alas, poor weaver, thy fond hopes of better days always prove abortive; distress and scorn is thy true companions; thy haggard and meagre looks plainly indicate thy hard usage and slavery, which knows no bounds.

29 January. I am now going to describe something quite un-common, for Podiham cotton-masters has made a grand advance of wages; they are rising at a surprising rate of 3d a cut.

1826. This year commences with very cold frosty weather; there is a great many people that is poorly about this time, and well they may be, what with hard work and mean food; but there are many without work and what must become of them? They must lie down and starve for anything that I know; for if they would beg, I know of none that will give anything; and if they would rob or plunder, they have the soldiers at Burnley ready to give them the last supper.

24 May. This day I got work of Mr Corlass, so now I hope through the mercy of God that I will be able to maintain life a little longer.

3 June. This day there is a general lowering of wages; they are now 1/3d a cut which has 64 picks in an inch. The poor weaver may now go to despair indeed, for if he has work, how must he get bread and there are a great number without work.

February 1827. The weather is uncommon rough and severe the whole of the month; sickness and disorders of different kinds prevail very much. The pox and measles takes off the children by two or three a house; and well may they die, for there is no aid, no succour to be had for them; the times is no better for the poor; hunger and cold are our true companions.'

The first decades of the nineteenth century are years of the most marked contrasts. On the one hand we can see the astonishing growth of the textile industry, with cotton predominating, and on the other we can see the growing resentment among the workers – resentment at ever-lengthening hours in the factories or at the disappearing work of the hand loom. It is a period when attitudes become so polarized that it is hard to realize that writers of different viewpoints are trying to describe the same phenomenon. Reading the papers of the time, the effect of polarization is very clearly seen. The pages of the *Bolton Chronicle*, for example, are full of reports of bad conditions, of mill girls forced into prostitution, of comparisons between the concern shown by Wilberforce and his supporters for 'black slavery' on the one hand and the lack of concern for the 'white slavery' of Lancashire, of new items in which it was the paper's 'painful duty' to report cuts in the wages of the 'unfortunate cotton-weavers'. The *Manchester Mercury* acknowledged the 'temporary suffering' caused by the introduction of the power loom, but added 'such no doubt must be the case', and then gave this simple philosophy of machines: 'There is, there can be, no other test of the intrinsic utility of a new machine, than whether it effects better or more cheaply, the purpose of that which has previously been in use. If it does, it ought to, and what is more, it surely will, force its way.'

The *Manchester Mercury*'s simple realism was generally accepted by the manufacturers, for the power loom did force its way, but it was far from an untroubled process. The existence of a great mass of unemployed weavers, willing to work at almost any rate, led to a systematic lowering of wages. Some objections were raised: at a meeting of manufacturers at Bolton-le-Moors in April 1826, a number of resolutions were passed including: 'This meeting highly disapproves of the conduct of those Manufacturers, who, to the manifest injury of the Weavers and fair Traders, take such an undue and unjustifiable advantage of the deplorable state of the depressed Weavers in the reduction of Wages, from what is given by other Houses.' As well as appealing to the decency of their fellow-manufacturers, they appealed to their common sense, arguing that they might well be pushing the weavers too far. Neither humanity nor reason was heeded, and in that same month Lancashire saw the rise of an army of angry weavers, who set about systematically smashing power looms and cloth-dressing machines. The press were unanimous in describing the events as a riot, and the perpetrators as an uncontrolled mob, and even the sympathetic *Bolton Chronicle* warned the workers that the smashing was being ordered by 'hired spies' and professional agitators. The machine-breaking raged through the manufacturing districts of Lancashire, but it is clear, even from the contemporary accounts, that, as with the Luddites of Nottingham, this was no disorganized rabble bent on indiscriminate destruction:

'On Wednesday, about a hundred of the rioters assembled between Haslingden and Rawtenstall, about ½ past 8 o'clock in the morning. They gave a shout at the north end of the hill leading to Rawtenstall, and immediately descended into the village, and commenced an active attack upon Mr Whitehead's factory, which was strongly barricaded on the inside, and occasioned them a delay of half an hour, before they could effect an entrance. On entering they immediately commenced the work of destruction, and in the short space of half an hour they completely destroyed ninety looms – all that the building contained. They did not attempt to injure any other machinery besides the looms. On coming out they gave three cheers, and proceeded to Mr Thomas Kay's of Long Holme.'

Wherever they went, they concentrated on the looms and left spinning machinery undamaged. On one occasion, after breaking looms at Rawsthorne's factory at Edenfield, they were on the move when 'recollecting that they had forgotten the dressing frame, they returned for the purpose of demolishing it; but on Mr Rawsthorne assuring them that there was nothing but spinning machinery, they retired without doing any further damage'. Hardly the action of an uncontrollable mob. Eventually, the military appeared and lives were lost. One small anecdote in a newspaper account shows the depth of the feelings of the weavers. As the cavalry came on the scene 'our informant saw a poor fellow lie down before the feet of the soldiers' horses: he said they might trample on him if they liked, he was starving to death, but he would persist in breaking the power looms'.

The machine-breaking led to an investigation into the weavers' distress, and this in turn led to some charitable hand-outs in the most depressed regions. But these actions were only the most violent expression of a growing movement among the working class. Strikes against reduced wages became more common, and employers and employed began to adopt the stances of rival armies. In Yorkshire, the woollen-workers struck when wages were reduced by as much as twenty-five per cent in 1829, and troops were stationed in all the major towns to guard against possible riots. Many of the strikes were long and bitter, lasting for months, and it was by no means only the working men who were involved. Although the writer in a Glasgow paper of 1831 adopted a condescending tone, it is clear from his account that the women workers of Scotland were perfectly capable of taking action on their own when faced by a manufacturer introducing machines likely to cause redundancy:

'This brought together several hundreds of honest wives and bonny lasses, to deliberate, not in secret, but in open air, on their grievances, and how they could be remedied. This was not a Quaker's meeting – for the time being precious, their business urgent, and their desires ardent, every one of them spoke fluently, and to good purpose ... after the practice of the Luddites and others in England, these fair ones "resolved unanimously" to inflict the utmost punishment of their law on this offensive machine, but not to injure its owner if he did not resist their decree ... Mr McArthur was not so ungallant and uncivil as to refuse compliance with the

82 The Cornish engine house. A complete set of buildings: engine house, boiler house and stack, at Wheal Busy

83 *Above* Inside the engine house of United Hills mine, Porthtowan. Grease from the bearings stains the arch of the massive bob wall

84 *Left* Mines in a wild setting at Porthtowan. The lower engine house is Wheal Ellen, the upper, United Hills

85 *Above right* The astonishing site of the lower engine house, Botallack, on a bleak February day

86 *Below right* The interior of the Levant whim engine house, which is unusual in having the whole of the beam, or bob, and fly wheel indoors

87 *Above* The beam of one of
Crofton's steam engines, showing
Watt's parallel linkage
88 *Right* The southern entrance to the
Tavistock canal tunnel
89 *Far right* The crude, but strong
construction of the Cornish engine
house is mirrored in this miner's
cottage at Botallack

90 *Left* Magpie lead mine, Sheldon. In the foreground is the whi engine house, behind the pumping engine house
91 *Below* Yorkshire miners' houses: Reform Row, Elsecar
92 *Right* The distinctive, tall, thin shape of the Beamish colliery vertical-engin house

93 *Far left* The mellow Cotswold stone of Egypt woollen mill, Nailsworth
94 *Left* Whiling away the workless days – carving on a window-sill at Shawford woollen mill, Somerset
95 *Below* Refinement in cast iron – a Venetian window at Stanley mills

96 *Left* The accumulation of years, but a unity of style at Dunkirk mill, Nailsworth
97 *Right* Avon mill, Malmesbury, with the sluice gate mechanism in the foreground
98 *Below* New mills, Wotton-under-Edge, seen across the mill pond

Halifax Piece Hall: 99 *Above* designed with an imposing entrance; 100 *Left* and an elegant interior, as a visible statement of confidence in an opulent trade

101 *Above* The glass roof lights of the cotton
weaving sheds at Whitehead's factory in
Rawtenstall – like an industrial market garden
102 *Left* Warehouses and mills line the Leeds
and Liverpool canal in Burnley

103 No escape: the factory at the end of the street lowers down on the workers' houses in the cotton town of Rawtenstall

104 Hebden Bridge's 'duplex' housing; two-storey on the uphill side, four-storey on the down

105 The Victorian industrial heritage – Huddersfield

pressing requests or peremptory demands of so many of the fair sex as had honoured him with a visit. The machine was demolished, and the fair ones were (as so often happens when such exertions are made) victorious.'

The great wave of agitation led to a number of half-hearted and even bizarre proposals being put forward. In 1826, Parliament set up a Select Committee on Emigration to look into the possibility of exporting the problem to the colonies, and their deliberations are interesting for the light they throw on working and living conditions. The Second Report, 1827, for example, produced the startling statement that in the Glasgow and Paisley districts there were eleven thousand hand looms in use and that the average wage of the weavers was 5s 6d a week out of which they had to find a rent of £6 to £8 per annum. Pamphleteers appeared who, expounding the theories of Malthus, explained that the whole problem could be resolved by reducing the numbers of the working class, and set out details of methods for contraception that sound as impractical as uncomfortable.

But while well-wishers, theorists and various benevolent institutions were looking for ways of effecting relief, a new group of militants was coming forward with a quite different message. John Wade dedicated his *Extraordinary Black Book* (1831) to 'the People':

'We are not of that number of those who inculcate patient submission to undeserved oppression. A favourite toast of Dr Johnson was, "Success to an insurrection of the Blacks". Shall we say – Success to the rising of the WHITES! We should at once answer yes, did we not think some measures would be speedily adopted to mitigate the bitter privations and avert the further degradation of the labouring classes.'

The radical leader, Francis Place, had fewer reservations, and stated the case more bluntly. When John Doherty sent him a pamphlet he had written appealing against a reduction of wages in April 1829, Place sent this uncompromising reply:

'A large portion of the printed address is worse than useless, in as much as it is an appeal to the humanity of the masters against their interest. The reasons given for the appeal are futile. The manufacturer looks only to his immediate profit, and cares little or nothing for what may be the state of trade hereafter, or what may be the profits of his successor. . . . Depend upon it, the working people never will, as they never have, obtain anything by such appeals. The struggle is a struggle of strength and "the weakest must go to the wall". Whatever the people either gain or even retain, is gained or retained, and must always be gained or retained by power.'

The gulf between masters and men had become so wide as to seem to many to be unbridgeable, and they could see no outcome but revolution. We know now that the revolution never came, and it is a futile exercise to speculate whether such a state of affairs need ever have come about in the first place, or whether, if circumstances had changed, a revolution might, in fact, have occurred. In one sense, a revolution did take place, but it was a social and economic revolution, not political. The changes that began in the eighteenth century and grew to immense proportions in the nineteenth, have left marks as deep and tangible as any left by a major political upheaval. The development of steam power changed the physical face of the country.

Rawtenstall in Lancashire shows the distinctive marks of the new generation of industrial town. The development was largely the work of the Whitehead family, whose looms were smashed in 1826. Higher mill had been built by Whitehead specifically to take power looms, and it was this building that was attacked. It is a comparatively small factory, and round it can still be seen the remnants of an older community in the tiny groups of cottages, such as those in Whitehead Street. But buildings such as this were soon overshadowed by new and far larger factories. Whitehead's lower mill is typical of the later developments – beside the great bulk of the spinning mill stand the long rows of specially designed weaving sheds where the power looms were housed. These have a distinctive sawtooth roof-line, with north-facing windows set on the steeper-pitched section to give a good even light to the workers below. The change in scale between the two sets of buildings provides an indication of how families such as the Whiteheads were able to ride out the storms of the 1820s, and go on to a period of expansion.

The pattern of change at Rawtenstall can best be illustrated by a look at developments along the Bacup Road. Coming in towards the centre of the town, one comes across a terrace of cottages, built in about 1800, of honey-coloured stone, with the long weavers' windows on the second floor. Beyond the cottages is the gaunt pile of a nineteenth-century cotton mill: where an eighteenth-century mill was tall and slender, this is built on a square plan and squats by the roadside, a dark and brooding giant of a building. Beyond that are the workers' houses, rows of back-to-backs, leading right up to the factory walls so that the dominance of the mill over the houses seems a physical expression of the dominant position of the mill in the workers' lives (plate 103). Standing here, it is easier to understand the reluctance of the country workers to give up their old way of life, even when faced by near-starvation.

One factor of life in nineteenth-century Rawtenstall that is now absent, is the permanent pall of smoke from the factory chimneys; but if the smoke has gone it has left its memento in the encrusting of soot on the older buildings. Further evidence that our forbears did not share the modern preoccupation with pollution can be seen in the river Irwell, which still retains an odd purple colour from the dye and print works.

Most of the developments we can see in the main cotton town of Lancashire and Scotland are Victorian, and so fall outside the scope of this book – most of the terraced rows, with names such as Paradise Row, which must have always been a bad joke, come from this later period. But enough remains from the early part of the nineteenth century to give us some idea of the scale of building that went on in those years. One obvious line of early development was along the banks of the canals. It used to be said that the finest view of a nineteenth-century cotton town was the view of Burnley from the embankment that takes the Leeds and Liverpool canal through the town. The embankment itself remains an impressive piece of canal engineering, but the view has changed, and old Burnley has gone. If one has any regrets for the passing of the old, it is that the planners have produced the type of anonymous architecture that belongs anywhere and nowhere. Whatever its faults, at least the old Burnley was very positive about being somewhere specific on the map of Britain. However, away from the new centre, you can still enter the world of nineteenth-century industry: follow the canal towpath away from the embankment, westward from the British Waterways yard, and you find yourself right back in the middle of it. Warehouses and mill buildings line the route on both sides (plate 102) – stark and uncompromising they may be, but they convey the power and scale of the new developments of their time as few other groups of buildings can.

Probably more has been written about the working conditions in mills such as those of Burnley than about any other aspect of the industrial revolution. The stories of long hours, brutality, and, above all the use of child labour, were discussed and argued over then and still are today. Doubt has been expressed about the validity of much of the evidence, particularly that of the famous 1833 Report on the Employment of Children in Factories, on the grounds that the commission was manned by proponents of the Ten-hour Bill, more concerned to prove a case than make an objective record of the facts. Certainly, the picture painted by the report is an appalling one, page after page repeating the same story. The account of a Leicester spinner: 'I have known the children hide themselves in the stove among the wool, so that they would not go home when the work was over, when we have worked till ten or eleven. I have seen six or eight fetched out of the stove and beat home', tells the same tale as that of a Lancashire overseer: 'After the children from eight to twelve years had worked eight or nine or ten hours, they were nearly ready to faint; some were asleep; some were only kept to work by being spoken to, or by a little chastisement, to make them jump up. I was sometimes obliged to chastise them when they were almost fainting, and it hurt my feelings; then they would spring up and work pretty well for another hour; but the last two or three hours were my hardest work, for then they got so exhausted.' The sheer volume of evidence is impressive, but other writers such as Ure denied its validity. He argued that the introduction of the new machines was heralding a new era of easy labour – 'in these spacious halls the benignant power of steam summons around him his myriads of willing menials'. But Ure's writings are full of contradictions – for example, he explains in one of his passages on the benefits of new spinning machines that a Stockport manufacturer had calculated that by introducing the machines he 'would save £50 a week in wages, in consequence of dispensing with nearly forty male spinners'. It does not seem to have occurred to Ure that the forty male spinners might not share his enthusiasm.

The machines that made possible the revolution in the textile industry are now museum pieces, and it is, thankfully, not possible to recreate the working conditions of the nineteenth-century mill. The question of whether the revolution brought a general rise or a general lowering in living standards for the workers is still a matter of hot debate. But the written evidence is not in dispute on one point – the revolution was accompanied by real suffering at least among some sections of the community. Given the standards of the times, it might be argued that such suffering was necessary if change was to come. Perhaps so – but that does not make the suffering any the less real. The physical evidence has its own story to tell of changes wrought on the landscape of Britain, and those changes can only be described as eventually leading to a deterioration.

Conditions may have always have been bad for the ordinary textile-worker, but the mills of Gloucestershire are better buildings in every way than the square begrimed and standardized factories of the late nineteenth-century towns. The houses built by Strutt and Greg are, on any reckoning, better houses than those put up by the speculative builders of Rawtenstall. The hand-loom weavers of Heptonstall may often have led wretched lives, but they did so in better surroundings than did the poor wretches in the damp cellars of Manchester. Travel out to the old weaving villages of Golcar and Linthwaite in the Colne valley, and then look back towards Huddersfield, where the valley floor is covered by the close-packed factories and houses of the woollen boom of the mid-nineteenth century (plate 105). In a very real sense, the move from Golcar to here can only be called a regression.

Traditionally the industrial revolution has been taken as covering a period from 1760 to 1832. All such dates are necessarily artificial, but certainly by the latter date Britain could be seen to have completed a revolution in its social and economic life. The powerful middle classes received official recognition of the change with the Reform Bill of the latter year, which gave the new centres of wealth their say in the government of the country. The year also roughly coincides with the beginning of a new stage of industrial development and the Railway Age. The story of the railways begins, as we have seen, in the eighteenth century, but it only reached its full importance in the years following 1830, so it has been deliberately excluded. One site, however, connected with the railway age will be taken as a conclusion, because it exemplifies many of the points that this book has been trying to make: that the ordinary, everyday buildings of the industrial revolution can be buildings of great quality, that they can often repay time spent on their study and that some, at least, are worth preserving. This site also shows that, at a time when working-class housing was notoriously shabby and drab, it was possible to build to a far higher standard.

The site is the Railway Estate at Swindon (plate XXIII), the houses built to the design of Sir Matthew Digby Wyatt for the workers at the new works and repair sheds of the Great Western Railways which reached here in the 1840s. It is an estate planned for people to live in comfort, with a decent amount of space around them. The houses are solid but neat stone terraces, planned with care, and originally laid out as a self-contained community, set among green fields apart from the old town. Today, these houses have been renewed and refurbished by Swindon Council, and we can see just how very fine they are. Historical 'ifs' are largely futile but Swindon demonstrates that the standard of Strutt's workers' housing at Belper could be repeated a century later, and it is surely not unreasonable to speculate how the appearance of Britain would have changed if only that standard had been maintained throughout and beyond the period of the industrial revolution. What an immeasurable gain that would have been.

Maps

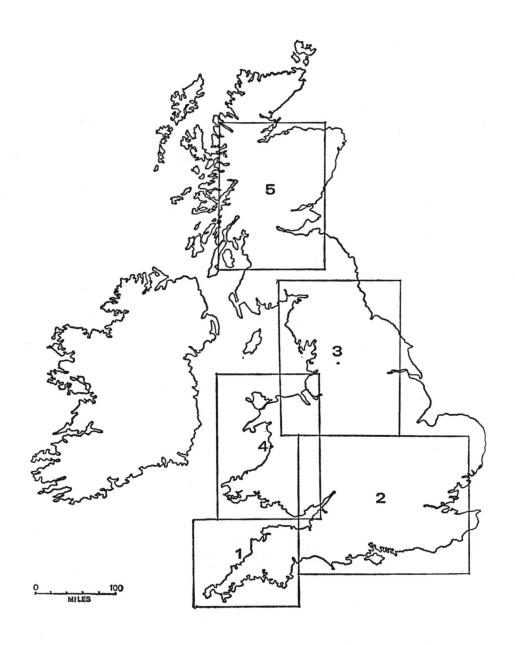

0   100
MILES

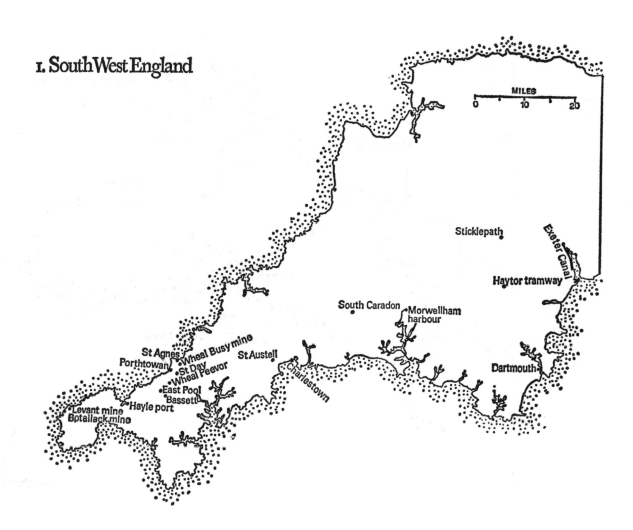

1. South West England

MILES
0   10   20

Sticklepath

Exeter Canal

Haytor tramway

South Caradon

Morwellham harbour

St Agnes Wheal Busy mine

Porthtowan St Austell

St Day

Wheal Peevor

Charlestown

Dartmouth

East Pool

Bassett

Levant mine Hayle port

Botallack mine

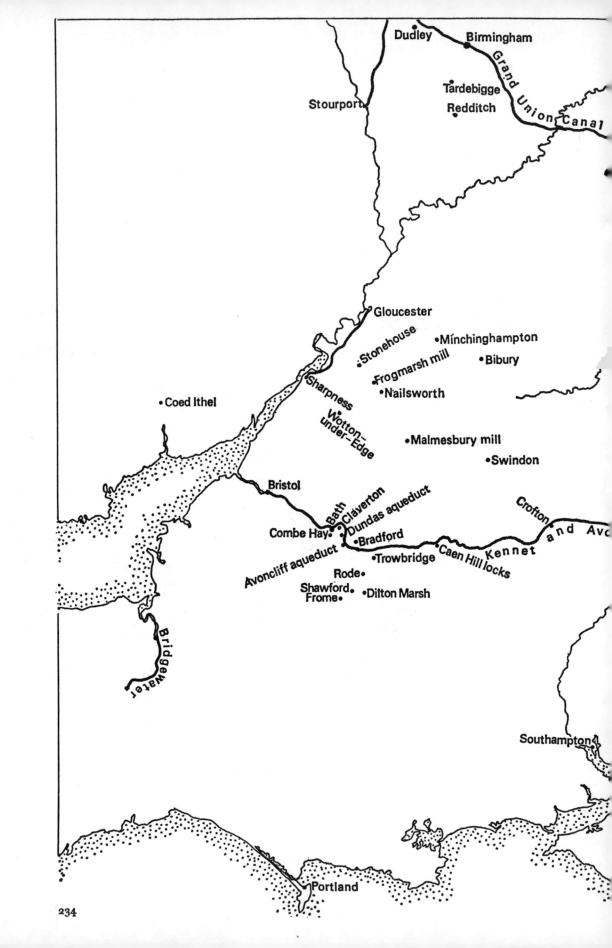

234

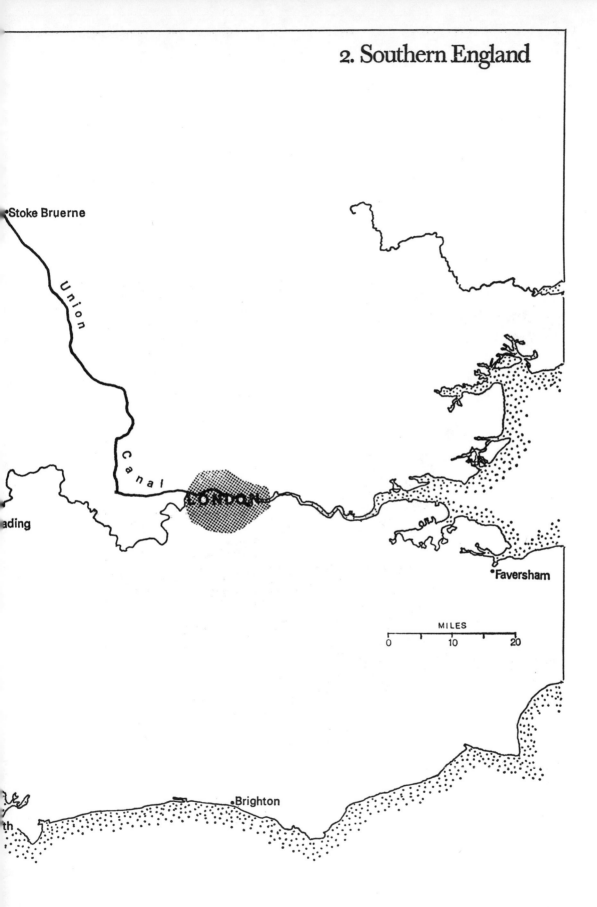

•Stoke Bruerne

Union

Canal

LONDON

ading

•Faversham

MILES

0   10   20

•Brighton

th

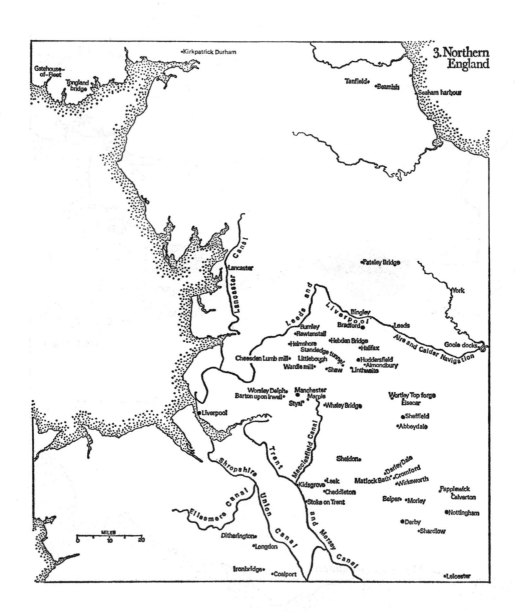

Kirkpatrick Durham

Gatehouse-
of-Fleet
Tongland
bridge

Tanfield
Beamish
Seaham harbour

Lancaster Canal

Lancaster

Pateley Bridge

York

Leeds and Liverpool

Bingley
Bradford
Leeds

Burnley
Rawtenstall
Helmshore
Hebden Bridge
Standedge tunnel
Halifax
Aire and Calder Navigation
Goole docks

Cheesden Lumb mill
Littleborough
Huddersfield
Almondbury
Wardle mill
Shaw
Linthwaite

Worsley Delph
Barton upon Irwell
Manchester
Marple
Wortley Top forge
Elsecar

Styal
Whaley Bridge
Sheffield
Abbeydale

Liverpool

Macclesfield Canal

Sheldon
Darley Dale

Trent

Leek
Matlock Bath
Cromford
Kidsgrove
Wirksworth
Cheddleton
Papplewick
Calverton

Shropshire Canal

Union Canal

Stoke on Trent
Belper
Morley
Nottingham

Ellesmere Canal

and Mersey Canal

Derby
Shardlow

MILES
0   10   20

Ditherington
Longdon

Ironbridge
Coalport
Leicester

4. Wales

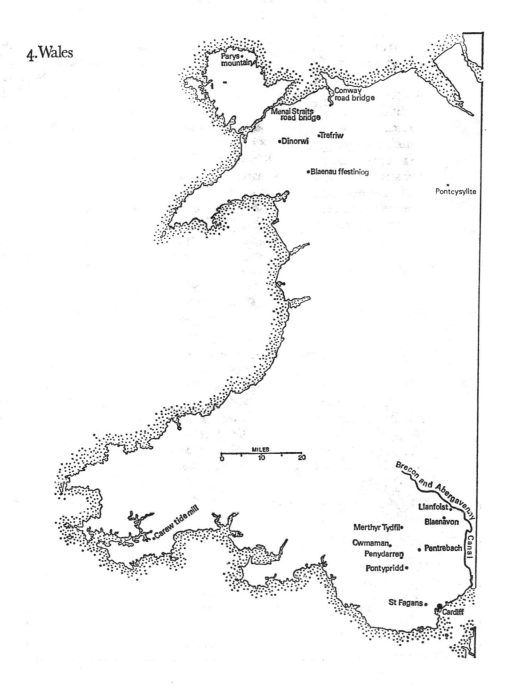

Parys mountain

Conway road bridge

Menai Straits road bridge

•Dinorwi   •Trefriw

•Blaenau ffestiniog

•Pontcysyllte

MILES
0   10   20

Brecon and Abergavenny Canal

Llanfoist•

Merthyr Tydfil•   Blaenavon

Cwmaman•   • Pentrebach
Penydarren

Pontypridd •

St Fagans •   Cardiff

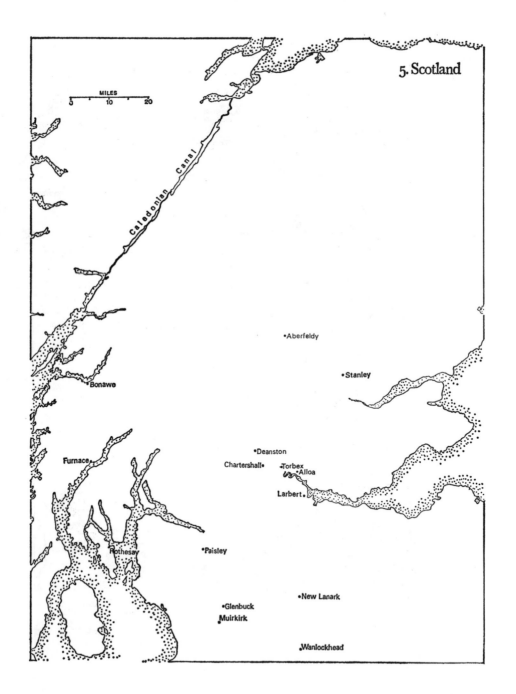

MILES
0   10   20

Caledonian Canal

5. Scotland

•Aberfeldy

•Stanley

•Bonawe

•Deanston
Chartershall•   •Torbex
•Alloa
•Furnace
Larbert•

•Rothesay

•Paisley

•New Lanark

•Glenbuck
•Muirkirk

•Wanlockhead

Gazetteer

The sites mentioned in the text are listed here and, where necessary, map references relating to the one-inch Ordnance Survey map are also given. A number of additional sites are also detailed, some of a rather later date.

South West England

1. Botallack mine (SW 362 333). See pp. 184–5, plates 85 and 89.
2. Levant mine (SW 368 346). See p. 186, plate 86.
3. Hayle port and foundry. See pp. 186–8. The remains of Harvey's foundry are at SW 558 372.
4. Wheal Peevor (SW 702 445). See p. 186.
5. East Pool. Two Cornish engines have been preserved here, *in situ*. A small whim engine stands, in its engine house, beside the main A.30. Nearby, on the other side of the road, is the engine house containing the massive 90-inch cylinder engine that pumped water from the Taylor shaft.
6. Bassett mines (SW 689 397). A late nineteenth-century mine, and well worth visiting as there is an unusually complete set of surface buildings, which now have an oddly monastic air.
7. Porthtowan: Wheal Ellen (SW 703 468) and United Hills (SW 698 474). See pages 183–4 and plates 83 and 84.
8. St Day mining village. See p. 188.
9. Wheal Busy mine (SW 741 449). See p. 182 and plate 87.
10. St Agnes. See p. 188. There are a number of attractive engine houses on St Agnes Head, and Wheal Kitty (SW 725 509) still has the count house where work was auctioned out.
11. St Austell. Centre of the china clay industry. The scale of works can be seen at the great open-cast site of Carclaze (SX 015 548).
12. Charlestown harbour. See p. 138.
13. South Caradon. The southern slopes of Caradon hill developed into a

rich copper mining area, and as well as the remains of surface buildings, the track of the Liskeard and Caradon mineral railway can be traced through the workings (SX 273 698).

14. Morwellham harbour, canal and inclined plane. See p. 187 and plate 88.
15. Sticklepath. On the A.30 between Exeter and Okehampton. In the centre of the village is a nineteenth-century water-powered forge – known perversely as Finch's foundry – where agricultural tools were made until quite recently. Now preserved. The banks of the same stream are lined with serge mill remains. See p. 13.
16. Haytor granite tramway (SX 762 778). A unique railway built on the edge of Dartmoor, on which, as the name suggests, trucks ran on stone rails.
17. Dartmouth. The home of Newcomen. A Newcomen engine has been re-erected here as a most appropriate memorial to a great engineer.
18. Exeter canal. The short cut along the river Exe is of historical importance, as it was the first waterway in Britain to use the 'new' pound locks.

Southern England

1. Combe Hay (ST 742 603). The locks on the now disused Somerset coal canal are a reminder of the importance once attached to the Somerset coal field.
2. Bristol. *SS Great Britain:* Brunel's famous ship, launched in 1843, and the first iron-hulled ship to be driven by propeller, is now being restored.
3. Claverton (ST 792 643). Like Crofton, a pumping station for the Kennet and Avon canal, but in this case a water wheel is used instead of steam to drive the pumps – a fascinating process by which water from the Avon is used to lift water from the Avon.
4. Dundas aqueduct (ST 786 626). See p. 96.
5. Avoncliff aqueduct (ST 805 600). See p. 96. Close by the aqueduct is an extensive weir across the Avon, with cloth mills on both banks.
6. Bradford-on-Avon. See pp. 13–14 and plate 1.
7. Rode. Once an important centre of the woollen industry, with many weavers' cottages. Nearby, is Rode mill on the Frome (ST 802 542).
8. Shawford woollen mill (ST 793 533). See pp. 202–3 and plate 94.
9. Dilton Marsh weavers' village. See p. 16 and plate 4.
10. Trowbridge. See pp. 16 and 201 and plate 31. There are also a number of fine clothiers' houses, for example in The Parade, and weavers' houses also at Timbrell Street and Yerbury Street.

11. Malmesbury mill. See p. 200 and plate 97.
12. Caen Hill locks, Devizes (ST 980 620). See p. 101.
13. Swindon Railway Estate. See p. 230 and plate XXIII. Within the same group, the original navvies' lodging house has been converted into a railway museum. The station has been recently 'improved' – about which the less said the better.
14. Crofton pumping station (SU 264 625). See pp. 174–5, plates XVIII and 87.
15. Fareham, Cort's iron-works (SU 550 070). See pp. 105–6.
16. London. Some fine late nineteenth-century industrial buildings, but less from the earlier period. One notable exception is St Katharine's docks designed by Telford, now undergoing development. Important canal connections include the Regent's canal and the Grand Union, which includes one well-known basin at Little Venice and another at Paddington. The Hampstead toll-house is described on p. 92. There are many important industrial remains in the Science Museum, South Kensington.
17. Faversham gunpowder mill (TR 009 613). Not a subject touched on previously, but a site well worth seeing. Few of these buildings survive – it being in their nature to disappear from the landscape, usually violently.
18. Oxford canal. The southern section from Oxford to Napton is a perfect example of contour-cutting. See especially Wormleighton bend (SP 430 550).
19. Sharpness. The southern terminal of the Gloucester and Berkeley ship canal (see p. 99). An impressive lock joins the canal to the river, and equally impressive nineteenth-century warehouses line the route.
20. Wotton-under-Edge, New mills (ST 737 929). See p. 204 and plate 98. Town mill, in the centre of Wotton, is unusual in being one of the few early nineteenth-century mills in this area to be originally designed as a steam-powered mill.
21. Nailsworth, Dunkirk mill (SO 845 005) and Egypt mill (ST 848 999). See pp. 200, 205 and plates 93 and 96.
22. Frogmarsh mill (SO 841 018). See p. 15 and plate 1.
23. Stonehouse, Stanley mill (SO 812 043). See pp. 206–7 and plates XX and 95. Nearby Ebley mill (SO 825 045) is another mill of great interest, with an odd *château*-style tower added to an otherwise traditional mill building.
24. Minchinhampton, St Mary's mill (SO 885 023). See p. 202.
25. Bibury, Arlington mill. See p. 18.
26. Gloucester docks. See p. 99 and plates 36 and 37.
27. Stoke Bruerne (SP 740 500). A warehouse on the Grand Union canal has been converted into a Waterways museum and there are a number of

other interesting points on the canal, including the entrance to Blisworth tunnel.

28. Redditch, needle factory (SP 050 680). See pp. 122–3 and plates XII, XIII and 54.
29. Tardebigge. Locks on Worcester and Birmingham canal.
30. Stourport. See p. 96 and plates VIII, 31 and 32.
31. Birmingham. The centre of Britain's canal network and in the centre of the city itself are a number of canal basins and warehouses; particularly interesting are Gas Street Basin and the canal-side development at the end of Brindley Walk – an area that has been given an imaginative face-lift by the council's architects.
32. Dudley. The Dudley tunnel on the Dudley canal has recently been re-opened and should, if possible, be travelled by boat, so that the cavernous excavations in the centre can be seen. The area surrounding Dudley, especially nearby Wednesbury, shows ample evidence of generations of coal-mining.

Northern England

1. Coalport pottery. See p. 138 and plate 71. Nearby is the track of the Hay inclined plane.
2. Ironbridge district. The area round Ironbridge, which includes the Coalbrookdale works, is part of a conservation scheme and a new and impressive open-air industrial museum has been opened at Blists Hill. See chapter 3 and plates IV, 17–21 and 28.
3. Longdon-upon-Tern. The site of the first iron trough aqueduct (SJ 618 156), the forerunner of Pont Cysyllte.
4. Ditherington mill (SJ 499 139). The first industrial building to be built on an iron framework.
5. Leicester. An industrial museum is being developed, based on the Abbey Lane Pumping Station (SK 586 060) – itself a splendid example of Victorian exuberance. Textile mills are found along the river Soar. Donisthorpe factory (plate XXII) has its entrance in Bath Lane.
6. Shardlow. Like Stourport, a canal town notable for its many excellent warehouses. It marks the junction of the Trent and Mersey canal with the river Trent.
7. Nottingham. Wollaton Hall has a small but excellent industrial museum which, as well as the horse whim (plate III), contains many examples of textile machines, including stocking frames.

8. Calverton. See pp. 23–4, 26, plate 10.
9. Papplewick. The remains of the cotton mill where steam power was introduced can be seen incorporated into the buildings of Grange Farm, beside the river.
10. Shropshire Union canal. The best example of the technique of cut and fill. See for example Tyrley locks (SJ 678 331) and the deep Woodseaves cutting to the south.
11. Stoke-on-Trent. Longton: Gladstone pottery, Uttoxeter Road; Elektra porcelain, Edensor Street; Aynsley china, Sutherland Road and Warren Terrace – see pp. 131–8 and plates XIV, 55–62; Burslem: Etruria works, see pp. 127–9, 138 and plate 59, also Wedgwood family house, now the Midland Bank, Swan Square. Potteries and associated buildings line the banks of the Trent and Mersey as it passes through the area.
12. Cheddleton flint mill (SJ 973 526). See pp. 138–41, plates 63–70.
13. Kidsgrove. The two Harecastle tunnels on the Trent and Mersey, Brindley's original and Telford's (SJ 840 540). See p. 95.
14. Leek. The preserved mill here has machinery installed by James Brindley (SJ 977 570).
15. Derby. Sir Thomas Lombe's silk mill (SK 340 360). Very little of the original 1717 building remains.
16. Belper. North mill and housing. See pp. 82–6 and plates VI, 26 and 27.
17. Morley Park iron-works (SK 380 492). See p. 114 and plate 48.
18. Wirksworth. As well as being an important centre for the lead industry the town has connections with textiles. Speedwell cotton mill (SK 283 539) was established by Arkwright.
19. Cromford. Mill building and houses. See pp. 73–82 and plates 24 and 25. There are also important transport remains here. From the Cromford canal, the Cromford and High Peak railway was built to Whaley Bridge. An engine shed and inclined plane can still be seen (SK 314 557).
20. Matlock Bath. Masson mill. See p. 77 and plate V.
21. Darley Dale. Two sough outlets can be seen here: Yatestop sough (SK 263 623) and Hill Carr sough (SK 260 636). See p. 33.
22. Sheldon village and Magpie mine (SK 173 682). See pp. 191–2 and plate 90.
23. Abbeydale, Sheffield (SK 325 820). See pp. 117–21 and plates XI, 52 and 53.
24. Elsecar, atmospheric engine (SK 388 999). Housing opposite entrance to colliery workshops. See pp. 52 and 197, plates 13, 14 and 91.
25. Wortley Top forge (SK 293 998). See pp. 117–18 and plates 50 and 51.
26. Whaley Bridge. The junction between the Cromford and High Peak

railway and the Peak Forest canal is marked by a unique covered inter-change – the canal goes in one end, rails come out the other.

27. Marple. Locks on Peak Forest canal. Oldknow warehouse (SJ 962 892). Aqueduct (SJ 955 900). Note also elegant 'snake' roving bridge on Macclesfield canal by Marple junction (SJ 962 883). The bridge carries the towpath across the canal and curls back under its own arch, hence the name snake.

28. Styal. See pp. 153–61, plates XVI, XVII, 77–80.

29. Barton-upon-Irwell. Only the abutments of Brindley's aqueduct remain (SJ 767 977), but next to that is the present, and no less remarkable, swing aqueduct.

30. Worsley Delph (SD 748 005). The entrance to the Duke of Bridgewater's mines and the beginning of his canal. See pp. 93–4, plate VII.

31. Cheesden Lumb mill (SD 825 161). See p. 145.

32. Helmshore higher mill (SD 781 210). See pp. 19 and 144, plates 8, 9 and 72.

33. Rawtenstall. Mills and houses are grouped in the centre of the town along the lines of the Bacup and Burnley roads. See plates 101 and 103.

34. Shaw. Dee mill engine (SD 945 093). A special type of steam engine was developed in the later nineteenth century for use in textile mills. This fine example has been preserved by the Northern Mill Engines Society.

35. Littleborough. Clough mill (SD 932 177). See p. 145, and plate 73.

36. Wardle. Wardle mill (SD 912 170) and many weavers' cottages, for example (SD 911 166) and later mill buildings. Remains of mill and extensive mill ponds (SD 905 160). See pp. 147–8.

37. Deerplay colliery, Bacup (SD 870 625). An early drift mine working, later more extensively developed with a still distinct tramway connection.

38. Burnley. Mills follow canal from end of embankment (SD 843 323). See p. 227 and plate 102.

39. Hebden Bridge. Oldest mill remains on course of river, westward from SD 989 291. See pp. 36, 146 and 215, plates 104, XV, XXI.

40. Standedge tunnel, Huddersfield canal (northern end SE 040 120). The most remarkable achievement in canal tunnels – 5,456 yards long.

41. Linthwaite. Weaving village with many examples of cottages and work-shops, e.g. SE 094 148.

42. Golcar weaving village. See p. 22.

43. Huddersfield. Main industrial concentration can be seen in Colne valley, spreading westward from the centre of the town.

44. Almondbury. Weaving community (SE 159 158). See p. 22 and plate 7.

45. Halifax Piece Hall. See p. 208, plates 99 and 100.

46. Bingley Five Rise (SE 108 400). Five-lock staircase on the Leeds and Liverpool canal.
47. Leeds. As in most large cities, many of the early industrial remains have disappeared. Interesting remains left include Burley mill, Kirstall Road, Marshall's flax mill, Marshall Street, an extraordinary building of the 1840s in the Egyptian style, and the Middleton colliery railway, the site of the first rack and pinion railway and now run, with steam locomotives, by a railway society.
48. Goole docks. Most of the early dock buildings have gone, but Goole remains an interesting example of a Company town, and also marks the terminal of the important Aire and Calder Navigation. See p. 34.
49. Pateley Bridge. Foster Beck mill (SE 148 664). Now used as a restaurant, this flax mill is notable for its huge breast-shot wheel.
50. Lancaster, Lune aqueduct. See p. 96 and plate 33.
51. Seaham harbour. See p. 46 and plate 12.
52. Beamish colliery engine house (NZ 220 537). See p. 194 and plate 92. Nearby is the Beamish Open Air Industrial Museum.
53. Tanfield, Causey Arch (NZ 201 559). See p. 46 and plate 11.
54. Killhope, lead-crushing mill (NZ 827 429). Ore-crushing was an important part of the mineral processing. The buildings here are comparatively well preserved and still have a large overshot water wheel.

Wales

1. Coed Ithel furnace (SO 527 027). See p. 28 and plate 11.
2. Llanfoist, tramway and canal interchange (SO 280 130). See p. 102 and plates ix and 41.
3. Blaenavon iron-works (SO 248 090), also company housing at Upper and Lower New Rank (SO 245 096). See pp. 106–9 and plates 42–5.
4. Dowlais. Very little remains of the original works, though some older buildings, such as the pattern shop, have been incorporated into the modern works.
5. Ynysfach. See pp. 109–10 and plates x and 46.
6. Pentrebach housing (SO 059 042). See p. 109 and plate 47.
7. Penydarren. The beginning of the tramway which leads down to Abercynon (ST 088 958). The track can still be followed along which Trevithick ran his steam locomotive in 1804.
8. Pontypridd. A notable eighteenth-century road bridge crosses the river.

From here up the Rhondda valley, the landscape of the coal-mining industry dominates.

9. St Fagans Folk Museum (ST 118 771). A complete eighteenth-century fulling mill is included in the museum.
10. Cardiff. There are a number of industrial remains in the National Museum, and Bute West Dock is being developed as a maritime museum site.
11. Cwmaman furnace (ST 004 992). The remains of a charcoal blast furnace.
12. Hirwaun (ST 959 057). See p. 113.
13. Carew tide mill (SN 046 038). One of the rare mills where tidal water is used to provide the power. This mill, built close to the walls of Carew Castle, is a good as well as a romantic example.
14. Pont Cysyllte aqueduct (SJ 270 410). See p. 97 and plate 35.
15. Blaenau ffestiniog. Moelwyn mill. This fulling mill has iron stocks, probably the last fulling stocks to be used in Britain.
16. Dinorwic slate quarries (SH 593 598). Once an important local industry, now finding a new life as a tourist attraction – not strictly within the scope of this book but an interesting site and a perfect example of the theory that old industrial sites can appeal to the general public.
17. Menai Straits road bridge. See p. 90.
18. Parys mountain (SH 450 910). See p. 176.
19. Conway road bridge. See p. 90.
20. Trefriw mill. In the centre of the village on the B.5106. The Welsh woollen mills were often small, but this is one of the larger, and particularly interesting as it is still in use.

Scotland

1. Gatehouse-of-Fleet, cotton mills. See p. 162, plate 75.
2. Tongland bridge. See p. 90, plate 29.
3. Kirkpatrick Durham. See p. 16 and plate 6.
4. Wanlockhead. This, with nearby Leadhills, has been an important centre of the Scottish lead-mining industry for centuries (see p. 192). The area contains many remains, including waggon ways, shafts and ruined smelters. A water-powered beam pump still stands (NS 870 131). There are many workers' houses, but the majority of the remains date from the modernization programme of the 1870s.

5. Muirkirk. Ironworks are at NS 697 268. Bell pits stretch away to the south. See pp. 40 and 116 and plate 49.
6. Glenbuck. See p. 116.
7. New Lanark. See pp. 164–9 and plate 81.
8. Paisley. This developed into a major centre of the cotton industry during the nineteenth century. The very grand Anchor mills (NS 490 635) show just how far the development went.
9. Rothesay. See p. 162.
10. Larbert. Carron iron-works (NS 880 824). Little of the early works survives apart from the canal system, though there are some late nineteenth-century structures. See pp. 115–16.
11. Chartershall. A small group of nailers' cottages with a workshop survive beside the new road development.
12. Torbex. Weavers' cottages. See p. 16, plate 5.
13. Alloa. The glass industry was established here, in the Clackmannan coal field, over two centuries ago. Some fine glass cones remain (NS 880 924).
14. Deanston cotton mill. See p. 162.
15. Furnace. Extensive remains of a charcoal blast furnace, comparable in importance with those at Bonawe (NN 026 001).
16. Bonawe (NN 010 317). See pp. 55–6, plates 15 and 16.
17. Stanley cotton mill, with mill housing. See p. 162.
18. Aberfeldy bridge. Probably the best example of the many bridges built by General Wade in his road-building programme in the Highlands in the early eighteenth century.
19. Caledonian canal. Telford's canal represents, as a whole, the greatest engineering feat of the canal age. The most spectacular section is the flight of locks known as Neptune's staircase (NN 114 770), but the most difficult section to construct was the deep Laggan cutting between Loch Lochy and Loch Oich.

Suggestions for Further Reading

Two excellent introductions to industrial archaeology have recently been published: R. A. Buchanan, *Industrial Archaeology in Britain*, and Arthur Raistrick, *Industrial Archaeology*. These supplement the earlier works: Kenneth Hudson, *Industrial Archaeology*, J. M. Pannell *The Techniques of Industrial Archaeology*, and R. A. Buchanan (ed.), *The Theory and Practice of Industrial Archaeology*.

A series edited by R. R. Green, *The Industrial Archaeology of Great Britain* (David & Charles), looks at the subject on a regional basis, and each volume has an extensive gazetteer. The areas dealt with to date include: Bristol, Cornwall, Dartmoor, Derbyshire, East Midlands, Hertfordshire, Isle of Man, Lake Counties, Lancashire, Peak District, Scotland, Southern England and the Tamar Valley.

Different aspects of the aesthetics of industrial remains are dealt with in Francis D. Klingender, *Art and the Industrial Revolution*, and J. M. Richards, *The Functional Tradition* – the latter notable for Eric de Maré's photographs.

Two periodicals deal specifically with industrial history – *Transactions of the Newcomen Society* and *Industrial Archaeology*.

The following are recommended for reading on specific industries.

Textiles

Duncan Blythell, *The Handloom Weavers* (1969).

Stanley D. Chapman, *The Early Factory Masters* (1967).

Frances Collier, *The Family Economy of the Working Classes in the Cotton Industry 1784–1833* (1965).

W. English, *The Textile Industry* (1969).

R. S. Fitton and A. P. Wadsworth, *The Strutts and the Arkwrights 1758–1830* (1958).

Herbert Heaton, *The Yorkshire Woollen and Worsted Industries* (2nd ed. 1965).

J. de L. Mann, *The Cloth Industry in the West of England* (1971).

Kenneth G. Ponting, *The Woollen Industry of South-West England* (1971).
Jennifer Tann, *Gloucestershire Woollen Mills* (1967).
Jennifer Tann, *The Development of the Factory* (1971).

Metal Industries

D. B. Barton, *A History of Tin Mining and Smelting in Cornwall* (1967).
D. B. Barton, *A History of Copper Mining in Cornwall and Devon* (2nd ed. 1968).
Roger Burt (ed.), *Cornish Mining* (1969).
W. K. V. Gale, *The British Iron and Steel Industry* (1967).
W. K. V. Gale, *Iron and Steel* (1969).
Arthur Raistrick, *Dynasty of Ironfounders* (1953).
Arthur Raistrick and B. Jennings, *A History of Lead Mining in the Pennines* (1966).

Coal-Mining and Steam Engines

T. S. Ashton and J. Sykes, *The Coal Industry of the Eighteenth Century* (1929).
Frank Atkinson, *The Great Northern Coalfield (1700–1900)* (1966).
D. B. Barton, *The Cornish Beam Engine* (2nd ed. 1969).
H. W. A. Dickinson, *A Short History of the Steam Engine* (1938).
Eric Robinson and A. E. Musson, *James Watt and the Steam Revolution* (1969).
Sir Arthur Trueman, *The Coalfields of Great Britain* (1954).
George Watkins, *The Stationary Steam Engine* (1968).

Transport

B. Baxter, *Stone Blocks and Iron Rails* (1966).
Anthony Bird, *Roads and Vehicles* (1969).
Anthony Burton, *The Canal Builders* (1972).
Charles Hadfield, *British Canals: An Illustrated History* (3rd ed. 1968).
J. P. M. Pannell, *An Illustrated History of Civil Engineering* (1964).
L. T. C. Rolt, *Navigable Waterways* (1969).

Index

Numbers in italics refer to black and white illustrations; Roman numerals refer to colour illustrations

Hall, J. C., 121–2
Hampstead, 92, 239
Harecastle tunnel, 95, 239
Hargreaves, James, 69, 71–2, 73
Harveys of Hayle, 178, 186, 187
Hawkins, John, 35–6
Hayle, 178, 186, 187, 188, 239
Haynes, John, 20
Haytor tramway, 240
Heage, 114
Heathersage, 122
Hebden Bridge, 36, 146, 215–16, 244, xv, xxi, 104
Helmshore higher mill, 19–20, 144, 244, 8, 9, 22, 23, 72
Henson, Gravener, 25
Heptonstall, 36, 215–16
Heron, Robert, 162–3
Hill, Francis, 200–1
Hill, Thomas, 106
Hillcar Sough, 33
Hirwaun iron works, 113, 246
Hodgson, Rev. John, 195–6
Holland G. Calvert, 120–1, 122, 123
Holland, John, 41, 47, 52, 196–7
Holyhead Road, 90
Hopkins, Thomas, 106
Hornblower, Jonathan, 177
Hosiery industry; 23–6, 72–3, 81, 83; and frame-breaking, 219–20
Housing: weavers', 16–17, 21–2, 145, 3–7, 73; coal miners', 53, 196–7, 91; iron workers', 56, 108–10, 116–17, 121, 123, 45–7; cotton workers', 80–1, 83, 146, 158–9, 161, 164–5, 169, 227–9, vi, xvii, 25, 74, 78–9, 81, 103, 104; lead miners', 32, 191; potteries, 137–8, 60, 61; tin miners', 188–9, 89; railway workers', 230, xxiii;
Huddersfield, 229, 244, 105
Hugh, Thomas, 72
Huntsman Benjamin, 119

Iron industry; 102; charcoal smelting, 26–9, 55–7; coke smelting and the Darbys, 57–67; Ironbridge, 62–4, iv; puddling, 105–6; South Wales, 106–13; Staffordshire, 113–14; Derbyshire, 114–15; Scotland, 115–17; forges, 117–120; grinding, 120–3

James, John, 11, 22, 209
Jessop, Williams, 97

Kay, John (of Bury), 69–70, 73

Kay, John (of Warrington), 72
Kelly, William, 162
Kennet and Avon canal, 96, 101, 174–5, 238
Kennet Navigation, 34–5
Kenyon, John, 162
Killhope lead mill, 245
King, Gregory, 10
Kirkpatrick Durham, 16–17, 246, 6
Knaresborough, 89

Lancaster canal, 96, 245, 33, 40
Lead mining, 31–3, 191–2
Leadhills, 192
Lee, James, 24
Lee, William, 23–4, 26
Leeds, 210–12, 245
Leeds and Liverpool canal, 98, 101, 208, 227–8, 245
Leek, 243
Leicester, 218, 228, 242, xxii
Lemon, Sir Charles, 190
Levant mine, 186, 239, 86
Lichfield, John, 190
Linthwaite, 229, 244
Littleborough mill, 145, 244, 73
Llanfoist tramway, 102–3, 107, 241, ix, 41
Lombe, Thomas, 71, 239
London, 14, 24–5, 40–1, 241
Longdon-upon-Tern, 242
Longton, 131–3, 137–8, 239, 61
Longhead Sough, 33

McAdam, John, 91–2
Macclesfield canal, 38, 39
Maclean, Donald, 207
Madeley Wood furnaces, 65–6, 20
Malmesbury, Avon mill, 200–1, 241, 97
Manchester, 93, 217–18, 222
Marple, 148–53
Marple aqueduct, 62, 102, 243–6
Matlock Bath, Masson mill, 77, 243, v
Mellor, shop, 152–3
Menai Straits bridge, 90, 246
Merthyr Tydfil, 108, 109–13
Metcalfe, John, 89
Minchinhampton, St Mary's mill, 202, 241
Morley Park iron works, 114–15, 243, 48
Morton, W. G., 176, 187
Morwellham harbour, 187–8, 240
Muirkirk, 40, 116, 247, 49

Nailsworth: Egypt mill, 200, 241, 93; Long-fords mill, 202; Dunkirk mill, 205–6, 241, 96